Chicken Soup
for the Soul®

My
Cat's Life

Chicken Soup for the Soul: My Cat's Life
101 Stories about All the Ages and Stages of Our Feline Family Members
Jack Canfield, Mark Victor Hansen, Jennifer Quasha. Foreword by Wendy Diamond.

Published by Chicken Soup for the Soul Publishing, LLC   www.chickensoup.com
Copyright © 2011 by Chicken Soup for the Soul Publishing, LLC. All Rights Reserved.
No part of this publication may be reproduced, stored in a retrieval system or transmitted in any form or by any means, electronic, mechanical, photocopying, recording or otherwise, without the written permission of the publisher.

CSS, Chicken Soup for the Soul, and its Logo and Marks are trademarks of
Chicken Soup for the Soul Publishing LLC.

The publisher gratefully acknowledges the many publishers and individuals who granted Chicken Soup for the Soul permission to reprint the cited material.

Front cover photo courtesy of Getty Images/Photodisc, © Arthur Tilley. Wendy Diamond photo on back cover courtesy of Wendy Diamond. Back cover photo courtesy of iStockphoto.com/rouzes (© Michal Rozanski). Interior photos courtesy of iStockphoto.com/Kirillov (© Konstantin Kirillov).

Cover and Interior Design & Layout by Pneuma Books, LLC
For more info on Pneuma Books, visit www.pneumabooks.com

Distributed to the booktrade by Simon & Schuster. SAN: 200-2442

Publisher's Cataloging-in-Publication Data
(Prepared by The Donohue Group)

Chicken soup for the soul : my cat's life : 101 stories about all the ages and
  stages of our feline family members / [compiled by] Jack Canfield, Mark
  Victor Hansen, [and] Jennifer Quasha ; foreword by Wendy Diamond.

   p. ; cm.

   Summary: A collection of 101 true stories from people about all the ages and stages
of living with their cats. Stories are personal anecdotes, ranging from funny to sad,
dealing with issues of life, love, family, perseverance, joy in life, death, friendship, and
other human emotions.
   ISBN: 978-1-935096-66-5

   1. Cats--Literary collections. 2. Cats--Anecdotes. 3. Cat owners--Literary collections. 4. Cat owners--Anecdotes. 5. Human-animal relationships--Literary collections.
6. Human-animal relationships--Anecdotes. I. Canfield, Jack, 1944- II. Hansen, Mark
Victor. III. Quasha, Jennifer. IV. Diamond, Wendy. V. Title: My cat's life

PN6071.C3 C455 2011
810.8/02/03629752   2010938813

PRINTED IN THE UNITED STATES OF AMERICA
on acid∞free paper
20 19 18 17 16 15 14 13 12 11   01 02 03 04 05 06 07 08 09 10

Chicken Soup for the Soul®
My Cat's Life

101 Stories about
All the Ages and Stages
of Our Feline Family Members

Jack Canfield
Mark Victor Hansen
Jennifer Quasha
Foreword by Wendy Diamond

CSS

Chicken Soup for the Soul Publishing, LLC
Cos Cob, CT

www.chickensoup.com

Contents

❶

~Irresistible~

❷

~Eat, Play, Love~

❸
~Do You Know How Much I Knead You?~

❹
~Who's the Boss?~

❺
~I Am Cat, Hear Me Roar~

❻

~It's the Cat's Meow~

❼

~A Purrfect Life~

8

~Are You Stalking to Me?~

9

~For All Nine Lives~

10

~Over the Rainbow~

⓫
~I'll Always Love You~

Foreword

What's your favorite stage of cat companionship? Is it when you first bring home your new kitten and she playfully swats at her new toy—right before the tables turn and the claws come out? We've all been there. Or is it when she turns into a feline "teenager" and her full-sized, trouble-making personality makes you worry terribly about just where she is—until she appears and twirls around your ankles, or drops a dead mouse she hunted at your feet. Maybe it's when your cat has hit his prime and settled into adulthood. Both you and he have a good sense of each other and your daily rhythms have adapted into a peaceful routine. Or is it the senior stage when your best friend has slowed down, and you can be quiet together and simply enjoy each other's company (usually sleeping)? And then there are the twilight years, when, as cat parents, we feel so needed. We realize that those tables are turned, and that we need to pay our best friends back for all those years of snuggling and unconditional love.

How can we choose our favorite stage? Well, we don't have to! We all know that every age and stage is special in its own way, and this book has unforgettable stories about every one of those special ages and stages.

Since I rescued my Russian Blue, Pasha, and my Maltese, Lucky, we have been through a lot of wonderful ages and stages together. Pasha has lived in New York almost as long as I have! And like many of us who have pets, it's fair to say that adopting mine changed my life. I had never felt unconditional love like that before. And after I saw how bad many animal shelters were, and how much love I felt for Pasha and Lucky, I knew I had to do something. Since then I have been truly blessed to be able to serve as an advocate for homeless animals.

What I do every day stems from when I adopted Pasha and Lucky. But as every parent of every dog or cat knows, we are all lucky, and this book illustrates so well the many blessings we have been given by our cats. Every story in this book reminds us how our cats have changed and positively contributed to our lives. The stories also remind us of the great gift it is to have our cats in our lives, the friendship we share, and how the human-animal bond makes us better people every day.

I promise you that in every chapter of this book you will love the stories.

Imagine reading Elizabeth Atwater's story about how she gave away her beloved kitten to her best friend to ease her friend's sadness the day she had to move away. Atwater never forgot her friend—or her cat. Imagine her surprise when, after the cat died, her old best friend found her to tell her about the cat's death and thank her for the great gift she had given her all those years before! I also love April Knight's story. She went, with a new kitten in hand, to a friend's house where they were gathering to bury her friend's beloved black cat that had been hit by a car. But, in the middle of the burial service, the supposed-to-be-dead cat jumped out of the bushes—probably to find out just *who* they were going to bury! Then, in Juliana Harris's piece, we read her incredible story of how her cat saved her from a gas fire in her kitchen by waking her up in the middle of the night. Imagine!

Then the teenage cat stories remind us of how sometimes our four-legged teens are kind of similar to the two-legged variety. Like some teenagers, cats don't understand that their crazy antics have consequences. Author Robert Chrisman shares the story of his sister who attempted to wash their family cat after it was skunked. The cat, after it was caught, trapped, and dunked, was so mad that it tore crazily after his sister until their mother finally opened the door to let her escape into the house! Nancy Kucik tells her inspiring story about how she and her teenage cat work together as an animal therapy team. Although few people think about cats as animals for pet therapy, she proves that some teenage cats can do it—and well. One of my favorite stories in this section is a humorous piece about the drama of getting a male cat neutered. It's a perfect example of why we shouldn't over-think everything we do! Especially in these days of pet over-population, sometimes you just have to do what you have to do!

In our adult cat chapters you will read stories about how our cats help us: to love, to be strong, and to laugh. Chicken Soup for the Soul's editors have selected amazing stories, such as Beverly Walker's tale of bringing home her deceased son's cat. The cat, at first scared and traumatized, wouldn't come to her. Then one day Beverly decided to listen to a CD of her son's guitar recital. When the cat heard his music, it walked right over to her for a snuggle. On the lighter side you will hear about the trials of a husband and wife who try to get medicine down their cat's throat—a situation that we have all been in! You'll also find a lovely story about a nervous couple who decide to adopt a cat the wife read about on a sign posted on a storefront window—and how it turns out wonderfully.

In our senior cats and twilight years chapters you will read stories which will prove to you why older cats really can make the best friends. You should definitely consider adopting an older cat from a shelter next time you are in the market for a new friend. Ruth Jones muses over the many wonderful years she spent with her cat as it moves into the twilight phase. Then Harriet Cooper tells the awesome story about how a vet told her that her thirteen-year-old cat with kidney disease would die soon—and then the cat lived for another six years!

Lastly, I promise, the stories on grieving and recovery will not depress you! They will inspire and empower you during a time that every pet parent dreads, the death and subsequent recovery from the passing of a beloved cat. Read about how Sallie Rodman and her remaining cat formed a bond after the other family cat died. And

Angela Marchi's story is pretty amazing! After she lost her beloved black cat, she proclaimed that she wouldn't get another cat unless an all white one, with one blue eye and one gold eye, happened across her path. Guess what? Two days later, one did!

As you can see, so many wonderful writers have opened their hearts and shared their stories with us about their beloved cats. So whatever your favorite stage of cat companionship is, one thing is for sure: cats don't go off to college, get married or fly the coop, so it's important to be the best cat parent you can be at all times. Relish every moment of pet parenting and relish these magnificent stories as I did. Each one is a reminder of how powerful, magical and life-changing being a cat parent really is.

~Wendy Diamond

My Cat's Life

Irresistible

Midnight and Stay Awhile

Cats come and go without ever leaving.
~Martha Curtis

"**M**olly's cat died," said Denise's tearful voice on the phone. "Midnight was hit by a car." Molly, Denise, and I had been friends for ten years and we all loved Midnight.

Denise explained that Midnight had somehow gotten past the fence in Molly's backyard and a car had hit him. A neighbor had found Midnight, put him in a box and taken him to Molly. Molly and Midnight had been together for eighteen years. I knew that she would be lost without him.

"Maybe we should go to her house and have a little funeral service," I suggested. "I'll pick up some flowers and make a little cross and put Midnight's name on it."

"I think that would make her feel better," Denise agreed, sniffing. "I'll miss that sweet old black cat. He was such a lovable thing, always purring and wanting to be held."

We decided to meet at Molly's house at four o'clock. I felt crushed. My own cat, Puff-Puff, had died from old age six months before. I missed him terribly, but I didn't have the heart to get another cat yet. I stopped by the flower shop and picked up a small bouquet of daisies. Then I decided Molly wouldn't feel like cooking dinner so I got three chicken dinners for us to eat after the funeral. There was a pet store on my way to Molly's house and I thought that they might have an appropriate sympathy card for the loss of a pet. In the pet shop was a small gray-and-black striped kitten in a cage. It was too soon to get Molly a kitten. After all you couldn't just replace one cat with another as if it were a broken dish. No, Molly would need time to grieve and mourn and heal and recover. In a few months she might be ready to get another cat but not now. Not yet. The kitten tried to climb the side of his cage to reach me and did a back flip and fell over, making me laugh.

"He's cute, isn't he? He's a real character. I don't know why no one has bought him yet," the store owner said. "I guess he is going to stay awhile."

"Stay Awhile," I smiled. He had just been named. "I'll buy him, and I'll take a cat carrier, too."

If Molly didn't want the kitten, I would keep him for myself even though I didn't feel ready for another cat. As I drove to Molly's house, the kitten meowed loudly.

"Be quiet, Stay Awhile, you're going to heal a broken heart today," I said, hoping Molly would accept the kitten. Denise and Molly were waiting for me.

"Molly, I know I shouldn't have done this without asking you first, but I saw this darling kitten and couldn't help myself. I know he can't replace Midnight, but if you don't want him, I'll keep him. His name is Stay Awhile," I said. Molly wiped her tears.

"Stay Awhile? What a silly, delightful name for a kitten!" She kissed the kitten's pink nose. "Of course I'll keep him. I couldn't bear a single night not having a cat in the house."

"We should probably—you know—bury Midnight," Denise said.

We solemnly dug a grave in the flower garden and gently placed the box in it and covered it up. I handed the flowers to Molly to place on the grave while Denise stuck the little wooden cross into the damp earth.

Suddenly, a cat leaped over the fence and landed at our feet.

"MIDNIGHT!" all three of us screamed.

Molly grabbed the black cat and lifted him up.

"It's Midnight!" She burst into tears of sheer joy.

"Molly, didn't you look in the box when the neighbor gave it to you?" Denise asked.

"No, I couldn't. I didn't want to see Midnight dead. The neighbor just handed me the box and said he found a black cat on the street and was sure it was Midnight," she said.

We all burst into hysterical laughter.

"Well, some poor stray cat just had a first-class funeral!" Denise said.

"What about Stay Awhile?" I asked.

"Well, he's a darling," Molly said, "But I don't think Midnight would share me with another cat. He's very jealous."

I was thrilled that I could keep the kitten. I had already fallen in love with him. A day that had started with tears ended in laughter, thanks to a cat who came to his own funeral and a kitten named Stay Awhile. I bought Stay Awhile to heal Molly's broken heart, but instead Stay Awhile healed mine.

~April Knight

A Cat Named Garbage

No one should be condemned as trash;
even a little stick can serve as a toothpick!
~Atharva Veda

The first cat I ever owned came from the county dump. I found her sitting atop several metric tons of detritus, licking one paw and rubbing her eyes with it like a sleepy baby. I fell in love with her on the spot and named her Garbage. I was seven years old at the time, and what I wanted most in the world was a pet. I had never owned an animal before and was anxious to try my hand at taking care of one. This cat would do fine, I told myself. First I had to clear it with Mr. Sprull, who owned the dump. He was a man with an overfed midsection and an eye-watering aversion to soap and water. He wore greasy overalls and walked with a whiskey lilt.

I hung around the dump a lot that summer. Often Mr. Sprull would hire me to pick through the trash for him. He didn't care much for grubbing about in the garbage himself, so he stayed on the bank while I burrowed through the tangle of muck and debris and retrieved anything that looked promising, such as old tools, copper wire, dead batteries, stained clothing, and radios that never made a sound. I would climb onto the piles of rubbish until I could reach down to wherever he was pointing. Half the time I was thigh deep in an odorous stew of rotten food, greasy car innards, and decomposing animal carcasses, but I didn't mind. When I told Mr. Sprull about the cat, he gave me a quizzical look.

"What you want it for, boy?" he asked.

"For a pet," I said. He stuck a pinch of tobacco under his lip and spit a long stream of brown juice.

"That critter is wilder than sunspots," he said. "I doubt you'll ever get within ten feet of it, let alone turn it into a house cat."

I told him I wanted to try, and so he gave me permission. As I crept toward the cat, my palms began to sweat. I felt dizzy, too, but that was probably because of the smoke. Mr. Sprull kept old truck tires smoldering to drive the mosquitoes away. The sickly sweet smell rose in a heavy brown fog and blanketed the entire dump. I drew closer. Garbage had matted fur and looked pitifully thin, as if she hadn't eaten in months. When I was a dozen feet away she made a little rumble sound deep in her chest and darted off. Mr. Sprull was right. That cat wasn't going to allow me to get anywhere near her. A better plan was needed.

I hurried down to the feed store and bought a bag of cat food with my last quarter. Then I returned to the dump to find Garbage sitting where I left her. I inched out over the trash. She moved away again. I opened the bag, held it out in front of me, and moved extra slowly. Before I knew it, Garbage was eating cat food out of a dented Nash hubcap while I gently scratched her head. She made a ratchety purr, like a diesel engine starting on a cold morning. Finally, she was mine. All I had to do now was convince my mother to let me keep her. I rushed home with Garbage in my arms and flew inside, letting the screen door slam shut behind me.

"Mom, Mom, I found a cat," I said.

"Don't you bring that animal into this house," she said. "It probably has fleas."

"Aw, Ma," I said, "she's a clean cat."

I brushed a flea off my arm and placed Garbage on the floor so my mother could get a good look. She reached down and stroked her fur. Garbage flipped onto her back, and twisted up like a question mark under her fingertips.

"She is cute," Mom said.

"Can we keep her? Can we, please?" I was begging for all I was worth.

"I'm afraid not," she said. "We can't afford to feed an animal when we can barely feed ourselves."

"But she doesn't eat much," I whined. "And she doesn't have a home. I ain't gonna take her back to the dump."

"Don't say ain't," Mom replied. "I didn't raise you to talk like a goat."

I looked down at my feet. Garbage had wandered off to explore the house.

That's when we heard a scuffle coming from the bedroom. Garbage made angry hissing and screaming noises, followed by what sounded like a shoe being thrown against the wall. Seconds later she emerged, carrying in her mouth the broken body of a large brown rat. It had two yellow teeth protruding over its bottom lip, and a long, pink tail. Mom screamed, causing my heart to skip a beat.

"It's a rat," she cried.

Garbage was making a low moaning sound in her throat, a strange combination of pleasure and revulsion. My mother climbed onto a chair for safety.

"We've got rats in our house," she shrieked. "Rats!" Nothing frightened Mom more than vermin.

"Garbage will take care of the problem," I said, proudly.

She stared at the cat for a long moment.

"Alright," she said, "you can keep her, on one condition. You have to promise that you'll eat all your vegetables from now on."

Like most families, we had vegetables for supper every night. And like most kids, I hated them. We had stewed tomatoes, steamed cauliflower, and lima beans with each meal, and I always felt the cold creeps as Mom would put some on my plate and tell me, "Just eat a little." Eating "a little" creamed corn, like vomiting "a little," was just as bad as "a lot." My stomach lurched sideways at the thought of it. But this was the deal of a lifetime, and I knew it would never come again.

"Alright," I sighed. "I promise."

Mom nodded. "Okay, you've got a deal."

It was a tough promise to live up to, but I ate my boiled carrots, fried okra, and raw cabbage without complaint. I ate so many vegetables I felt like Br'er Rabbit. But with Garbage chasing rats all day, and sleeping on my bed at night, it was worth every awful bite.

~Timothy Martin

Crippy

Attitude is a little thing that makes a big difference.
~Winston Churchill

n retrospect, Crippy probably wasn't the most politically correct name for the cat, but then again it was 1970 and political correctness wasn't, well, politically correct yet. My sister's godmother had given her a purebred Persian cat for her birthday three years earlier, and now the cat was having her first and, as it turned out, only litter of kittens. One by one the beautiful cream colored puff balls entered our world, each perfect and healthy. In no time at all the cat had calmly produced four little petite felines, but she wasn't done.

"What's up, girl?" my mother prodded gently. "You have another baby in there?"

The new mother cat looked up at all of us with round orangey, almost-beige eyes, as if to reply, but then with a few grunts and a screech, out came the final kitten, a male. In all, Buffy, who was now cleaning the kittens with her leathery, pink tongue, had produced three females and two males. But something was odd about the last kitten. His hind legs seemed to be double jointed or broken. Although the other newborns were clumsy, he was especially challenged as he fumbled about.

"That one may not make it, kids," Mom flatly said to us, her four children, ages four, eight, ten and twelve, with me the oldest. "Something's not right."

Everyone stared at the tiny, helpless cat with sympathy as he struggled to squirm about. His future appeared pitiful and dim. He survived the first two days, but needed special attention from his mother and from our family. Everyone rallied to the kitten's side. Then, a trip to the veterinarian disclosed that the cat was not dying, but was handicapped—crippled. The vet said it was a rare case of "radial hypoplasia," a disabling condition that normally affects the forelegs not the hind legs.

"Cats are amazing creatures," he said with a touch of awe in his voice. "He will adapt and adjust. He'll be just fine." Our family was assured that the kitten was not in pain, and everything else about him, including his internal organs, was fine and functional.

The cat, which we affectionately named Crippy, matured and grew like his brothers and sisters, but walked with an exaggerated limp and gait. He was a curious character, prone to snooping around secluded places and climbing into tight quarters. He was playful and upbeat, a happy cat despite his disability. We found ourselves being entertained by this cat and he quickly became everyone's favorite of the litter. When it was time to sell the kittens, we wondered if anyone would want Crippy. One by one his siblings were happily chosen, and eventually he was the only kitten left. A few people visited and looked at Crippy, but no one wanted him despite our best marketing efforts. Once they saw his hind legs they would glance at their watches and then politely exit our home. Crippy didn't mind; he had a home, and we were happy, too.

Crip, as we often referred to him, was not only a lovable and affectionate beast, but also an astute hunter. He would track down mice, birds or tunneling moles and come victoriously to the front door stoop and drop the dead thing like a big game hunter plopping down his fourteen-point buck. He spent hours in front of our rectangular fish aquarium digging with his paws at the smooth glass, determined to one day grasp one of those teasing, tempting goldfish that nervously patrolled the waters within. Frustrated, he would leave, only to return later to repeat the cycle. At Christmastime he would often retire under our Douglas fir, sometimes to sleep and sometimes to swat at the shiny ornaments and lights. He broke two or three every holiday season and would coolly slip away trying to look innocent.

At the conclusion of every school day, Crippy would be at the front door awaiting my brother, two sisters and me as we arrived home courtesy of the yellow school bus. He would welcome us home with an affectionate twirl between our legs, and then follow us around until dinner. He had missed us. The years passed and Crippy was an ever-present part of our family life. He was loved and he gave affectionate love in return. He participated in everything and wasn't a shy cat. He loved the limelight. And then right after his tenth birthday he became ill. I had just graduated from college and was living at home trying to calculate my next move. Crip had been making "mistakes" around the house, unable to contain his bowels and urine. Strange oblong lumps were also discovered along his stomach, and he seemed sensitive to touch in that region. We worriedly took him to the vet for a diagnosis.

"I'm afraid I have bad news," the vet began, peering over his spectacles with empathetic eyes. "Your cat has cancer. At his age, and considering the type, I don't think it's advisable to operate. We'd just be delaying the inevitable for a few months, plus it would be very expensive I'm afraid." And our family, a single income clan of six, was far from rich.

We took Crippy home to say goodbye to everyone. He was pampered and hugged, and I remember my mother crying. Two days later my brother, who was particularly close to Crip, and I took our beloved friend back to the vet to be put to sleep. We were somber during the ride and did not speak, grief already penetrating our hearts. Crippy, who often would move back and forth in the back seat and peer out the windows like an excitable dog, was quiet and rested. He looked at me and I knew he was uncomfortable and in pain.

I held him in my lap and stroked his back as the office staff administered the necessary needles. Crippy seemed at peace and looked trustingly up at my brother and me, before closing his eyes forever. I told him we loved him and I sobbed quietly but in torrents.

Seconds later the vet confirmed that Crippy was gone. Crippy taught our family a lot during his decade of life: living life to its fullest regardless of your limitations, hope for the hopeless, laughter often is the best medicine, and love, pure and unconditional, is powerful. Not bad for a handicapped cat. Not bad for any cat.

~David Michael Smith

Peas in a Pod

Are we not like two volumes of one book?
~Marceline Desbordes-Valmore

I'll never be sure if it was wisdom or folly that struck that day, but I would think a little of both. We had been happily living with one cat for a couple of years, a fairly large black-and-white English Shorthair named Smedley. It was time for his annual exam and shots, so off we went to our local veterinarian's office, puss in hand, or actually wrapped up like an Egyptian mummy to save us from his dreaded claws.

"Ah!" Doc Pete said, a twinkle in his eyes. "I'm glad you dropped in. I have a kitten out back that needs a home and I thought of you!"

Before I could stop him, his assistant brought out the tiniest marmalade tabby, weighing just over a pound, with a cast on his left front leg. He put him in my arms, looked up at me and said, "So what do you think?"

They say that a sucker is born every minute and that was my minute. We took one look at the poor little thing and then at each other and we were done for. We found out that someone had broken his leg and tried to drown him in the nearest canal. A Good Samaritan had rescued him and brought him to the vet's office.

"How will they get along?" I asked. "How do we go about introducing them to each other?"

"Oh, that's no problem," he said. "You just put him in a carrier, take him home, leave the carrier open and let Smedley think he is rescuing the kitten."

Well, it sounded good. As per instructions, once we got home, we left the kitten in the carrier in the middle of the room. Then we sat back to watch. Smedley circled the box and growled deeper than I had ever heard him before. The kitten, meanwhile, mewed plaintively while sticking a paw out of the holes in the side of the carrier. After about an hour, we decided to open the top of the carrier a little wider. Smedley walked up to the top, looked inside and was rewarded by a lightning strike from a small orange paw.

That was the last we saw of him that evening. I was convinced that the next morning would find us back at the vet's office returning the little tyke. However, the next morning, we were in for a surprise. As I got up to put on the coffee, I saw the two of them curled up together on the sofa as if they were one cat with two smiling faces. From then on, Smedley watched over the little one as if he had given birth to him, and they went everywhere together.

Doc Pete was right!

~Sue Young

Wedding Bliss

People who love cats have some of the biggest hearts around.
~Susan Easterly

I grew up in a house that was often referred to as the "Schoen Zoo." Not because we were a bunch of crazy animals, although that fit sometimes, but more because we took in or adopted lost and abused animals. Most of the time we only had them until we found their owners; occasionally they became part of our family. I grew up with three dogs, two Malaccan cockatoos, a Quaker parrot, hamsters, and fish. It was like living in a pet shop, and I loved it. As an only child I was never at a loss for a friend or companion.

When I moved to Orlando to live with my fiancé, we had no pets and I went through major withdrawal. I knew a dog was out of the question since we traveled too much, but I thought a cat was an option. I patiently kept planting the idea with my reluctant partner, but he wasn't budging.

On one Saturday afternoon in July, I was shopping for my wedding gown with two of my friends, one of whom was my fiancé's sister. We had been to the mall and were on our way to the showroom of the designer of my dream gown. He was based in New York and only had one other store in the state of Florida, and it just happened to be in Orlando. I just knew it was fate, and lo and behold I found the perfect dress.

As we were leaving the store I noticed a pet superstore two doors down. Outside the door was a large sign that said "Adoptions Today."

I looked at my friends, they looked at me, and they immediately shook their heads. "No way! Rich would kill us!"

"Please," I begged. "I just want to look. I know we can't get one now." They conceded, since I was the bride to be, after all.

When I entered the store my eyes were drawn to an energetic beige-and-white Bengal kitten. He was talking up a storm and running and jumping all over the cage. His brother wasn't nearly as entertaining. I asked to hold the kitten, at which point my friends knew it was over. They had lost and Rich was going to become the proud owner of an enthusiastic kitten. We bonded, and instantly I knew this was the one. He wasn't a regular independent, boring, opinionated, selfish cat. He had spunk and he had character. Rich would love him, I was sure. Besides, it had to be kismet — my dream gown and a kitten all in one little shopping strip. It was meant to be.

I found out that the kitten and his three brothers had been tossed into a dumpster at six weeks old, and that they were perfectly healthy but needed a lot of love, as most abandoned and abused animals do. I had plenty of experience. I knew that I was just what this little guy needed. I asked the man if he could hold him until I could check with Rich first. He agreed. My mission now was to convince my husband-to-be that this was the kitten for him. Not just any old cat, he was a running, jumping, climbing trees cat, a suitable companion for any guy.

In the end, Rich said yes and we were off on our new adventure with a little companion in tow. It seemed our family was taking shape. I not only married the man of my dreams, in the dress of my dreams, but I had the cat of my dreams as well. Wedding gifts come in all shapes and sizes, mine just happened to have four legs, fur, a heartbeat, and one super-sized character, but that's a whole other chapter.

~Francesca Lang

Mimi

*The most powerful agent of growth and transformation is something much
more basic than any technique: a change of heart.*
~John Welwood

I was attending a run-down martial arts school in New York one
summer. The place had no air conditioning. I don't think it
even had fans. Sweat was considered good and cold water was
considered bad. This was either based on ancient Chinese medicine
or just being macho. The windows provided a view of a dark alleyway.
Most of them were shut and locked, but one was kept open. That's
how an alley cat mom and her six kittens slipped into the school one
day and made the place their home.

The alley cat mom looked ready to attack us, and when we tried
to pet the kittens they ran. They would crawl underneath the dusty
couch in the corner of the school's main room where human hands
couldn't touch them. We didn't see the mother much. She would
usually escape out the window at the sound of human footsteps. She
had either judged that, although we were strange and untrustworthy,
we wouldn't murder her brood, or her parental instincts weren't all
they were cracked up to be.

Things went along fine when the kittens were hiding. We could
do our form and sparring unobstructed. All it took to keep them
around was a box of Purina in some dollar-store bowls, not getting
too close to them, and for our sake—a litter box. They cheered up
the school, and it was a happy system. That is until the kittens became

less afraid of us. Then we couldn't move without danger of stepping on a little creature running between our feet.

Members were asked to take them home. I wasn't a nurturing type. Insensitive and a tad brutish, most of my downtime was spent watching horror flicks on my discount VCR in an undecorated, stark abode. Nonetheless, I couldn't help noticing a little kitten that seemed to jump the highest, run the fastest, and have the most spunk. A week later she was in my apartment. I named her Mimi. I had heard about a PBS nature special that said felines interpreted a sound similar to "mimi" as friendly.

Mimi and I had an okay relationship until I tried to pet her. She let out a hiss and ran. I tried to calm her down by pressing her gently to my cheek, but she let out a scream of fear like I've never heard from cat or man. I think she believed I was going to eat her.

It took six months, but one morning I woke up in bed and Mimi was cuddled next to me, under my arm. Why? I'm not sure, but I guess she had gotten used to me. Soon Mimi was jumping onto my lap and falling asleep as I stroked her fur with one hand and managed the remote control to watch the *Arizona Chainsaw Monsters* or some such with the other. None of my movies' screaming or drama seemed to disturb her. She would relax in my lap, close her eyes, smile a little cat smile, and start purring. I began to feel downright mushy toward her.

Mimi saw me through a lot. She was there when my parents died, my mother passing from cancer, and my father of a heart attack a few months later. I cried into Mimi's fur. She was also there when I met my wife, Rosetta. Rosetta's a dog person, but Mimi was so friendly that she began to win her over.

When Mimi was at least fourteen years old she appeared to be a permanent fixture in our lives. I had stopped keeping track of her birthdays. I guess I didn't want to think about her getting along in years and the inevitable conclusion it would bring.

The end happened fast. One day, she was wobbling and having trouble standing up. Rosetta and I took her to the vet. Her kidneys had been giving out for who knows how long and were nearly defunct. That day, Mimi was put to sleep.

If you told me when I first noticed Mimi that I would be mourning the death of a cat, I wouldn't have believed you, but mourn I did. It took time and it wasn't like I didn't miss her. Rosetta the dog person cried openly about losing her. I cried more inside, like men often do, but one day I started laughing. I remembered Mimi's little cat smile, her purring, and her presence, and when I had first seen her running around as a kitten. My sadness was still there, but I felt good when I thought about her. I was just happy that Mimi had been alive and part of my life.

~David Alan Richards

A Bad Start

She clawed her way into my heart and wouldn't let go.
~Missy Altijd

A coworker knew I was looking for a kitten as a companion for my one-year-old cat. "My neighbor's cat had a litter," she said one day. "They're really cute, especially the gray one with white paws."

"I'll take it," I said, having always wanted a gray cat. "Let me know when the kittens are weaned."

A few weeks later, on my day off, I took the bus to work to pick up my new kitten. The cluster of women surrounding my desk told me my little fur ball had arrived. I edged my way in, expecting to see a fluffy, wide-eyed cutie. What I saw was a dun-colored animal with almost no hair, so skinny each rib stood out. Noting my expression, my coworker turned to me.

"My neighbor gave away all the kittens even though I told her you wanted the gray one," she said. "But a stray cat had a litter in a tree on her property, and this is one of the kittens. Unfortunately, she got a little scared on the ride in. I cleaned her up as well as I could, but…"

One whiff told me what had happened. Anger washed over me. I had not agreed to take a sickly-looking feral kitten that undoubtedly had fleas, worms and other parasites. But the workday was starting and, without food or a litter box, the kitten couldn't stay in the office. I sighed and got more paper towels from the washroom. I placed a layer on the bottom of the now-stained cardboard box the kitten had come in. Then, covering my hands in more towels, I picked her up and dumped her none-too-gently back into the box. She weighed almost nothing and her cry was as thin as her body.

The kitten mewled the whole way home. I got a lot of sidelong glances from the other passengers on the bus, but I refused to meet anyone's eye, pretending the odor emanating from the box had nothing to do with me. When we got home I went directly upstairs to the bathroom, where I had already set up a litter box and dishes for food and water. I opened the box and found the kitten shrinking in a corner.

"You're not staying," I told her, as I picked her up. "I'm going to clean you up a bit and then take you to a shelter. Then you'll be someone else's problem." She barely filled my hands and her body trembled with fright.

"It's okay," I said, keeping my voice soft, "I'm not going to hurt you."

The trembling subsided and she meowed softly. "No way," I said. "That 'love-me-I'm-a-kitten routine' is not going to work. As soon as you're cleaned up, you're leaving."

I wet paper towels and wiped off the rest of "her accident." Even with the smell gone, she was an unattractive sight. Small tufts of hair grew in patchwork over her body and her scrawny tail looked like it belonged on a rat rather than a cat. As I gazed at her, a black speck jumped off her back. Then another and another. Fleas. I crushed a few and hoped they wouldn't hop downstairs. After locking the kitten in the bathroom, I called my vet and made an appointment.

"What's her name?" my vet asked when the kitten and I showed up.

Thinking of fleas and worms, and looking at the salmon-colored skin that showed through the patchwork of gray and cream hairs, I replied. "Salmonella."

The vet raised an eyebrow. "That's quite a name."

"It doesn't matter. She's just a visitor. I want to get her in better shape, and then she's off to the shelter. The way she looks now, nobody in their right mind would adopt her."

The vet nodded and began her examination. "She needs food, which will help with her coat. And something for the fleas. Oh, and we'll need a stool sample because she probably has worms. But I'll bet she's going to be a cutie once we get her healthy."

"I wouldn't bet on it," I said, glancing at the kitten. "Besides, she's at least part feral. Not what I had in mind."

As the vet tickled the kitten under her chin, I mentally added up the bills—examination, flea shampoo, fecal tests. A lot of money for a kitten I was giving away. Still, every animal deserves a chance. Someone would be willing to give her a home. Just not me.

Back home, I dumped the kitten in the bathroom sink and turned on the water. The moment the warm water touched her body, she shrieked and scrambled out of the sink, up my arm and over my shoulder. Then she dug her claws in the back of my shirt and held on.

After a few minutes of twisting and turning, I managed to dislodge her. This time when I turned on the water, I kept a death grip on her. By the time I finished shampooing her, the water was reddish brown from flea detritus. I rinsed her until the water ran clear to the accompaniment of yowls and shrieks.

Wrapping her in a towel, I took her into the den where I sat down on the couch, still holding her in my arms. Her body shook with fright and she whimpered softly. I rubbed her gently and began to murmur the meaningless sounds all mothers murmur to their young to ease their fear. Her body relaxed and the whimpers turned to sighs.

Just before she fell asleep, she gazed up at me. Gold eyes locked onto mine and the hard knot of anger that I had been robbed of the perfect kitten began to soften. "Maybe you're not so bad after all," I said. "I guess you can stay. But I think I'll shorten Salmonella to Sammy."

A tiny purr answered me. Her eyelids fluttered and in that

moment between fear and trust, I knew she had claimed me for her own. The visitor stayed for sixteen wonderful years.

~Harriet Cooper

The Legacy of Boo Radley

A black cat crossing your path signifies that the animal is going somewhere.
~Groucho Marx

It had been raining the day Nicole, one of my students, showed up in my classroom at lunch. Earlier, I had seen her wearing a heavy wool poncho to keep her warm and dry. Now she had it folded carefully across her forearms, and she held it out to me.

"Ms. Murphy, look," she said, her long blond hair, damp with rainwater, framing her face.

I lifted a corner of the fabric and peered into a dark woolen cave. A tiny black kitten with huge ears and glassy eyes stared out at me. In class, we had been reading Harper Lee's novel, *To Kill a Mockingbird.*

"Hey, Boo," I said.

"Can I please stay in here with him during lunch?" Nicole begged. "Some boys were throwing rocks at him and trying to kill him."

The high school had a farm, and Nicole had been preparing for a horsemanship class when she heard a commotion. The boys gleefully admitted they were trying to "kill it" because it was a black cat.

"Of course," I told her, and she settled in on the floor to comfort the terrified kitten. When the bell rang to go to class, she looked at me. "Just leave him here," I said.

"I'll come get him right after school!" she gushed. "I know my mom will let me keep him." And off she went. But when she returned two hours later, she was sobbing. Her mother had met her in the parking lot and would in no way give permission for one more passenger.

"Can you take him, Ms. Murphy, please?" she begged.

How could I refuse? I already had one black cat at home—Calpurnia—a fluffy, fussy thing who had her own special blanket atop my bed. I gave Nicole back her poncho, nestled the kitten inside my jacket to keep him warm and dry, and drove home.

Once there, I poured some cat food in a shallow pan in the bathroom adjoining my bedroom. I set the kitten down near the food and a dish of water. I also arranged a small litter box nearby. The little cat ignored it all, turned slowly, and crept into the bedroom, crawling under my bed, where he sat trembling. I reached under, stroked him gently on his neck, and then left him alone.

Four hours later, he hadn't moved. I didn't think he would survive. He was skinny, undernourished, and definitely in shock. I went to bed, expecting to find a lifeless kitten in the morning, but I awoke in the night to the sound of cat food crunching, then a faint scratching in the litter box, both hopeful signs. I had brought Boo home on a Friday, and that weekend he remained in hiding, creeping out only to eat and use the litter box. When he was still alive on Monday, I took him to my vet. Dr. Olmstead was a kind, gentle woman who loved anything furry. She spoke to the flea-bitten, worm-ridden, half-wild cat as if he held some rare pedigree, telling him he was quite handsome, while in asides to me she explained the special needs of feral cats.

"So you think he'll live?" I asked.

"Oh, he'll live a wonderful life!" she exclaimed.

I was skeptical. But she was right.

It was weeks before Boo would come out. At first, I would come home from work, crawl halfway under the bed, and just talk to him, scratching his neck. After the first week, I began to scoop him up and sit him in my lap while I worked at the computer, to get him used to the idea that human hands could be kind. Finally came the day that he decided, I suppose, that life wasn't all that terrifying. I was at the stove, making a Sunday breakfast, when suddenly he appeared in the kitchen.

"Meow," he said, pronouncing the syllables precisely, as if he'd read them in a book.

"Meow, Boo," I replied.

"Meow," he said again.

And this became our morning ritual. He would return my greeting as many times as I said it to him. That day, he strolled casually over to a sun-swathed patch of tile, flopped over, then rolled on his back. Safe and happy.

Boo grew into a stunningly beautiful cat with a shiny black coat and gorgeous bright green eyes. He looked like a miniature panther, although few people ever saw him. Over the course of the next decade, I don't know how many times friends said to me, "I thought you said you had another cat," followed by, "How come I've never seen him?"

True to his namesake, he remained reclusive, only emerging from the safety of my bedroom closet when the house was relatively quiet and he felt safe. He loved to go outside and creep around in the neighbor's very overgrown yard, and he became a mighty gopher hunter. For some reason, he loved going out in a light rain. He would return to the house and jump in my lap, waiting to be toweled off, the smell of all things wild and woodsy on his paws.

When Boo was eight, Calpurnia died. She was sixteen. For all but the first three months of her life, she had spent every night curled up next to my feet. I missed her terribly, but didn't want to wait too long before getting another cat, since I didn't want Boo to be an only child. Six months after Cal passed, I visited a local pet retailer with an adoption center. There, amongst the tortoiseshells and tabbies, was a small black cat with stubby legs and a chopped off tail. "Sugar Plum" was her name.

"She's been here a long time," a volunteer from the rescue group told me. "Black cats are very hard to place."

When allowed out of her enclosure, Sugar Plum walked straight over to me and jumped in my lap.

"I've never seen her do that," the volunteer told me, "She's usually a bit wary of strangers."

Like her brother, I thought to myself. Of course, she came home with me. And like Boo, it was clear that Sugie had experienced some trauma before her rescue. Boo was only with me for ten years. I miss him every day. But Sugie is here, and when the time is right, I have no doubt that another black cat will find us.

~S. Kay Murphy

Taken by Storm

Kittens can happen to anyone.
~Paul Gallico

All we wanted that day, as we headed out to the pet store, was a jar of tropical fish flakes. The furthest thing from my mind was that an hour later my daughter and I would walk out of the store with not just one cat, but two.

As we entered the store, we had to walk around a ridiculously large cage that almost blocked the entrance. We could hardly avoid looking at its contents.

"Oh, Mom. Look at that adorable black kitten," Emilie said. "Can I pick him up?"

I hesitated. I hadn't even laid eyes on the kitten and knew that it was a bad strategic move to let her handle it, but to my amazement, I found myself saying, "Well, I guess it wouldn't hurt to just pick him up."

Handling the kitten required the help of a sales associate, and he of course aided and abetted twelve-year-old Emilie in her quest to become a cat owner.

"We just got these kittens this morning, and lots of people have been looking at them," Joe said casually. Kittens? It was then that I actually looked into the cage and discovered that besides the tiny black kitten that Joe was retrieving, there was a second, much larger, gray kitten with spiky fur and tufted ears.

"Can I hold the other one?" I asked.

It was here that I sensed intuitively that I had just crossed the point of no return. Because, in addition to the softest, silkiest fur I had ever felt, the gray kitten had a beguiling way of wanting to be cradled in my arms, baby-style, and looking up at me with enormous owl-like golden eyes. It was love at first sight.

I had always wanted a cat when I was a kid, but my parents wouldn't let us get one. Instead we had to be satisfied with a series of turtles and gerbils. They were fun in their own way, but definitely not as much fun as I imagined a cat would be. Somehow the longing for a cat of my own had gone dormant but had not died entirely. As I was scratching the gray kitten under the chin, and he began to purr, Emilie turned to me.

"Could I get this kitten, Mom?" she pleaded. "Please? I promise I'll take care of him."

I didn't doubt it. She'd been a wonderfully responsible pet owner for a dwarf hamster and now fish. But was she ready for a cat?

"How are we going to keep the cat away from the fish?" I asked, trying to buy time, but even to my ears my question sounded lame. The bigger concern was that, unlike hamsters and fish, cats lived a long time. Long after Emilie grew up and moved out of the house, the cat would still be with us. Was I really ready to make such a big commitment? I thought not.

"I'm sorry honey," I said, as gently as I knew how. "I think we'd better just sleep on this. Let's get the fish food and go home and talk to Dad. If it's meant to be, the cat will still be here tomorrow. And that's if Dad says yes," I cautioned.

"Why don't you call him right now?" Emilie asked, reasonably enough. Figuring it was better to get it over with, I did.

My husband thought I had temporarily taken leave of my senses.

"I've never heard you mention you wanted a cat before," he remarked incredulously. "Are you sure you're not just being impulsive because the kitten is cute? Why don't the two of you come home now and we can talk about it?"

That would have been the sensible thing to do, but when are

people ever sensible when they've already fallen in love with an animal they have always wanted to own? I put Emilie on the phone and she wheedled Daddy into agreeing to the cat. And then because we couldn't possibly pick between the two, and it was a shame to separate littermates…

"How much is it for the pair?" I asked Joe. And with that, the deal was clinched. It turned out that the kittens were free to a good home. However "free," as it turned out, was a relative term. The cats needed to be neutered and get their shots, and then there were the cat scratchers, toys, food, cat carrier, litter box, and the dozen and one other things kittens needed. But of course none of this mattered as we headed joyfully home with our darling new kittens.

Smokey and Shadow took our lives by storm. Nothing in the house was safe from these tiny bundles of energy. First the fish had to be moved to a room with a closed door. Then the household plants joined them. Suddenly it was as if we had toddlers in the house again. Smokey ate anything he could find, from rubber bands to the shoelaces on our shoes. In fact, the only good thing that could be said about Smokey's predilection for consuming random objects was that in no time, he had trained us to keep the house clean.

Shadow, the smaller and more nimble of the two, turned his attention to climbing. He soon discovered that it was great fun to climb up the grasscloth wallpaper in the entryway and then slide his way down. The same trick worked on screens and drapes too. As our curious little kittens explored their new digs, we constantly scrambled to stay one step ahead of them. But our biggest problem was still to come when Shadow slipped out the door one evening that first summer and, try as we might, we couldn't find him.

"Mom, we've got to find him tonight, or the coyotes could get him," Emilie insisted frantically.

The roaming pack of coyotes in our neighborhood picked off any unwary housecat that was unfortunate enough to be caught out at night. But trying to find a black kitten who didn't want to be found, at night, was a bit like looking for a needle in a haystack. Reluctantly, we put off the search until daylight. The next morning I was awakened by a piteous cry outside my window. Shadow was home.

It has been eight years now since we first acquired our frisky little bundles of fur. As I predicted, Emilie has gone off to college, leaving the cats at home. Shadow still tries to slip out the front door every time it opens, Smokey still thinks anything on the floor is fair game to eat, and our sofas are a bit worse for wear. But whenever I sit down to write and Smokey or Shadow climbs into my lap, purring rapturously, I forget these things.

~Cara Holman

My Cat's Life

Eat, Play, Love

Please Remember Me

A friend is one of the nicest things you can have,
and one of the best things you can be.
~Douglas Pagels

When Grandma's cat had kittens I was thrilled that Mama let me choose one for my very own. "You'll have to take care of it," she warned sternly. "I have too many babies to worry about whether a cat has been fed."

I barely heard her words as I gingerly picked up a tiny orange kitten. She reminded me of sunbursts and rainbows, with her orange fur and luminous green eyes. I thought she was the most beautiful creature I had ever seen. I kissed the top of the kitten's head and she mewled softly. My heart was bursting with love for her already.

"I'll take good care of her," I said, grinning with joy. "I'll love her always." I called her Cookie.

Susan was my next-door neighbor and my best friend. She was an only child and she always got anything she ever wanted. As soon as she saw my kitten, she wanted one too. She laughed at Cookie's name, saying it was a silly name for a cat. A few days later she showed up at my door holding a fluffy white Persian kitten that she, of course, had named Fluffy. I stared at the small white kitten in her arms, wondering how she could possibly think that this plain white creature could compare with the magnificent colors of Cookie.

"Half the white cats in the world are named Fluffy," I said sarcastically, recalling how she had laughed at Cookie's name. "The other half are named Snowball. You must have had a hard time choosing between the two names." Susan sniffed.

"Fluffy has a pedigree. Daddy said your kitten is a plain old alley cat."

I asked Daddy what the difference was between a pedigree and an alley cat.

"Money," he said wryly. He looked at Cookie as she lay on her back playing with an old ball of yarn. "Cookie is happy, affectionate, and amusing. You can't buy that."

Susan and I and our kittens played together every day. We would sometimes dress them up in doll clothes, with Fluffy struggling defiantly and Cookie languidly allowing me to tie tiny bonnets on her head and put her in doll dresses. She would even allow me to push her around in my doll stroller, while Fluffy would jump out and run away and hide, refusing to suffer such indignities.

The first really sad day of my childhood came when Susan tearfully announced that they were moving away. Her dad had gotten a promotion and they would have to relocate to another state. We played together every chance we got, but the specter of her imminent move put a damper on our play. In our childish innocence we promised to be friends forever.

Susan normally walked over to my house to play because my house was filled with kids, noise, laughter and freshly baked cookies. One morning when she failed to come over, I walked next door, clutching Cookie, as always. Susan's mother opened the door and looked down at me with solemn eyes.

"Fluffy died last night," she said. "Susan is very sad right now, but maybe she'll feel better when she sees you and Cookie."

I found Susan lying across her bed, looking lost and forlorn. She reached for Cookie, and buried her face in the kitten's back and cried. Cookie purred softly and endured Susan's display of grief until she was ready to surrender her to me.

"I'm going to lose you as my best friend," she said in a small voice. "And now I've lost Fluffy too. I'll be all alone in our new town."

I bit my lip, uncertain what to say, because at seven years old I didn't know how to comfort her or help her feel better.

The day before Susan was to move away I lay on the floor and watched a sappy movie that Mama wanted to see. A young soldier was going off to war and his pretty sweetheart pressed a locket in his hand. "I want you to have this to remember me by," she said tearfully on screen.

I went through my things, wondering what I could give Susan to help her remember me. The only jewelry I had was a cheap pair of pink plastic pop beads that I got when Susan and I went to the fair last summer. Everything that I had, she had better. All of her dolls were prettier, larger, and better dressed than the few I had. I had nothing to give to her that wasn't far inferior to what she already had.

Susan and her family were inside their car, packed and ready to go when I walked over to say goodbye one last time. I carried Cookie so she could say goodbye to her too. Susan and I hugged and kissed with Cookie pressed between us. She gave a sharp meow to let us know that she was being squeezed. Susan laughed and stroked her back.

"I never told you before, but I've always thought that Cookie was the best cat ever. I'm going to miss her almost as much as I'll miss you," she said. Our eyes locked and I saw the intense pain of being separated from everything familiar in her face. I pushed Cookie into her arms.

"I want you to have her. You need her more than I do now," I said.

Susan looked at me in disbelief, but her arms wound around Cookie. "Do you mean it?" she asked breathlessly.

I nodded, blinking back tears. "You'll have something to remember me by."

Susan looked at her parents. I hoped that they would refuse to let Susan take Cookie, but I knew that they could never say no to her.

"That's the kindest, sweetest thing I've ever known anyone to do," Susan's mother said, with tears in her own eyes.

Time passed, and I eventually stopped grieving for Cookie, although I never forgot her. I sometimes wondered if Susan ever thought of me. Initially, we sent a few letters to one another, but as Susan made new friends the letters eventually stopped.

When I was a junior in college I got a letter from someone in Seattle. I tore open the envelope, certain that I knew nobody in Seattle. Inside was a typed letter and a picture of a fat orange cat held in the arms of a pretty young woman.

"I found your old address," the letter said, "and I hope you still live there. Daddy got several promotions since I last saw you, and we live in Seattle now. Cookie died of old age recently and I feel compelled to let you know. She was the best gift anybody ever gave to me, and I loved her more than I can tell you. When you gave her to me I was too young to understand the sacrifice you were making for me. Now that I do, I am overwhelmed by what you gave up for me. I've never had another friend like you. Let's reconnect." And we did.

~Elizabeth Atwater

Fearless Emma Pie

Prowling his own quiet backyard or asleep by the fire,
he is still only a whisker away from the wilds.
~Jean Burden

I live in the country and looked out my bay window one day to see what looked like a moving mud ball. I walked across the street and saw that it was a small mud-covered kitten. All I could see were four tiny feet, a little tail, and sad eyes. She had been dumped. I took her to the vet, and the vet dewormed her, bathed her, gave her shots, and stitched up her tail, since something had gotten hold of it — it was a tad short. When I picked her up, she was a beautiful little tiger kitten, a few pounds short of perfect weight, and she purred and cuddled on my lap the whole way home. I gave her a Victorian name, Emma, because she liked to hide under the lace on tables and chairs and in lace clothes. In no time, with the right food and the right care, she became a part of my family that included three other cats: two Ragdolls named Andie Pandi Dandi and Perceval Puttie Tat, and one black female named Olivia.

I soon found out that Emma had some traits that were uniquely her own. For one thing, she loved jumping into pies when they were cooling on the stove. She did not discriminate between fruit, pudding or candied — all made a nice whooshing and squishing sound as her little paws whooshed down and squished through them. This earned her the second name she went by: Emma Pie.

One day when Emma was eleven weeks old, she followed me

out the back door, which faces a wooded area. We ran right into a coyote. I don't think the coyote was particularly partial to me, but Emma thought otherwise. She bushed right up, every tiger stripe tip in the air, shaped her body like an upside down "U," and hopped forward on all four paws toward the coyote. I froze, not knowing what to do, but Emma was in full military stalking mode.

The coyote lowered itself down toward the ground, and Emma hopped forward a few more steps. She looked much bigger than her eight pounds. This kept up for what felt like hours, but must have been minutes. Finally, Emma spit right on the coyote, and I guess that topped the tank since he was gone in a second into the woods.

I hugged that little cat with all my heart, and gave her a special cat treat when we were inside, a custard pie all her own to stomp through. I was still shaking off the adrenaline while making that pie, but I looked over and Emma was calmly grooming herself and preening like all was right with the world.

When my husband came home that evening, I told him the story of Emma Pie and the coyote and he picked out a new nickname for her — the "Ripster." She has been part of our family now for three years, and she still dashes across the floor after an imaginary mouse, and still stomps in pies. She is my little foundling that risked her all for me — I guess it was providential and meant to be that I looked out the window that day to see that little mud ball in the street.

~Pamela Tambornino

The Mysterious Meowing

There is no more intrepid explorer than a kitten.
~Jules Champfleury

When I was seven years old, my kitten, Butterfinger, ran away. None of us could figure out how he did it. He was little, bright orange, and not very fast. But somehow he had managed to get outside past us, or so we assumed. After all, we hadn't seen him in two days. I was taking a bath, pondering my kitten's whereabouts, when I heard a tiny noise. It was so quiet I thought it was only in my head at first. But then I heard it again, and again. A faint meowing was coming from the wall. I rushed downstairs to tell my dad, who, despite his protestations and false claims, loved cats. He ran upstairs, my sister Heidi and I in tow. He put his ear to the bathroom wall, and heard nothing, at first, but then his bushy eyebrows shot up. "I hear it," he told us excitedly.

All of us scattered, putting our ears to various walls of the house so we could pinpoint the kitten's exact location. Though we could hear him in the bathroom, he sounded very far away. I put my ear to the wall in the hallway, and down in the basement, while my dad listened in the living room. It was Heidi who finally pinpointed his location. In the downstairs bathroom we could hear him perfectly. We all gathered around the toilet listening intently. There it was, the meowing, and it sounded close, right on the other side of the wall.

I looked up at my dad, and asked, "What do you think, should we cut in?"

"Nah, it's no good," he said. "We've got pipes running down behind this wall for the washing machine and the upstairs bathroom. We'd have to cut through all the pipes, too."

We all stood there silently, listening to the pitiful meowing, wondering if Butterfinger had been stuck there the whole two days. Then Heidi posed a question:

"Dad, how did Butterfinger get back there in the first place?"

"I don't know, sweetie."

"Well maybe we can get him out the same way he went in," she said.

Heidi was always the smart one, even at ten. We spread out once again, and this time I checked under my bed, in my closet, in the kitchen, beneath the sink, and even Heidi's room. I couldn't imagine how the kitten got in there. Then I heard Heidi call out, "Found it!" My father and I rushed into the upstairs bathroom, where it all began, and found Heidi kneeling in the bathroom closet.

"Back here," she said.

We knelt too, and looked. On the closet floor, in the corner which wasn't even visible unless you crawled into the closet, a whole plank of the floorboard was missing. How did we not know that? We'd lived there for five years and had never seen it. My dad knelt, crawled in, and reached his arm into the hole. "No good," he said. "Can't fit."

Heidi, ever the fearless one, said, "Let me try! I'll bet I could crawl in."

My father protested at first, but relented, and Heidi lowered herself into the hole, after my father tied a rope around her waist so he could pull her back if need be. I watched Heidi's feet disappear into the black hole, and saw her flashlight beam dancing down into the dark. After a few minutes Heidi called back to us, "I can see him, I just can't reach him! He fell down a hole!"

My stomach pretzeled. Was Butterfinger going to starve to death? Or was he already dying from the fall? Soon Heidi was extracted feet first from the hole by my father, like watching a videotape on rewind. Heidi's face was dirty. But again, she had an idea.

"Dad," she said. "Give me a blanket. I can drop it down the hole, and the kitty can grab it, and I can pull him up."

"That won't work," I argued. "Let me crawl down, and I can climb down the hole."

"The hole's too small," said Heidi.

"I can squeeze!" I said, on the verge of tears. I desperately wanted to be part of Butterfinger's rescue.

"Just let me try," she said. Down she climbed once again, blanket in tow. My father and I waited tensely as the minutes passed, listening to the faint meowing coming from the hole, and the sound of Heidi crawling farther away. Soon Heidi's voice floated to us. "I got him!"

Heidi emerged with tiny, dusty Butterfinger, his blue eyes bulging like kittens' eyes do. Heidi handed him to my father, who expertly tugged all his legs and even his tail for good measure. He placed Butterfinger on the floor, and his little orange tail shot straight up like a flag pole as he trotted out of the room toward his cat food dish downstairs. Two days in total darkness, crammed in the cramped shaft between water pipes and sheetrock, and Butterfinger was up and about as if he had been relaxing the whole time.

~Ron Kaiser, Jr.

Mutual Trust

To err is human, to purr is feline.
~Robert Byrne

The little black-and-white Manx kitten reached out from the cardboard box with her yellow eyes and captured our hearts. "We'll take her," we told the woman who had advertised her free kittens in a newspaper ad. It was spring and we were living in Aumsville, Oregon and finishing up classes at a local college. We had just bought our first house—a small gray three-bedroom—and were looking for a pet for two-year-old Jeremy and four-year-old Jason. We carefully placed the kitten in Jason's arms as we drove home, amazed at how calm, gentle and trusting she was as she rested. Jason's eyes gleamed as he held the kitten. We knew immediately there was something special about the cat, but little did we know how amazing she would turn out to be.

We named the kitten Patches and set about making her feel at home in our cozy house. The two boys fell madly in love with her from the first day, arguing over who got to play with her, and incessantly rigging up stringy toys that would capture her eye. She was never lacking for attention. The minute Patches heard voices in the morning she would come running, eager to interact with humans. She had an unusual way of communicating, almost as if she understood us on an emotional level. If we felt sad, Patches would be there, kneading her paws into our arms and looking lovingly into our eyes. She was a giver and a nurturer, and as she grew into a beautiful full-grown cat, she had an uncanny ability to be there whenever we needed a boost. If the boys cried or got hurt, Patches was right there meowing and fretting over them just like a second mother.

Although we tried to keep Patches indoors, inevitably she snuck out the door. One day she disappeared when the boys went out to play in the yard. Fearful that she had run away, we spent the afternoon searching and calling for her. We hardly slept that night, but the next morning she was at the door asking to come in. We were overjoyed and vowed to keep a closer eye on her from then on.

As nature would have it, we noticed Patches' belly begin to grow early in the spring. Before long it was evident that she was pregnant. I knew I would have no trouble giving away her kittens if they looked like her, and I also believed it would be a wonderful opportunity for our two young children to learn about the miracle of birth. I explained the process to the boys, who stared wide-eyed at Patches, then gently put their small hands on her belly to feel the tiny kitten kicks. They became gentler with her from then on, and she became even more affectionate with them.

As the time for the kittens' birth drew near, my father became very ill and we were forced to drive the 300-mile trip to Idaho see him. We were perplexed about what to do with Patches, knowing that she would soon have the kittens and not knowing how long we would be gone. So we decided to take her along with us. We fixed up a box, filled it with soft blankets, and loaded up the car with our suitcases for the long trip down the Columbia River Gorge. Hours later we descended the long hill into Troy, Idaho, and pulled up beside the town park to stretch our tired legs before continuing on to my parents' house. Weary from sitting, the boys were eager to run and play. They forgot about Patches sleeping in the box between them as they tumbled out of the car toward the swings in the local park. I followed the boys closely to the swing set and started pushing them alternately. "Higher," they yelled. "Higher, Mommy!"

We were so engrossed in our fun after the long drive that we didn't notice the car door was left open.

"Oh no," I thought, as I remembered Patches in the back seat. "I'll be right back," I told the boys as I ran for the car.

But I was too late. By the time I got there, Patches was gone. When Jason and Jeremy found out, they sobbed. We searched the neighborhood around the park, but couldn't find her anywhere. It began to get dark, so we drove, hesitatingly, to my parents' house and spent a restless night worrying about our cat. The next morning I drove to town and posted ads in all the store windows about our lost cat. I couldn't forgive myself for letting her run off. I thought of how frightened she must be and felt sick. I knew the dangers she and her kittens might encounter on their own, and I prayed that someone had found her and taken her in. Even if we never found her—I hoped she was safe. Two days later my parents' phone rang.

"I think we have your cat," the man on the phone said. "I'll be right there," I said.

I arrived at the tiny house about one block from the park and knocked on the door. A middle-aged kind man answered.

"She's under the house," he said. "She had her kittens underneath that tree, then carried them underneath the house. I don't know how many there are."

My heart began to pound as we rounded the house to the crawl space opening. I got down on my hands and knees and peeked into the musty, dirty space giving my eyes time to adjust to the darkness. My stare was met by two glowing yellow eyes.

"Patches?" I said. "Come here girl. I'm so sorry."

In an instant, Patches was beside me, rubbing against me—forgiving me for my mistake. As I ran my hands over her, I noted how thin she was now.

"Where are your babies?" I asked her as we cuddled. "Can you bring them to me?"

What happened next still stuns me. As if she understood what I'd said, Patches went back under the house and came back with a tiny ball of fur between her teeth. She gently dropped the kitten in my hands, and then went back for another and another. After she delivered all three kittens to me, she sat and looked at me as if to say, "Can we go home now?"

The man who lived in the house had watched the scenario in stunned silence. "We thought she was wild," he said. "We couldn't get near her at all."

I placed Patches and her three kittens into our travel box and drove her to my parents' house.

"You'll never guess what I found," I said to Jason and Jeremy when I went in the house. We spent an evening of awe watching the love of a mother cat for her children—both feline and human. Patches' kittens were beautiful calico specimens and we were able to give them all away. It was hard to see each one go, but we knew that they had the best mother any kitten could ever have. Long after our beloved Patches was gone, I remembered how she trusted me with her own babies, just as I had trusted her with mine.

~Cheryl Dudley

A Tale of Two Suckers

There's a sucker born every minute.
~P.T. Barnum

My cousin Becky isn't easily rattled. She is, after all, head nurse on the oncology ward of a prestigious hospital. She's as capable as they come. Calm, controlled, in charge. She is not, in any circle, considered a sucker.

But one very hot day at her home in central Indiana, even Becky lost her cool. She was washing dishes when her daughter Jenny raced into the kitchen.

"Mom! Mom! There's something wrong with the kitten!" she said frantically.

Becky dried her hands and followed her six-year-old outside. The kitten lay in his customary spot, his calico fur warm in the sun. He looked content so Becky leaned closer, and then recoiled, pushing Jenny behind her to shield her from what she had seen. On the kitten's soft abdomen was a rounded protrusion—a rusty chocolate color, like old blood. Becky had been a nurse a long time and knew that a dog must have savaged this kitten, for its abdomen had been torn open and its intestines exposed. Periodically, the poor beast bent to lick the wound, and then flopped onto his side as if he were completely spent.

"Find your brother! Hurry!" Becky said.

Attica was sixty miles away, and Becky knew the kitten probably wouldn't make it to the vet's. It was too badly hurt. In spite of all the things her job demanded of her, Becky couldn't help this kitten. Indeed she couldn't even make herself examine the gaping wound. She ransacked the house for a way to transport him, finally settling on an old Nike shoebox. Then she wrapped him in a dishtowel and placed him in the box, lid ajar.

"The kitten's going to be okay, right, Mom?" her son, Jamie, asked as he and Jenny peered into the box.

Becky put on a brave face, not wanting her children to know the gravity of the kitten's condition. She didn't want to lie, but for now, she had to.

"Sure, honey! He'll be fine," Becky said. "But we have to hurry. Get in the car."

They hadn't gone a mile when the cat started to scream out in pain, its voice muffled by the box. Becky looked into the rearview mirror at the kids. Their eyes had gone wide.

"Don't let the kitty out, sweethearts. He might hurt himself some more." Becky shuddered, visions of cat guts smeared on the car's interior popping into her mind. What would that do to the kids? She stomped the gas pedal hard.

The cries continued, now accompanied by raking sounds as the frantic cat tried to break free. Jenny clamped down the lid, eyes wide, for the kitten's agony seemed to have given it Hulk-like strength. Suddenly, the lid popped off, and the cat dashed for freedom, careening across the back seat, into the front, then the back again.

"Roll up the windows! Quick! Before he jumps!" said Becky.

The kitten raged through the car, bouncing off windows, howling, hissing, and finally retching. Becky wanted to join her daughter and cry too. Finally, the kitten came to rest on the floor, exhausted, panting, only bending once to lick the bloody bulge.

"Should I pick him up and put him back in the box, Mom?" Jamie said tentatively.

"No!" said Becky. "He's fine where he is, honey. Just let him rest."

But the kitten wasn't ready to rest. He scratched at the back seat, then shinnied under it until he was beneath the driver's seat, his wailing harmonizing with Jenny's. If this cat didn't die on the way to the vet, it would have to be put down. An animal that sounded like that was too injured to survive. How would the kids take it? In the back seat Jennifer had begun to whine.

"Mom! Mom! I'm hot, Mom!" said Jenny, raising her T-shirt to show Becky her tummy covered with angry pink pinpoints. Jenny had prickly heat.

The vet's office was both efficiently modern and cozy. After wrestling the cat from the car, he was now lying on the exam table, the wound exposed to Doc's professional scrutiny, purring as if he hadn't a care in the world. Apparently, he didn't know he was dying.

"Becky, come here," Doc said.

"Just do what you have to do," she said, shooting a quick look at the children. "Kids. Go outside." She watched them leave and then turned to Doc. "I know you can't save him. I know how badly he's hurt. I mean, for God's sake, his guts are exposed!"

"Becky, come here," the doctor said again.

"Not exactly a medical word, guts, but you know what I mean. Just do what you have to do. It'll be fine. I'll be fine. I'll explain to the kids, though I don't know how," she said and started to cry.

Doc had been around for a long time and seen it all. Becky had known him for years. He knew all about her career. He knew her children, her husband. More importantly, he knew her parents, and when Doc spoke, Becky was inclined to obey. But this time she just couldn't. "Just put the poor thing out of his misery!"

Doc kissed the kitten's calico head and sighed. He turned to Becky and crossed his arms over his chest.

"Someone needs to be put out of her misery today, but it sure isn't this kitten," he said. He took Becky by the arm and dragged her to the examination table. She squeezed her eyes shut.

"Open your eyes, Becky."

Slowly, she did. The kitten gazed up at her, eyes at half-mast as he succumbed to sleep. The poor thing was still purring. Doc turned the kitten over so Becky could get a better look at the exposed intestines. A feeling of surprise washed over her. Then relief. Then the most pained embarrassment of her nursing career.

"You can take this kitten home," he said. For there on the kitten's abdomen, where earlier Becky believed she had seen protruding intestines, was a half-eaten Tootsie Roll Pop—chocolate, in fact. She watched the kitten bend over and give the sucker a long, satisfied lick.

~Leslie C. Schneider

Sidney the Wonder Cat

The cat does not offer services. The cat offers itself.
Of course he wants care and shelter. You don't buy love for nothing.
Like all pure creatures, cats are practical.
~William S. Burroughs

Sidney came into my life when I moved into a studio apartment in San Francisco. It was my first time living on my own, and a friend at the advertising agency where I worked decided that I needed a kitten from her cat's recent litter. The cutest one of the bunch was an orange-nosed American Tabby whom I named Sidney, after the Chairman of the Board of the agency.

The two of us quickly settled into a regular routine. At night, when I put my key in the lock, I could hear Sidney meowing me a welcome home. He would have his evening repast of Cat Chow while I prepared my supper and then we would settle in for an evening of reading or television viewing. When I opened my hide-a-bed, Sidney would wait until I was settled under the covers before hopping up and nestling under my chin for a whispered goodnight.

Sometimes, when I was feeling lonesome and a tear or two trickled down my cheek, he gently dabbed them away with his paw before heading down to the foot of the bed where he curled into a ball of purring contentment.

Some six months after we had become roommates, I was roused

from a deep sleep by Sidney frantically tugging at my blanket. I looked at the clock. It was 3:15 in the morning. "Sidney, what on earth are you doing?" I yelled as he leaped off the bed and headed around the corner toward the kitchen. I threw the covers off and ran after him in a fury. "If you think I'm going to feed you at this hour, you're very much mistak…" Terror cut off my words, leaving me speechless. An eerie light filled the room. A sheet of flame was hovering beneath the stove.

In a panic I rushed to the phone and dialed the fire department.
"Who do I report a gas leak to?"
"Well, lady, you want to call Pacific Gas and Electric."
"The reason I'm calling is there's a sheet of flame under my stove."
"WHERE ARE YOU, LADY?"
As soon as I hung up, I heard a siren and, before I knew it, my tiny kitchen was filled with six huge firemen.

"It's a good thing you called us when you did, ma'am. I don't know what caused this stove to ignite, but you've got one helluva gas leak here. If you had tried to fix it yourself, you could have blown yourself and the whole building to kingdom come. And, if you had closed all your windows on a cold night, you would have woken up dead."

I will never know what caused that stove to ignite. But I do know that a certain orange-nosed American Tabby was, from that night onward, forever known as Sidney The Wonder Cat.

~Juliana Harris

Bathing Beauty

A man of wisdom delights in water.
~Confucius

There are those who say that you don't choose a cat but the cat chooses you. It doesn't matter, since Miss Bess is here and that is what matters. I picked her out of a litter — or she picked me. She was the runt, tiny with a splotchy coat of black, white, brown and orange marking her as a calico. Her skinny body showed her ribs, since the other kittens wouldn't let her feed regularly from her mother. I knew I had to have her. I named her Miss Bess since nothing else seemed to fit.

She grew into her paws and became a beauty. I laughed at her antics and her curiosity. She was forever getting into things. Once I found her playing with my costume jewelry. She had a tangle of gold bangles around her neck, and pearl necklaces decorated her body in loops of purple and blue. Rhinestone combs had gotten twisted in her fur and hung at strange angles. She looked at me hopelessly from the clutter as if to beg for forgiveness, asking to be relived of her excess indulgence. I delighted in making her toys and brought others home for her. She never tired of feathers and little mice filled with catnip, although wicker balls were her favorite. As the days passed we grew to know each other's idiosyncrasies and became very fond of each other. I thought I had learned all I could about her, but I couldn't have been more wrong.

One night when I was drawing a bath I forgot to close the door.

Miss Bess, never one for privacy, nosed her way past the door and into the bathroom. Upon seeing me in the tub she jumped onto the toilet and then onto the counter to have a better view of what I was doing. I like bubbles and they mesmerized her. With nose quivering and head bobbing, she moved closer to get a better look. After jumping from the counter to the floor, she bounded up again this time onto the tub's edge. She peered at the bubbles and brought her nose closer to sniff their scent. I laughed when her nose hit and the bubbles popped. My chuckles set the water in motion and she stared at the ripples. She pawed one only to find that her paw made more ripples. She slapped the water, following the rings with her eyes. Only when they quieted did she regard her paw and the moisture there, licking it until the water was gone. She began to pace the edge of the tub with the grace that all cats possess. As she was meowing her reaction I watched her become more agitated and I couldn't understand why she was getting upset.

And then it happened. Suddenly she jumped into the bath, her whole body launched through the air, and after a tremendous splash she was with me in the tub. Luckily she had landed near the faucet end of the bath. If I hadn't been so concerned about her, I would have been in fits of giggles since Miss Bess is a cat who displays her emotion in her eyes and on her face. What I saw was a mixture of complete shock and sheer joy. She swam around the tub, droplets of water hanging off her whiskers. She looked like she was having the time of her life. I was perplexed to say the least, since I had never heard of a feline who liked water. We stayed in the tub, and I let her enjoy the water for another thirty minutes.

I decided to get out of the tub since the water had gotten cold and my hands were wrinkled. I dried off, dressed, and ran a comb though my hair. I thought that at some point she would have jumped out, but she just puttered about the tub basking in her newfound toy. Finally I pulled the drain, thinking the sound of the water escaping would draw her out but it didn't. I tried to pull her out but she skittered to escape my grasp. I grabbed a towel and waited for all of the water to drain before trying again. Reluctantly she agreed to the rubbing of her fur to get most of the water out. Though she was clearly perturbed to be separated from her newfound love, I coaxed her with promises of more baths. I kissed the top of her head and let her go on her way. She was not dry but I knew that she would lick her fur into a better condition than the towel could. I cleaned up the spilled water from the bath and put the towel in the laundry.

I found her in my bedroom lying on my pillow, a huge wet ring underneath her. Clearly I was not getting to sleep anytime soon, since at night Miss Bess would not sleep anywhere but above my head. I decided to use a hair dryer to dry her off faster, and hoped that the sound would not scare her. I started with a low setting but I didn't need to worry. Miss Bess loved the warm air and being brushed. Soon she was dry and we were both asleep. Later that same month I found out that Miss Bess liked showers too. I thought she would get soap in her eyes and the droplets would annoy her, but they didn't. She just closed her eyes, drew in her whiskers and let the warm water rush over her. She would stay there all day if I let her. When it is time to get out and I shut off the water she scowls at me. Fortunately if I give her a treat she forgives me.

I have often wondered why Miss Bess, with her love of water, did not once tackle the toilet. I am very glad she didn't!

When guests come to visit us I always explain about Miss Bess and her love of the water. I tell them that the best way to make sure they are not bothered by her is to check the bathroom first, as she has been known to hide in the wastebasket, and then close the door tight. Of course this will not protect them from her loud wailing outside the door when she hears the sounds of the shower or bath and complains about being left out. She will ignore whoever has shut her out of the bathroom for the rest of the day.

I don't know who picked whom, but I do know I would not be the same had Miss Bess not come into my life. I love her quirky character and her moods and I wonder what other discoveries we will make along the way.

~Tracie O'Braks

The Ballot Box

The ballot box is the surest arbiter of disputes among free men.
~James Buchanan

My fourteen-year-old son, Steven, thought Britney Spears would be a good name for the new kitten. She didn't really look like a Britney Spears or even act like a Britney Spears. In fact, she couldn't dance or sing, but Steven liked the idea of Britney Spears living in his house. Unfortunately, my husband, Sam, didn't like it.

"Come up with something better," I said.

"Cleo," Sam said, "short for Cleopatra."

"She doesn't look like a Cleopatra," said seventeen-year-old Jeff, who normally couldn't be bothered with family decisions but had taken a sudden interest in naming the cat. "I think she looks like a Kenshin."

"He's not naming the cat after a Japanese cartoon character," said Steven, referring to Jeff's interest in Japanese animation. "That's a dumb name. I'm not naming my cat a dumb name."

"Britney Spears isn't dumb?" asked Jeff, not waiting for an answer.

"It isn't as dumb as Kenshin, the cartoon guy who can't talk English unless he has subtitles," Steve battled back. "You're not naming my cat after a dumb cartoon guy who carries a cartoon sword."

"Look at her face," said Jeff. "She even has markings like Kenshin. See the stripe? That's like Kenshin's scar."

"I don't like it," I said, backing up Steven.

"So, you have a better idea?" asked Sam.

"Of course, I do. I think we should name her Trouble. She has been a pest since we brought her home." I was thinking of how little work I'd gotten done since this kitten, who likes to watch computer screens while being stretched across my chest, entered our life. I was thinking about how she hadn't been declawed yet and how she climbed up my furniture. I was thinking of how miserable she'd been making our older, more set-in-their-way cats, who were simply putting up with her until they were hungry enough to eat her. I was thinking about her level of energy and her inability to find a place to sleep.

"Trouble is a dumb name," the men all said at once.

Thus, the dilemma of naming the new kitten began. But with every dilemma comes a solution. We decided to let everyone who came to see the new kitten vote on a name. We would put Britney Spears, Kenshin, Cleopatra, and Trouble on a ballot. We would even leave a space for a write-in vote. The name with the most votes would win. I set the deadline at 5 p.m. Sunday.

The voters started arriving. First, Steven invited everyone he knew in the neighborhood and from school to vote. Mothers and fathers of his friends came in to meet the new kitten and vote.

"Her name is going to be Britney Spears," he said confidently, as each vote entered our ballot box that looked strikingly like a Reebok box. Then Jeff started arriving home after school and after work and after karate class with a different girl or girls.

"This is Megan," I'd get, as his newest female interest would squeal, "Oh what a cute kitten, Jeffrey."

"Doesn't she look like a Kenshin?" he'd ask.

"Kenshin?" she'd ask, as he pushed a ballot in front of her and guided her hand toward the right hole and helped her fill in the circle with the arrow pointing toward it. I was amazed at how many Megans my son knew. And Crystals. And Stephanies. And Melissas. And Jennifers. And Andreas.

Thanksgiving was a tumult. No one was watching the ballot box, but when I asked my husband if his relatives all voted, he smirked and said, "Looks like it's going to be Cleopatra. "By the way, that was great STUFFING," Sam added.

On Sunday, we watched the clock. At five o'clock, we took the box and began to open it at the kitchen table. A few minutes later Steven arrived. "I have one more friend who wanted to vote," he said waving another ballot.

"Sorry," I said. "Five o'clock deadline and it's ten minutes after!"

"That's not fair," Steven said, "it's only a few minutes late. Every vote should count. In a fair election, every vote should count."

We sat around the kitchen table a long time. We held the ballots up to the light to make sure we were reading each vote correctly. We argued about whether it was confusing with the circles being so close together. We argued about legibility and intent. We argued if one ballot was for Kenshin or if it was a coffee stain. Another ballot had two votes and we decided to throw that ballot out, even though my husband insisted it was chocolate syrup and not a vote for Britney Spears. We argued if we should count the mail-in votes from Grandma and Cousin Bob even though they hadn't met the cat. We thought it would be too close to call, but one name got three more votes. We counted the votes again. The vote came out similar, but not the same. We counted the votes a third time and fourth time until we were convinced we were close enough to have a name. Unfortunately, Steven has voiced a formal protest and said he is taking it to the Supreme Court, so the count is still not official, even though it's been certified by the veterinarian. Her name is Cleopatra, Queen of Denial.

~Felice Prager

A Fallen Blessing

Some people come into our lives and quickly go. Some stay for a while, leave footprints on our hearts, and we are never, ever the same.
~Flavia Weedn, *Forever*

T uffy literally dropped into our lives. It was a Friday morning in early December when I got a phone call from my neighbor about a kitten stuck in a tree in front of our subdivision's clubhouse. With my reputation as the "cat lady" of our neighborhood, it didn't surprise me when I occasionally got calls from neighbors when they found a stray cat.

When I got to the clubhouse I saw a very small gray-and-white kitten squawking pitifully about thirty feet up a very large oak tree. He tried to come down when he saw me, but he didn't know how to back down the tree and his attempts to go headfirst were too frightening for him.

"Come on, boy, you can do it. Come on down," I cajoled. He did a one-step-forward, two-steps-back dance on the limb. "Here, kitty, kitty. Here's some nice tuna. Yum! Come on down."

I waved the tuna can in the air, trying to get the smell to waft up to where the kitten huddled, hopeful that his hunger would draw him down, but it was to no avail. Finally I had to go home to wait for my ten-year-old son, Dylan, to return from school. I left the tuna on a paper plate on the ground at the base of the tree.

Later Dylan, his friend and I went back to the tree with more food and a ladder. The boys held the ladder while I climbed up as far as I dared to go, trying to tempt the kitten with the canned tuna. However, I couldn't get close enough to him and, with a look of complete fear in his eyes, he refused to budge. I grabbed a long branch from the ground to try to use as a bridge for the kitten to climb onto to get to me. It made sense in theory, but I couldn't get the branch close enough for the kitten to dare to step on it. I tried to push him off his perch with the branch, knowing that his fall would be broken by the thick juniper bushes, but he successfully evaded my awkward, swishing tool.

After an hour of trying to convince the kitten to come down, the boys were cold and bored by the unsuccessful rescue attempt. We started home, casting a reluctant backward look at the pathetic creature.

I had a meeting to go to that evening and on my way home I decided to stop and see how the kitten was doing. I hoped that he had found his way down from the tree, but he hadn't. There he was, shivering in the cold wind and meowing miserably. I called to him for several minutes, but then, cold myself, I started back toward my car to sit and think about what to do next. As he saw me leaving, he cautiously stepped farther down the branch, crying, as if to say, "Don't leave me." I thought that he might get desperate enough to jump if he saw me leave, or he might fall because of his fatigue and hunger. I got into my car, started the engine, and waited. Sure enough, his cries reached a frantic pitch. As he ran down the branch toward me, he slipped and hung onto the branch with his front paws.

"Fall! Fall!" I yelled, willing him to drop from the branch. Then fall he did, plunging into the leaves and bushes below with a soft crunching sound. I yelled with joy as he scrambled to the plate of food at the bottom of the tree. He made slurping, guttural noises as he ate. He was so famished that he didn't miss a bite as I picked him up along with the plate of food and put them both in the back seat of my car.

"Honey, guess what I have?" I called upstairs to my husband. Both he and our son came downstairs to see. My husband had that

"You're not thinking about keeping it, are you?" look on his face, but my son was overjoyed that I had rescued the kitten. I was a hero.

Inside, the kitten wasn't fearful. He sniffed and walked around his new surroundings, purring loudly. He had faint tiger markings in his dark gray fur and his paws and chest were milky white. His new-kitten fur had the soft, downy feel of feathers. Our three cats came slinking around to see what all the excitement was about. Sasha, our mothering cat, seemed more curious than upset. Lexie, our wild tiger cat, was all hissy and nervous as she discovered the intruder and would have nothing to do with him. Georgie, our big Russian Blue, looked haughty and miffed at the scrawny little puff's presence in his house. However, our little guest wasn't intimidated by the other cats; he was too busy checking things out. We discussed naming the kitten and came up with Tuffy since he had weathered a long fall and seemed like a pretty tough little guy. Tuffy wandered around some more and then settled into a box with blankets that my son had put together for him. Exhausted from his long ordeal, Tuffy was soon asleep.

We made a "Kitten Found" sign the next day, posted it at the front entrance to our subdivision, and waited. Tuffy was a delightful houseguest—very grateful, curious and friendly. He slept with my son at night and they played "soccer" together, batting a small ball back and forth to each other across the floor. We got a call a couple of days later from some neighbors who had seen our sign. It wasn't their cat, but if we didn't find its owner, they would take him. Their old cat had recently died and they wanted another cat in the house. We waited a few more days to make sure the owner wasn't coming forward and then called them.

"Just a couple more days," my son pleaded. He was enjoying Tuffy and didn't want to give him up. But it was time. We explained to Dylan that three cats were enough for our household, and that our neighbors were lonely since their cat had died and they needed a new cat to love. Also Tuffy needed a home where he would feel comfortable and get the attention he deserved.

Our neighbors offered to come over to pick up Tuffy, but I

wanted Dylan to give him away so he would feel some ownership in the process. I didn't want Dylan to feel like Tuffy had been taken from him, rather that he had willingly given the cat to them. A small distinction, but one I thought would help Dylan understand about doing the right thing. That night, we put Tuffy in the cat carrier and took him over to our neighbors' house. Dylan was tearful and sad on the short car ride over.

"You're very brave and considerate, Dylan," I said, grasping his hand. "I know this is very hard for you." Dylan nodded, looking at me with tears in his eyes.

When we got to our neighbors' house, Dylan very slowly took the carrier from the back seat of the car and even more slowly trudged up to the house. As we entered the kitchen, Dylan pulled Tuffy out of the carrier, held him up like a prize, and proudly said, "This is Tuffy!"

Our tough little kitten took it all in stride, sniffing and meandering around his new surroundings in the clumsy, delightful manner of a kitten. We stayed for a few minutes chatting with the neighbors, and then Dylan became solemn as we got ready to leave. He held back his tears as he said goodbye, kissed Tuffy, then asked the owners if he could visit sometime. They assured him that he was welcome anytime, and that made him feel better. We reminded Dylan that Tuffy was now our neighbor and lived just down the street from us.

In the car on the way home, I reiterated to my son how brave and selfless he had been, and what a good thing he had done for both Tuffy and our neighbors. He was silent for a while, thinking it over, then he smiled. I saw compassion in my young son, which greatly encouraged me. I knew he would grow up to be a caring person, not only to other people but to animals as well. And I saw that the lessons we need to learn about empathy and sacrifice can come from the most unlikely of sources—from a needy little cat who fell into our lives.

~Luanne Porper

The Rescue

Nobody has ever measured, not even poets,
how much the human heart can hold.
~Zelda Fitzgerald

I hadn't planned to go anywhere that day. However, at 3:30 on Friday afternoon I found myself in rush hour traffic on Interstate 5 in Portland, Oregon. What pulled me away from my peaceful day on my small farm in Yamhill County? A year-old orange calico kitten named Buddy. I'm a widow of fifteen years, and after raising our two daughters on the farm I found myself alone. Sure I have other cats. What farm doesn't have more than one? But none had ever entered my life the way Buddy had. Buddy had been one of five feral kittens that had emerged from our woods last September, following their mom into our freshly cut hayfield. Buddy would become something special.

My older daughter had come for a visit, and we had managed to trap three of the kittens. We took them in to be spayed and neutered. She took the two girls and I kept the boy, Buddy. Throughout the long cold lonely winter it was very comforting to come home to someone waiting for me, someone who needed me. Buddy would cuddle with me near the woodstove. He eventually started following me everywhere, so as spring arrived and chores began outside, he became more like a loyal loveable dog than the classic independent cat. When I called his name he came running.

A few months later, a friend of mine needed a place to stay, and she moved in with me for a short spell. She was traveling a lot over the summer, and on one beautiful summer day, she was getting ready for another trip and packing up her car. I was outside stacking wood, with all the cats close by watching. Of course, Buddy the kitten was doing some of his crazy antics like running back and forth and darting between the stacks of wood. After a while, I went in the house to fix something to eat. After my friend finished loading her car for the weekend trip to Seattle, she said goodbye.

"Please check your trunk for any sleeping cats," I hollered out the window.

"Okay," she replied.

Three hours went by and I continued to work outside, but didn't think too much about the cats not being in sight. It was naptime. As it began to get hot, I went into the house to check for phone messages. To my disbelief my friend had left me a message saying that Buddy had jumped out of her trunk at the first rest area in Washington off Interstate 5. He took off through the wooded area of the rest area.

"I couldn't believe my eyes," she exclaimed in the phone message. She went on to say that she stayed in the area trying to get Buddy to come to her, but to no avail. My heart cried for the loss. What was I to do? Questions ran through my head. Did someone catch him and take him home? Did he run away from the cars and trucks? Or did he run into the path of a moving car or truck? Already I felt empty.

After the anger and the reality of the phone message sunk in, I needed to decide what to do. Should I wait for my friend to stop there on her way back to look for him, or drive to the rest area and look for him myself? I grabbed a cat kennel and cat food. Minutes later, I was on the road.

The traffic was bumper to bumper. I started to question if I was crazy for driving three hours, using a tank of gas, and creating this much stress for myself, all for a kitten that might never be found. But even if it seemed crazy in my mind, my heart said it was the right thing to do.

As I drove, I continued to say a little prayer that I would find him, and when I neared the rest area my anxiety was high. There were so many cars, semi-trucks, trailers, and motor homes. What were the chances of me finding a kitten that had been running on his own in a new area for more than five hours? I pulled into a parking spot and realized I had no idea where my friend had been. What direction would Buddy have gone? It was feeling like a futile trip.

I grabbed a can with dry cat food in it and walked into the wooded area. Shaking the can, I kept calling Buddy's name. After fifteen minutes on the car side of the rest area, I headed toward the truck side. In the little wooded area between sections I could hear the trucks idling and the vehicles on the freeway whizzing by. I continued to call his name and rattle the can of food.

Suddenly I heard a faint meow. Where was it coming from? I said his name again, and I heard another meow. It was coming from the left side of the trail. Then I heard yet another meow. I called his name again, and this time I saw him. As Buddy ran to me, I fell to my knees, crying with relief and gratitude.

~Deborah Van Dyke

Chapter 3

My Cat's Life

Do You Know How Much I Knead You?

Summer of Skooter

The power of love to change bodies is legendary, built into folklore, common sense, and everyday experience…. Throughout history, "tender loving care" has uniformly been recognized as a valuable element in healing.
~Larry Dossey

I fell in love the instant I saw him. He scooted across the room and hopped into my lap. With one little eye open, he fit in the palm of my hand. He was the cutest, tiniest, most mischievous-looking, pink-and-black nosed tuxedo cat that I had ever met. The kitten was the last remaining of a litter that had lost their mother, and my friend, who wasn't much of a cat lover, was looking for a home for him. That summer I worked full-time, and, because my home life was so miserable, I took on as many extra shifts as I could, often working six or seven days a week.

My live-in boyfriend, John, stayed home every day in our secluded, three-bedroom house. His only hobbies were playing video games and consuming drugs in an attempt to drown out the desolation and emptiness of his life. The more he was alone, the more depressed he became, and in turn, this only made him seek isolation even more. It was a vicious cycle. It was lonely in our big house, and the kids were away, hiding from the angry, empty atmosphere my partner and I had created. I thought of all this as I climbed into my van with my little passenger curled up in my lap for the drive home.

He was so tiny, and with no mama cat to feed him, he was voraciously hungry. I was the only mother he had, and he did what any hungry baby would do—he looked for something to suck on. He found my thumb, and my heart melted. I was floating with happiness when I introduced the kitten to John. With a scowl, he told me that I couldn't keep him. I convinced him to at least let me wait until after work the next day before taking him back. I was nearly heartbroken, but glad to be allowed to keep him for one night.

The kitten seemed to think that he was a furry little person. He followed me everywhere, and copied me while I watched TV, sitting on his rear end, front paws at his sides as if they were his arms. That night he stayed in our bedroom with us. The night was long since the kitten woke me up every couple of hours, trying to nurse, sucking my hand, telling me it was feeding time. John grumbled every time I got up to get the kitten's milk, and complained that it wouldn't be soon enough when I took the kitten back to my friend.

However, something changed in the morning as I was leaving for work. When I popped my head into our bedroom after my breakfast, I announced, "Okay, I'm going now." As soon as the words left my mouth, the kitty scooted to the end of the bed with a frightened and sad look, and emitted the tiniest and saddest little meow, as if he understood. It was irresistible. John's face softened for a moment and then he smiled.

"Awww, that's so cute, he's crying for you, Betty," said John.

It was the first genuine smile I had seen from John in months. Right then I knew my little tuxedo cat was staying. When I arrived home that evening, it was to an excited John telling me all about his day with the kitten. Happily demonstrating all the games that they played and how the kitten would hunt John, thinking that if he stood very, very still he was invisible and John wouldn't see him. John announced that we should come up with a name. I thought for a few minutes, watching the kitten race around the house chasing him.

"Skooter. He's a Skooter-cat," I said.

That summer was long, lonely and difficult until Skooter came along. He helped us both smile at least once a day, whether it was because I couldn't break him of his sucking habit—he salivated at the sight of any exposed human flesh, and he mauled me when he had the urge to suck—or his fascination with watching the water in the toilet swirl around. He loved it so much that he figured out how to flush the toilet himself just so he didn't have to wait for a human to do it. John spoiled Skooter, feeding him only the best cat food we could find, and caring for him as if he really were an actual human child. And Skooter saved John. I knew John's drug use, chronic depression and self-imposed isolation were driving him crazy. On more than one occasion, John has told me that he had been suicidal before I brought Skooter home. Then, in this tiny kitten, he could see the beauty and wonder in life again.

John and I have since parted ways, healthier and happier. John went off to a rehabilitation program and cleaned up, and I'm enjoying a peaceful life with my two kids, who no longer need to escape their home to find love. When Skooter came into our lives, he fit in the palm of my hand, not even weighing one pound. Today, he is three years old and weighs a whopping twenty-five pounds. He isn't fat—he's just a big healthy guy who still thinks he's a baby. Yup, he still tries to suck on my thumb.

~Louise Nyce

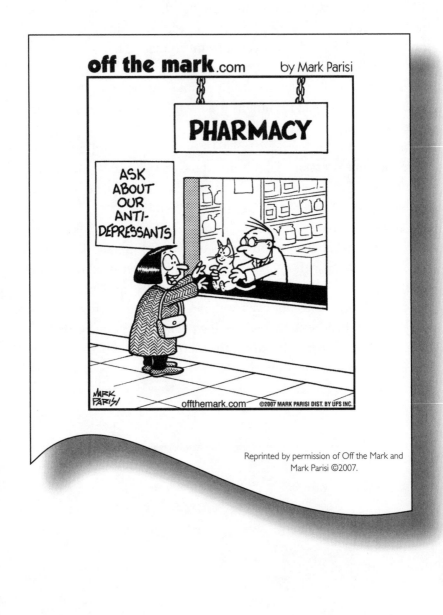

A Feline Friend

The language of friendship is not words but meanings.
~Henry David Thoreau

The petite, gray-haired woman wore mismatched clothing, as if she had dressed with little concern for her appearance. In the waiting room of the emergency veterinary clinic, she sat holding an animal wrapped in a thin blanket. I was waiting for my daughter and her new kitten. A few days before, my daughter had found a sickly kitten next to her college apartment's dumpster. She had scooped up the little feral and begun to nurse the newly named "Lizzie" back to health. Unfortunately, my daughter thought rich food, and lots of it, would revive the weak kitten. Within no time, Lizzie's health was spiraling downward.

"Mom, she's vomiting and has diarrhea," she said to me over the phone. "What do I do?"

Because she was only two hours away, I told her to meet me at a veterinary clinic in a nearby city. Having made the trip in record time, I sat alone and observed others in the crowded room. The aged woman occasionally lifted the worn blanket and whispered to the occupant. There was no way to tell what was hidden in there, but no doubt that the little pet was in crisis. The woman's face told me more than I wanted to know.

Sometime later my daughter arrived with her own crisis wrapped in a sweatshirt. She revealed a kitten barely clinging to life.

My daughter, a cat person like me, would be devastated if she could not be saved.

"You need to be prepared," I warned her. "This little one may not make it." She nodded sadly in agreement.

A short time later, the anxious older woman was called in. I sensed her tension as she brushed past, but I refocused on my daughter, who probably would soon need all the comfort I could muster.

Finally, our turn came, and one of the staff gently lifted Lizzie and carried her away. With Lizzie out of sight, my daughter and I stood silently in a sterile hallway where we had been told to wait. Within moments, an examining room door opened, and the little woman stepped out. Maybe she recognized me as a cat person, but mostly I think she couldn't contain the pain any longer. With no one else to whom she could turn, she walked straight to me and began choking on words, "They're putting my cat to sleep. They can't do anything more for her. She's too sick." And she broke into heart-wrenching sobs.

"I'm so sorry," I said feebly.

"She's been my best friend for eight years," she cried. "Eight years. The best friend I've ever had. What am I going to do without her?" I felt pity for this person whose life was so empty that she had resorted to a cat for friendship. Although I loved cats, I had never considered a cat a friend. In the short time that followed, I offered the old woman kind words but not the hug she so obviously needed. As she lowered her head and shuffled away, I felt immediate regret for not doing more to console her.

Our turn with the doctor came, and the prognosis was not good.

"This kitten is very sick," he said as he touched her almost lifeless body. "With ferals, even if they recover from something like this, they often have physical problems." The only glimmer of hope he offered us was a dropper bottle of medicine, which we accepted with the intent of willing this kitty to live. As I stepped into the night air, I tried to shake off the gnawing feeling that I had failed the old woman by only feebly acknowledging the depth of her loss.

My daughter and I jointly determined that Lizzie would go

home to live with me because the kitty's frail state of health required consistent monitoring and care.

"Keep this sweatshirt, and wear it backwards with the hood to the front so she can always be close to you," my daughter instructed. I did as suggested, and Lizzie gradually began to recover after being "worn" daily as a papoose inside the hood under my chin. Hour after hour, she snuggled and slept while I worked at the computer. She watched as I washed dishes at the sink. She read with me at night. Lying against my chest, she felt my breath and heard my heartbeat for days on end.

As she grew stronger, she began to explore her new world but never ventured far from me. She became part of the rhythm of my life. When I arose, she arose. When I went into a room without her, she cried mournfully if she were shut out. She seemed to live only to be at my side regardless of the activity. From writing and painting to cooking and cleaning, I did nothing without her.

"Cats don't care about people the way dogs do," I heard a television news announcer say, following a dog segment one day. I looked down at Lizzie, who was engrossed by my bed sheet changing skills.

"He never met you, girlie," I said.

Her attachment to me at times was amusing, for she often mimicked my actions. For example, when I bathed, she sat on the side of the tub and gave herself a tongue bath. When I ate, she scooped out her own food with her paw, as if using a spoon, thereby joining me in a meal. And early in her life, she even began copying me by sticking out her tongue. It began one morning when she was staring at me so intently that I stuck out my tongue at her. She tilted her head, focused on my mouth and stuck out her tongue, too. She even allowed my husband to witness this copycat activity. It was amazing to me that she was so in tune with me that she even copied my facial expressions.

Sadly, however, the same love that kept her focused on me also caused her to pine when I was away from home. If I had to be gone overnight for work, my husband said there was no consoling her. She would roam upstairs and down and wail for me. And frequently she carried one of my bedroom slippers to the door through which I would re-enter. If my husband tried to move the slipper, she stubbornly returned it to the same.spot. Of course, when I wore those slippers, I was settled at home with no plans to leave, and, in Lizzie's mind, that's just what she wanted.

In the years since I carried Lizzie in a sweatshirt hood, her devotion continues to claim the heart on which she once lay. It is ironic that my, dare I say, "friendship" with Lizzie began on the same day that the aged woman suffered the loss of her best friend. No doubt someday I, too, will have to say goodbye to my faithful companion. But, hopefully, on that day, some kind soul will offer me the comfort of empathetic arms. And may it be someone who, unlike me in an earlier place and time, understands the importance of a feline friend.

~Joan McClure Beck

Second Chances

We all have big changes in our lives that are more or less a second chance.
~Harrison Ford

The "Free Kitten" sign was nailed to a tree outside a rundown stone farmhouse. Carol and I drove in. Our four children, ages two to seven, were squeezed in the back seat like a litter of kittens in a shoebox. It was our first summer married, each of us bringing two children from first marriages. People predicted we wouldn't make it. Too much baggage on both sides, they said. Too much harm had been done to everybody involved. Damaged goods. Don't jump into something like this. Give it time to be sure. What they were really saying was give it time to die. But we were not dead inside. If you love someone, you should go for it with all you have. We got married before the ink on the divorces was dry, scraped together a minimal down payment for a handyman's special house, and now wanted a family pet to help bond our blended family. We had decided there would be no stepchildren in this family, no "her" children or "my" children, only "ours." A kitten would be a life that belonged to all six of us.

The farmwoman searched the barn without luck, then hollered for her nine-year-old daughter. When the girl appeared, the woman said, "Where's that dang cat of yours?" The girl pulled a dirty gray fur ball from her jacket pocket. The tiny kitten lay limp. Crumbs and pocket lint clung to it. Its mother had been run over and killed by a truck. The plucky girl had fed the litter of three-week-old kittens with an eyedropper, but they wasted away and died one by one until only this kitten remained. He came from barn cats, probably had fleas and worms, and was about as damaged as goods come. But he was gentle from being handled and could now lap milk. Our children cooed and giggled as they passed him around. Like us, he needed a second chance.

In our kitchen sink, we lathered him to kill fleas and to clean off the grunge from the pockets he'd been carried in. The grime rinsed away to reveal bright orange fur. He was like a little orange sun in our drab kitchen. When we dried and fluffed him up, our oldest, Cindy, said, "What'll we call him?"

"How about holding a family meeting to decide?" I suggested.

"Let's do it like Indians!" our second-oldest, Amy, said. We had been pretending we were a Native American tribe with names like "Tiger Lily" and "Princess Moon Flower" to help bond us.

"Indians don't have meetings," Cindy said.

"They have powwows," I said. "They sit in a circle by the fire and vote to make decisions."

"And they eat cake," my wife added, to encourage enthusiasm.

So we sat in front of the fireplace, happily eating "buffalo" cake while the orange kitten scampered inside our circle. He jumped after strings and spun tiny paws as he skidded across the wood floor. "What'll we name him?"

"Cake!" our youngest, Jeremy, said.

The three girls groaned.

He tried again. "Truck!"

"You can't call a cat 'Cake' or 'Truck'," Diana sighed.

"Now, girls," I said. "In a powwow everybody has a chance to speak."

"Let's call him Powwow!"

"Yeah!"

Powwow? Carol looked at me and I looked at her. A ball of fluff named Powwow would represent our new family? I'd hoped for a name with more zing or glitter, but the looks on our children's faces told me this was exactly what we wanted. They solemnly passed little Powwow around the circle, each kissing him on the head.

We've brought fourteen other cats into our home since then; all but one were strays or orphans. Almost all have now passed on, but Powwow lived with us for twenty-three years. That's a lot longer than anyone would have guessed. He attended many naming powwows for other kittens. He supervised three litters, and unlike most male cats, he let kittens climb over him and wrestle his tail. If one annoyed him too much, he would only rest a paw on its head to hold it in a gentle time-out for a few seconds, then lick the kitten to let it know he forgave it, like a good father. I needed to be reminded of that at times during the next twenty years. Maybe he was grateful for the kindness of that little farm girl. Maybe it was just his nature. But he taught us that since we are all thrown together in this world, we ought to care for each other and not be stingy with second chances. Several times he even brought home stray cats for shelter and food. For him, strangers were simply family you have not met. That was a good message for our blended family.

Powwow saw our children off to kindergarten and college and was there when they returned on vacations, standing in line with them for a sample morsel of turkey before dinner. When a boyfriend turned sour, when Carol was in a car accident, when any of us needed comfort, Powwow sensed our distress and curled close, pressing his warmth into us. He visited the neighbors and sometimes stayed for a meal and slept in bed with them. He was a sociable guy who made up for lost family by liking everybody. He taught us that the world was our family. And that second chances can be the best thing that ever happened to you.

~Garrett Bauman

Destiny

Nothing else matters much—not wealth, nor learning, nor even health—
without this gift: the spiritual capacity to keep zest in living. This is the creed
of creeds, the final deposit and distillation of all important faiths:
that you should be able to believe in life.
~Harry Emerson Fosdick

By that October I had been out of the convent for almost a year, and I was living alone in a tiny little house in a tiny little town. During the day I worked as a coordinator for people with disabilities. By night, I was simply a person searching, wondering who I was and who life was calling me to be. I could not remember how to have fun, how to relax, how to play or laugh. It was a quiet lonely time.

My friend Carol called me on a Monday. She said that she had a kitten she wanted me to meet. The little gray soul had followed her friend's family as they walked to church the day before, and had been waiting for them on the sidewalk when they came out afterward. They took the kitten home, only to find that their youngest son was acutely allergic. They gave him to Carol, but her cat was unhappy with the new houseguest, so she thought of me. I agreed that the kitten could come for a visit, but I insisted that it be only a short visit. I had had a childhood allergy to kittens, and I was unsure of my own life's direction. I asked myself how I could possibly take on the responsibility for another life when mine was in such turmoil.

Carol came for the short visit and brought the cutest kitten that

I had ever seen. His round apple-shaped head was almost bigger than his fuzzy gray body, and his copper eyes danced like sunlight reflecting on a pool of water. He was only as big as a handful of grapes, and was playful, clean and healthy looking. I knew immediately that this was not some random stray kitten. I asked Carol to return to the church neighborhood to see if she could find the kitten's family, and in the meantime, I would think about adopting him. I called Carol a few days later to let her know that I had decided to give the little kitten a try. I figured that I didn't have anything to lose. When she answered the phone, I heard the hesitation in her voice. She had found the kitty's family that very afternoon, and had reluctantly left him in their care. I thanked her for thinking of me. Though I realized this kitten was not intended to be mine, I was sad at letting go of the possibilities he had awakened within me.

The next evening I was sitting alone in my tiny little house watching TV. Suddenly, my friend Paula arrived on my porch step with a little gray kitten in her hand. I gasped. Here was my little kitten again, brought back to me by a different friend. She asked me if I would be willing to adopt this little kitten, and seeing the shock on my face she quickly began to explain. She told me that she had just pulled up to the neighborhood convenience store when she was met by a young man holding a kitten who had just run out from the center of the busy intersection. He had been walking by and had seen a little gray kitten in the middle of the intersection, frozen in terror as the cars sped by him. The young man ran into the traffic and scooped up the kitten even though he had no idea what he was going to do with it. The first person he saw was Paula, and he asked her if she knew of anyone who might want a kitten. She said I immediately came to mind. I couldn't believe it. It was the same kitten that had been at my house a few days earlier. I knew in an instant that this was of much more than this earth. He had come to my house twice, and I did not need a third invitation. I said yes with my whole heart.

I named him Destiny, and quickly realized that he had already adopted me. He taught me again how to have fun, to relax, to play and to laugh. My quiet, empty home became one filled with love and chatter. There were no more empty lost moments. Destiny called me to the present moment again and again, and together we passed the next fifteen years as partners in mischief, delight and unconditional love. In the midst of it all, I found my new direction without seeking and struggling. The path was laid out before me simply by living life on its own terms and in the present. If ever again I begin to wonder if God is truly going to provide me with what I need to live and give life fully, I remember the miracle of Destiny, brought to me twice before I knew enough to say yes, bringing with him more gifts than I ever could have thought to seek.

~Cate Adelman

Reprinted by permission of Off the Mark
and Mark Parisi ©1997.

Living with Louie

There is something about the presence of a cat...
that seems to take the bite out of being alone.
~Louis J. Camuti

After my twenty-year-old son, Matthew, died in a car crash, I felt like my own life had ended. For weeks I couldn't breathe, eat, or sleep normally. For months, my emotions were a mess. I couldn't focus on anything and had sunk into a deep, dark depression. I withdrew from others and spent most of my time alone, with only my grief and my memories. Matthew was my baby, my joy, my reason for living. He made me laugh, and he was the one person on earth the most like me.

Friends and family suggested I should consider getting a pet. I thought the idea ridiculous—as if a pet could replace my child. I started going to a grief counselor who also made the suggestion that I get a pet. She talked to me about pet therapy and its benefits. Since she was a professional, I considered it, but the apartment complex where I resided didn't allow dogs. I expressed my dislike of cats, although I had never had one. People suggested a fish, which to me was not a pet.

After months of considering it, I said a prayer, asking God for guidance. I explained to Him that I didn't want a cat that climbed on curtains, clawed my furniture, napped on the dining room table, and other things that I knew to be typical cat habits.

The next day, I called the local animal shelter and was advised that they currently had 300 cats and kittens. I wondered how I would ever choose from so many, if indeed, I felt inclined to get one of the little creatures. When I arrived at the shelter, I explained my situation to them, and told them I was only considering adopting a cat, and that I wasn't really sure I wanted one. They led me to the room which contained the cats under a year old. I spotted a very handsome young male kitten. He was steely blue-gray, with white tuxedo markings. His large green eyes seemed to call to me from his little prison cage. He poked his tiny white paws through the wire door as if reaching out to me. I asked if I could hold this little fur ball named Louie, figuring he was as good as any of them to start with.

When I held him close to me, I could hear him purring loudly, his small body vibrating with pleasure. He stared into my eyes for a long time, as if studying me. I always wear a heart-shaped locket around my neck, which holds a photo of Matthew. After staring into my eyes, he reached up and put his tiny paw on my locket. In that instant, I knew he was my new friend. It was as if he knew my pain.

Within a few short days, we had settled into our routine. We made up games that we played together, and against my own protests, he started sleeping in my bed. I enjoyed feeling his warm little body cuddled up next to mine in the night. Even though he was "just a cat," I felt less lonely with him there.

The next week I told my doctor that she should have written me a prescription for a kitten instead of the medication I was taking. With the aid of this tiny kitten, I was starting to feel like I had a reason to live again. He needed me.

Louie is four years old now, and we are great friends. We have been through good times and bad times. He knows my moods and is always there for me. When I cry, he comforts me by wiping my tears with his paws or his own face. If he makes me laugh, he repeats the behavior to try to make me laugh again. I am grateful to the people who kept insisting that I needed a pet, and so thankful that I finally listened.

~Regina K. Deppert

The Hollyhock

What greater gift than the love of a cat?
~Charles Dickens

everal springs ago I planted a hollyhock flower underneath our family room window. Every spring without fail the hollyhock would push forth a strong green stem from its earthy winter resting place. Its dark red flowers would open up to claim its rightful place in the sun. My husband would sit in his favorite chair watching TV with a perfect view of the hollyhock as it gently swayed in the summer breeze.

"That is my favorite of all the flowers you planted," he said.

I tended to it faithfully in hopes it would live forever and provide him with one of life's simple pleasures. That following May, without warning, he passed away, forcing me to live in a world full of fear, pain, and loneliness. My life and my children's lives were shaken to the core as the pillar of our small family was suddenly stripped from us. My world was shattered and I wondered if I could ever pick up the pieces and continue my own existence. Even though I had four children, they had their own lives, with children, jobs, and their own homes to tend to, leaving me with the feeling that I had no one left to care for.

With nothing but time I went outside to brush away the dead leaves and other debris left by the winter from around his favorite flower. I was anticipating its reliable bloom to sway once again in the summer breeze as if it would bring his spirit to life again.

"I don't know how to live without you," I whispered while brushing away the tears that would not stop falling. My heart was heavy, and my soul lonely and scared.

Just as I reached to grab the dead leaves I heard a hiss coming from behind the stem. Startled, I jerked my hand away. My heart pounded, and my vision was blurry from the tears that filled my eyes. I feared there was a snake under the leaves. I quickly stood up to leave the creature alone in hopes it would eventually move on. Blinking several times to force the tears away, my vision cleared. My fear vanished and compassion rushed into my heart instead. What I thought was a snake turned out to be a tiny black fur ball trying to scare away its intruder. I reached for the kitten and it hissed again. Without hesitation I picked it up and began to stroke its tiny head.

"Poor little thing, what are you doing under there?" I said as I carried it into the house.

"Where did you come from and how did you get all the way here?" I said as I tore up lunchmeat into tiny bite-size pieces. The little cat growled like a large lion as it devoured the food. I laughed at this tiny cat with a fierce heart. "Poor little thing, you must be starving."

Since I had never had an inside cat, I took him back outside after his meal. Unfortunately he found the outside drainpipe, decided to explore and got stuck. After much chaos and dread, he was finally retrieved with some assistance. Realizing how vulnerable he was, I decided he would share my home and gave him what I thought was a fitting name, Piper.

Piper has become a magnificent animal with a shiny, sleek coat and he has filled some of the void in my life. He provides me with company on those lonely nights when the house is quiet except for the sound of the TV and his purring as I stroke his head. On days when my world is dark he lightens my heart and makes me laugh, because to this day, even though he is big and strong and is provided with all the food he needs, he still continues to growl while eating. His strong will and determination inspire me to carry on with my life the best I can.

At the time it seemed strange that a little kitten would appear under the hollyhock that my husband so loved. But what better gift was there to give someone who felt so alone in the world, and who was able to give a tiny creature a loving home? Piper and I needed one another more than either of us knew. The hollyhock never bloomed again. It was as if it was transformed into a tiny kitten. Perhaps the kitten was a gift from my husband to give me something to care for and to give me pleasure, just as the hollyhock did for him.

~Patricia Sabengsy

Better than Medicine

If purring could be encapsulated, it'd be the most powerful
anti-depressant on the pharmaceutical market.
~Alexis F. Hope

Against my better judgment, I visited the cat room at the shelter. Given free rein, I would have filled my pockets with kittens. It didn't help that my husband, John, and I had recently euthanized Abby, our seventeen-year-old black, orange, and white calico. From the day Abby joined our family, John said she was better entertainment than television. I saw how much he missed her.

We took Abby's remaining food and litter to donate to the shelter and I ventured into the cat room, where three white-mittened black kittens climbed the cage bars and reached out as kittens often do. Sitting primly in the midst of the chaos of the three boys was their sister, a white, gray, and sand-colored calico, a pastel version of Abby. She looked like a real lady, not inclined to climb curtains and upset houseplants.

I coaxed John to come and look at the little calico I had spotted.

"If you want the cat, get the cat," he said.

I took her out of the cage and handed her to him.

"What's this smudge on her nose?" He rubbed her nose with his thumb and then handed her back to me. "If you want the cat, get the cat."

"That's not dirt on her nose. It's a little spot of gray fur. Do you want to think about it over the weekend?"

"Here," said John as he reached for his wallet. "She may be gone on Monday."

Smudge promptly proved me a bad judge of kitten character. Her prim lady act in the shelter cage could have garnered an Academy Award. One evening we heard her crying but couldn't find her. Somehow she had opened a bathroom vanity drawer, climbed in and wiggled until it glided shut. Several days later, she opened the same drawer, but this time it didn't shut. It blocked the door and barricaded us out of the bathroom. We kitten-proofed the drawers. She pulled towels off the rods and piled them in the sink to use as a comfy bed. She hid her toys in our slippers at night, pushing them down into the toes so we would have a real wake-up call in the morning. John encouraged her wild behavior, like her racing up and down halls and stairs that we dubbed "the evening zips." He would put her in a plastic grocery bag and drag it on the floor. She loved it.

Several weeks after Smudge's adoption, severe back pains felled John. Medication and rest did nothing to improve his condition. After two weeks, he could no longer go to work, even for a short time. Stoic, John spent the day lying on quilts on the den floor. Before I left for work each morning, I would assemble a box of Smudge supplies: sheets of aluminum foil for John to make into balls, ping pong balls, shoelaces, and a yardstick notched for a string, to which John could tie ribbons or feathers for his kitten to chase. When I came home at noon to get John's lunch, I would crawl around to retrieve and re-box the Smudge supplies.

John's condition worsened. Physical therapy exacerbated the pain that was misdiagnosed as sciatica. A month went by and the pain traveled to his leg as well as his back, and narcotics helped him rest at night. Smudge grew and slept with John on the floor. Tucking herself between his arm and chest, she snoozed when he did and played when he needed diversion. Several more weeks passed with additional X-rays, an MRI, and then the true diagnosis. The head of the femur was dying and collapsing in a condition called aseptic necrosis. He needed a hip replacement, but his loss of weight and muscle strength over the preceding months forecast a lengthy recovery.

The day after surgery, John had a bad reaction to the medication and stopped breathing. After two days in critical care and further complications, his physical therapy was behind schedule. I stayed with him fourteen hours a day, sleeping in a motel near the hospital, dashing home to tend to mail and to check on seven-month-old Smudge. I would find her in the sphinx posture on John's recliner or on his quilts on the floor where they had spent the days. She ate but had no interest in her toys or in me. She mewed when I called to her but held her position on John's territory. I could have cried over her obvious distress at the change in her life. Ten days after surgery, John was transferred to a nursing facility closer to our home to catch up on rehabilitation. The next morning I walked into his room.

"Good morning," I said.

"Where's my cat?" he answered.

I felt cold fear. Was there lack of oxygen after surgery? Did he have brain damage? Didn't he know where he was?

"John," I began quietly. "Smudge is at the house. You're in a nursing home."

"I know that," he said. His eyes had a touch of the old mischief in them. "I checked. If a pet has all its shots, it can come and visit. Go get her."

I raced home, grabbed health papers, put Smudge in her elastic harness and then in her carrier. The harness would ensure I wouldn't be chasing her down the hall or fishing her out from under the bed. But how would she react? Would John be upset if she panicked? I put the carrier on John's bed and opened the door. Smudge crept out cautiously. John spoke to her and extended his hand. Smudge walked up to him, sniffed his face, and then lay down at his side between his arm and chest, just like she did during those long weeks on the floor at home. She spent the next four hours on his bed catnapping with him, chasing a ribbon, and amusing the staff. John's blood pressure dropped to a near normal level. He needed fewer pain pills. Smudge made several more visits before John came home to continue treatment as an outpatient. It was May. Smudge had been his emotional therapy since January. A month later John was back on his garden tractor.

And Smudge? She is now six years old and regularly clears counters of anything she is capable of moving. Jar lids become hockey pucks on the hardwood floors. Shake out a plastic bag and she leaps into it for a ride, still not in the least inclined to be a lady.

~Ann E. Vitale

A Gust of Fresh Joy

Once in a young lifetime one should be allowed to have
as much sweetness as one can possibly want and hold.
~Judith Olney

Charlie and I noticed the very pregnant black-and-orange calico scampering away from the food dish we kept full for our feline "regulars," cats that were too wild to catch, but smart enough to return for their daily meal. We wondered if she might choose our shed to have her kittens. A week passed and Charlie saw a much thinner version of the calico carrying something in her mouth as she crossed our roof. We figured that she'd had her kittens and was moving them to safety. The next day we heard a faint mewing inside the house. We looked everywhere but couldn't find the source of the pitiful cries. Relentlessly, they continued, and we realized that they were coming from inside our wall. It struck us that this would be an excellent time to have our air conditioning system checked. Mike came right away and wasn't fooled by our "check the air ducts" alibi. He had heard the faint mews as soon as he entered the house and had seen our concern focus on the area they seemed to be coming from.

"Want me to bring you anything I find while checking your system?" he asked, grinning.

He went right to work. While he was on the roof servicing the unit, he managed to contort his big muscular body just enough to

A Gust of Fresh Joy : Do You Know How Much I Knead You?   95

peek under the eave. He was in this awkward position when he discovered a hole just wide enough for a cat to squeeze through.

Mike marched through the house and followed the sound that had become fainter after two days without its mother's milk. Charlie and I were trailing hopefully behind when Mike announced, "I've pinpointed the kitten's location behind your bedroom wall. If we're lucky, I'll be able to lift him out through a pocket door. If not, how do you feel about a new hole in this wall?"

Our quick glance at one another led to a telepathic agreement. In unison, we murmured "Do it."

Mike had discovered the pocket door when he saw a tiny paw trying to poke through the opening. Wrestling with the seam, he levered the door open just wide enough to grab hold of the paw. A high-pitched feline squeak was followed by silence as he gently eased the kitten out of its dark prison. Charlie and I were like two kids on Christmas morning. Mike cupped the dusty little feline with his second calloused hand. Unlike its black-and-orange calico mother, the kitten was charcoal gray with distinct black stripes. We just stared at it for a few moments before Mike asked us if we needed anything else looked at. No, we assured him, he had found what we were looking for.

I wrapped our new baby in a soft towel and just held it while Charlie rushed off to the pet store. A half hour later I was still on the sofa holding onto our now-quiet visitor. Charlie had cans of kitten formula and tiny doll-size bottles for feeding. In our first feeding attempt, we discovered that "he" was "she," and we were encouraged by her appetite and ability to drink from the bottle. This began our round-the-clock feeding schedule which we, being in our eighties, never expected to revisit. What should have made us tired seemed to invigorate us. We couldn't stop talking about the things she did, the sounds she made and the games she played. We loved the way she began to hold her bottle while we fed her, and her angry protests when we removed an empty bottle from her grasp.

It's funny now to think that we went through each day with our regular routine, never guessing that what we needed was the excitement of a new dependent. Coming through our bedroom wall via our burly air conditioning repairman, the little kitten managed to blow a gust of sweet joy into our lives. Naturally, we named her Candy.

~Charles and Patria Pettingell as told to Marsha Porter

Chapter 4

My Cat's Life

Who's the Boss?

Surviving Charles

The troubles of adolescence eventually all go away —
it's just like a really long, bad cold.
~Dawn Ruelas

"Having a pet is just like having a child," my mother reminded me when I announced my intention to adopt a cat. I knew that pet ownership came with its own set of responsibilities, yet after several years of pet-free apartment living, my husband Bill and I were anxious to welcome the pitter-pat of four paws into our new house. So, ignoring my mother's warning, Bill and I went down to our local no-kill animal shelter and selected Charley, a small, friendly, black-and-white tuxedo cat just shy of his first birthday.

It was love at first sight between Bill and our new pet. I, on the other hand, had certain misgivings about our latest addition right from the start. All the other cats that fate had previously brought to my doorstep had been large, lazy, older tabbies—the type of cat that wakes up in the morning, waddles over to his food dish, eats, burps, and then waddles back to bed to recuperate from the exhaustion of it all. Immediately, I could tell that Charley was different. He was lively, curious, and always moved front and center, ready to experience whatever life had to offer regardless of the risks.

To Charley, an open window held all the allure of a diving board to Greg Louganis. The roof of our tool shed soon became Charley's personal Mt. Everest, from which he needed to be air-lifted several times. Our bed turned into a feline trampoline, and Bill's sock drawer provided a handy hideout whenever Charley needed a few hours of peace away from his human parents. Outdoors, under my supervision, I watched as Charley regularly faced off with our backyard's community of squirrels. Once, I swooped in and grabbed him just as he was about to rush a stray opossum. Charley knew no fear.

As a result of our cat's joie de vivre, Bill and I spent more time at the local animal emergency center with him than my sister-in-law spent at the hospital emergency room with her three rambunctious boys. During his first two years with us, Charley managed to knock out a front tooth, sprain his back, and break a leg. His spirited personality exasperated me. Yet, in between swinging from the drapes and vaulting from the china cabinet to the dining room table, Charley was sweet and loving, always at the ready with an appreciative purr each time Bill or I tickled his head or rubbed his back. Every afternoon when I came home from work my little kitty ran to the door to greet me, and as I sat reading in the evening, he lay across my feet. Weekends, he watched me attentively as I tended to the garden. I felt his love in each corner of our house, and it was that love that really helped turn our new house into a home.

Eventually, I came to accept that our cat had a split personality—the loving, sweet Charley and the mischievous, troublemaking Charles. With that in mind, I decided to ignore his more unnerving behaviors. I decided to ignore them, that is, until he sent me bumping down the basement stairs on my derrière after an hours-long search for him unexpectedly revealed Charles hiding at the top of the darkened landing. Motivated by my bruises, I embarked on an all-out mission to find solutions for bad-cat behavior. I searched the Internet and sought counsel from my library's wealth of books, magazines, and videos on the subject. In accordance with their advice, I tried changing his diet, limiting his free rein of the house, and even administering relaxing cat massages. Nothing worked. Charles still climbed and clawed, somersaulted and swung.

One day, as our veterinarian, Dr. Andrew, patched up one of Charley's less serious injuries, I posed my concerns. "I've never had such a lively cat," I began, choosing my words carefully. "Do you think Charley might benefit from... um... tranquilizers?"

Dr. Andrew laughed and pointed toward the cat age to human age comparison chart that hung on his office wall, "Charley's just going through his teenage years. Give him time. He'll calm down."

Not quite convinced, I took a deep breath, packed up Charley, and headed out. As I drove home, I continued to doubt Dr. Andrew's words. Teenage years? A cat? During my lifetime, I had had eight other cats. Wouldn't I have noticed this phase with any of them? But, they had all been older rescues. They were probably so worn out from their freewheeling younger years that by the time they got to me, they were grateful for the quiet atmosphere I provided for them. Suddenly, our veterinarian's words made sense to me. However, I still had a dilemma. Dr. Andrew had provided an explanation, but he had not provided a solution. So when I arrived home, I phoned my mother.

"How did you get through our teenage years?" I asked her. She breathed a deep sigh. "Well, there really wasn't a whole lot I could do about them," she said. "I just held on and waited until they were over."

This time, following her advice, I did the same, and eventually my frantic feline did calm down. Now, at the ripe old age of thirteen, Charley may occasionally attempt a half-hearted back flip off the bed or surprise me with his unusual choice of a hiding spot. For the most part, though, his turbulent times are behind him. These days Charley can usually be found at floor-level, lolling in a lazy ray of sunshine, or curled up, snoring in Bill's lap as we watch television in the evenings. Sometimes I look at him and wonder how he ever survived his teen-age years. Mostly, though, I wonder how I survived them. My mother had been right. Having a pet is a lot like having a child. Like most parents, though, I see my sweet, little boy now and realize I would never have traded him or his terrible teens for anything.

~Monica A. Andermann

Let Stinking Cats Lie

Some people say man is the most dangerous animal on the planet.
Obviously those people have never met an angry cat.
~Lillian Johnson

"**S**omething stinks," Stevie said, waving his hand in front of his face as he crinkled his nose. We looked around and saw my cat, Black Cat, standing behind us. My sister walked out the back door and her first words were, "Which one of you two wrestled with a skunk?"

We pointed at the cat. "It's him."

Being a teenager who didn't always think clearly, my sister decided to wash the cat. Stevie and I agreed that her plan had one serious flaw: the idea that the cat would like a bath. We knew from experience how much cats hate getting wet, but we kept our mouths shut. She disappeared down the basement steps and reappeared with the garden hose and a washtub to set up a cat washing station in the backyard. She brought dishwashing liquid from the kitchen and soon the tub filled with sudsy water.

"I got some gloves so I can hold onto a wet cat," she said emerging from the back door with rubber gloves on her hands. "Now all I need is the cat."

We took seats on the cement stairs that led to the garden, the perfect place to watch what would happen. My sister approached the cat with gentle cooing. He lay down on his side for her to pet him. She knelt beside him and stroked his fur a few times. He relaxed.

Before he knew it, she had picked him up by his legs, his front ones in her left hand and his back ones in her right hand. My sister rushed to the tub and dipped him. The first time he surfaced, he looked stunned as if someone had caught him by surprise. Then she dipped him again. This time he surfaced a snarling, wriggling mass of mad cat. She dipped him a third time, and when she raised her hands, they were empty. The cat had disappeared.

My sister stood up and leaned over the washtub, uncertain as to what to do. Then suddenly the cat rose straight up from the water as though levitated by some evil force. He bared his teeth and laid his ears back against his head. He stared at my sister and started running in midair like a cartoon character. My sister gasped and took off around the house. The cat followed, yowling and hissing. Stevie and I sat and watched. My sister streaked by us screaming, followed by the angry cat. After three circumlocutions of the house, my sister's cries for help drew my mother to the back door. She surveyed the scene. The next time my sister ran past, my mother yelled, "I'll hold the door open for you."

Sure enough, my sister found refuge the next time she ran around the back corner of the house. Black Cat stopped. He walked over to the back door where he sat down and began grooming himself. Every time my sister or my mother started to open the door, he hissed at them. Stevie and I lost interest because the chase was over. My sister and mother yelled at us to come inside.

"That cat's crazy," Mom said. "It'll attack you. Both of you get in this house. Go to the front door!"

We looked at each other and shrugged and then wandered off to play. We knew the cat was mad at my sister, not us. We knew to let stinking cats lie.

~Robert Chrisman

Clothed in Love

*I am thankful for the piles of laundry and ironing
because it means my loved ones are nearby.*
~Nancie J. Carmody

We got Princess Beta Goldeneye, "Princess" for short, when I was in sixth grade, which made us both kittens. She was a wide-eyed calico with a strong affinity for scratching posts and shoulders, which she often confused with one another. My sister, Sarah, saved her from a cardboard box on the side of the highway when she caught the package in her high beams coming home one night. She found Princess wet and shivering but alive. The rest of her litter weren't so lucky. It wasn't long, however, before Sarah left for college.

"Take good care of Princess," she told me. "She's used to a lot of attention."

It was a direct order from my big sister, so I went out of my way to make sure that Princess felt properly loved. When I got back from school, I would tell her how my day was and fill her in on all the high school gossip. Princess had grown to be something of a grouch—she would knock all the pens and books off my desk if I forgot to feed her—but she remained the best listener I had ever met. Talking to her helped me sort out what had transpired over the course of my day, and I think that Princess enjoyed it, too. At any rate, she didn't complain.

Most of our bonding had to do with household chores, specifically laundry. While some people hate the mindless task of washing clothes, there was nothing Princess viewed with more anticipation. Even after she stopped playing fetch with cat toys, presumably due to the pride that comes with feline adulthood, she would still help me sort clothes fresh from the dryer. My job was to fold all the warm laundry, and her job was to generally disrupt my efforts by snuggling in between the towels and furring my dress pants. Eventually Princess would get herself tired, at which point she would take on a more digni-fied posture, watching me with sphinx-like stillness except for her serpentine, black and orange tail, which thrashed across the floor in appreciation.

"It's not a very efficient system," my dad told us.

"I'm not saying it's efficient; I'm just saying it works for us."

The cat's silence seemed to indicate agreement. We made a good team.

But six years after Princess Beta Goldeneye became my charge, I was following in my sister's footsteps, moving to Boston for college. Although I was excited about higher education, I was disappointed to hear that there were no pets allowed in the dormitories—something I should have remembered from when Sarah left for college. College life was exciting and engaging, and I would be lying if I said that I missed Princess enough to make those first few weeks unbearable. But as I got settled into the college routine, I began to think of her more and more often. The worst was when I had to use the com-munal laundry machines. I would haul the load to the end of our hall and wait next to the humming appliance with a paperback. It was a nice chance to get some reading done, but there was something miss-ing. Something with wide eyes and a penchant for clambering up my back to claw at my shoulder. Folding my clothes back in my room was positively depressing. It got to the point that I considered going without fresh clothes, just to avoid the empty feeling that washed over me when I got out the detergent.

"She really misses you," Dad said when I called home.

"How can you tell?"

"I can just tell," he told me, and we left it at that.

It turned out that Dad had been withholding some significant details. When I came home for a weekend in October of my freshman year, I planned on wearing the clothes I had left behind—old pants and shirts I hadn't bothered to move to my dorm. But after I trekked home from the train station, greeted my parents, and dropped my bag on my bed, I turned around and saw that a small, concentrated tornado had swept through my room, or at least my wardrobe.

"Dad, what happened to all my clothes?"

"Princess was scratching at your dresser," he said. "She kept raking her claws over it and mewling at odd hours of the night. We tried keeping her out of your room, but she'd just camp outside the door and scratch at that. Eventually, your mother and I gave in and opened your drawers. Why? Did she do something?"

She did. Somehow, Princess—who, as far as I knew, weighed no more than nine pounds—had managed to pull nearly all of my jeans, shirts, socks and underwear out of the open drawers and scatter them across the floor. I was baffled. That kind of physical exertion seemed like the sort of behavior fit for a dog, not the kind of work you'd expect from a cat. Especially Princess. She was royalty, after all.

It didn't end there. Dad had said that Princess missed me, so I was surprised that she didn't come to wind herself around my ankles when I was home for the first time in nearly two months. Once I began to pick up my clothes, I found out why. Princess had been fast asleep between a green sweater and a pair of old khakis I had left at home. When I took the sweater off to reveal her fluffy form beneath, she stared up at me as if to say, "There you are! Can't you see how busy I've been without you here to help?"

Apparently, she'd been sleeping in my clothes ever since my folks relented and let her have the drawers. I scratched behind her ears, and she purred the way she used to when she was just a kitten. "Good cat," I said.

The funny thing was that I actually forgot to do laundry that weekend, so the clothes I wore home were still in the wash when I returned to Boston, and I had to sift through my older threads for something that still fit. I wound up in those very same khakis that

Princess used as a cushion when I caught the early Monday train back to college.

"Dude, what happened?" my friends asked. "Why are you covered in fur?"

I told them it was my cat, but I left out the details. I didn't tell them that I was clothed in love.

~Peter Medeiros

The Wander Years

It is in the nature of cats to do a certain amount of unescorted roaming.
~Adlai Stevenson

Waldo liked to wander. And wander he did, much to the chagrin of his owner, my cousin Mary. He would sometimes be found in the oddest of places: lounging in an abandoned baby carriage on a neighbor's property; sunning himself outside the door of the bakery located in a strip mall across the street; and once, after a three-day search led by Mary's scent-sniffing German Shepherd, Waldo was found locked in the garage of a nearby gas station. With her house so close to a main road, Mary took pains to keep Waldo indoors, yet his wanderlust could not be contained. So deft was he at negotiating closed doors and windows that my cousin frequently wondered if her big, black-and-white tom-cat with the crooked tail and roar like a mountain lion was a direct descendant of the famed escape artist, Harry Houdini. Or perhaps, she once joked during holiday time, Waldo had trained at the North Pole with Santa Claus, where he learned to make his mysterious exits and entrances by shimmying up and down the chimney.

Regardless of his methods of egress, the bottom line was that Waldo went missing on a regular basis, generally returning when the rumble of his empty stomach sent him packing homeward. The fact of this pattern did little, however, to reassure his concerned owner during his extended absences and Mary frequently called me to vent her distress.

One day, a typical phone call came.

"Waldo's missing," my cousin said.

"Don't sweat it," I told her. "He always comes back."

"I know, but I'm worried about him. He's been gone since Grandma's funeral."

I paused. That was cause for concern. Our grandmother's funeral had taken place well over a week earlier. As I listened to my cousin's muffled sobs on the other end of the line, I recalled how difficult the event had been for Mary, whose family shared a home with Grandma. Only months earlier, my cousin, barely out of her teens, had lost her father suddenly to a brief illness. Shock engulfed her and her family. During the times that followed, Waldo had been her comfort, her confidant, easing the ordeal in a way that only a beloved pet can. My stomach sunk at the thought of another loss.

"Don't worry, Mary," I encouraged. "We'll both pray that Waldo comes home soon."

Almost daily, I phoned my cousin for an update on Waldo's whereabouts. Each day, the answer was always a quiet, sad, "He's not back yet," followed by a hopeful, "But I know he'll be back soon."

After several weeks of this same response, it seemed clear to me that this time Waldo was gone for good and it broke my heart to watch my cousin wait in such a hopeless limbo for his return. The next time we spoke it had been a month since Waldo had disappeared. I started slowly, "Mary, I think you might just have to accept that Waldo is not coming back."

"No!" my cousin cried into the phone. "He's coming back. I'm still praying for it."

That night, as I laid my head on my pillow, I said my prayers too, this time for my cousin to somehow find the strength to accept one more loss.

The next afternoon I received a phone call. It was Mary.

"You'll never believe who's back," she sang, a smile in her voice.

Exactly one month after his mysterious disappearance, Waldo had returned home.

Apparently, that afternoon the adventurous kitty simply walked across the backyard, stood at the screen door, and demanded in his trademark roar to be let into the house. Mary's mother was first to spot the bedraggled ball of fur. Had it not been for his roar, she said, she would have never recognized him. His once ample frame had become bony from lack of food and the white fur that once caused a bright contrast against the black had turned an odd shade of bluish-gray. My aunt called for her daughter and Mary ran to the back door for a tearful reunion with her cherished pet. It wasn't until Waldo got his fill of hugs and kisses that he finally sauntered over to his food bowl.

Soon after, we learned from neighbors that Waldo had been spotted near the funeral limousine as it deposited mourners at Mary's house after our grandmother's burial. Family lore has it that he must have jumped into the vehicle, only to be transported to its next destination in another county, his homing radar eventually bringing him safely back to his worried owner. While we never will know for sure what happened that day or what transpired in the month that followed, we do know that the experience changed Waldo. He lived another ten years, to the remarkable age of twenty-one, but he never once wandered away from home again.

~Monica A. Andermann

"We could use someone with your independence."

The Teenage Years

*It's difficult to decide whether growing pains are something
teenagers have — or are.*
~Author Unknown

A dopting Iggy, a three-year-old orange male tabby, turned out to be a bit like bringing a teenager into the house. He was way past the cute and cuddly kitten stage, but was still young enough that he needed some mothering. Only he didn't know how to ask for it.

"He was rescued from a house with multiple cats," the volunteer at the shelter told me when I stopped in front of Iggy's cage. "He was fostered for a couple of weeks and now needs a permanent home. He's a good boy."

I didn't know how good a boy he was, but I did know that his slightly crossed, wide-set eyes reminded me of a sad clown. Since he was used to living with other cats, I figured I wouldn't have to worry about him fitting in with my three. Still, bringing in a three-year-old male when I already had a male and two female cats might be asking for trouble. I moved closer to the cage and Iggy edged forward to greet me. When I put my fingers through the bars, he sniffed them with a wet, pink nose and then rolled over, baring his tummy. As I rubbed his tummy, he closed his eyes and purred.

"So, Iggy, what bad habits have you picked up from your former friends? Are you going to be a good cat or a bad cat?" I asked. Iggy's answer was to purr louder. I turned to the volunteer.

"Can you take him out of the cage? I'd like to hold him." The volunteer grabbed the orange tabby and handed him to me. The moment he was in my arms, Iggy stiffened, pushing away with his front legs.

"So, you're not a cuddler," I said. "At least you're not trying to bite or scratch me." Iggy kept on purring. As I held onto him, I remembered my introduction to my third cat, which resulted in blood—mine—when she was startled and scratched my face, knocking off my glasses. With time, a lot of care and a tube of anti-septic ointment for my scratches, she'd gone from a psycho cat who terrorized me, visitors and even my vet, to a loving one. Maybe Iggy would be easier. Or maybe this would be a big mistake.

"Okay, Iggy, you're coming home with me," I said. Iggy just purred.

For the first week, Iggy was a perfect tom. He showed respect to my other cats, ate whatever I fed him, and slept on my bed, near my right hip.

"Iggy," I said, scratching him under the jaw, "bringing you home was the right decision." I spoke too soon.

Two weeks after I brought him home, he went from well-behaved young man to teenager from hell. He took turns sleeping in the other cats' favorite spots, but fought off anyone who tried to sleep in his cardboard box. He chased his "brother" and "sisters" around the house and got into fights with all of them. He decided he was too old to sleep with me, aka his mother, but not too old to attack my feet while I was preparing his meals.

In short, he was testing his limits—and mine. If he had been a real teenager, he would have been piercing one or more body parts, dyeing his hair purple, and getting a tattoo. I couldn't "ground" him since he was already an indoor cat. Saying "no" to him had the same effect it has on most teenagers—none. And taking away his toys wouldn't work because everything was a toy for him, including paper clips, pens and anything else he could steal from my desk.

"Iggy," I said, when he stayed still long enough for me to talk to him, "I have one nerve left where you're concerned, and it's getting pretty frazzled." Iggy gave me that teenager look that said, "Like I care."

I reminded myself that all cats, even "teenagers" deserve second, third and fourth chances. I hung in there but made sure I always wore shoes when getting the cats' food ready. The worst of his teenage phase lasted six months. Then he began to follow me to bed each night. He would lie on the floor and look up at me, slightly cross-eyed, but obviously trying to tell me something. Then he'd roll over.

"Aha," I said, "my teenager isn't so independent. You still need some mommy time."

I would sit down on the floor and he would roll around near me, never quite touching me, but close enough that I could lean forward and rub his tummy. He'd purr softly and then try and bite my hand. Since he was younger and quicker than me, he often succeeded. However, he never broke the skin.

By the end of his first year with me, although he still disliked being picked up, he started to sit on the other end of the couch, close but not within petting distance. He would sleep with me at least once a week, though it often meant fighting his way past one or more of my other cats. And during our nightly tummy rubbing sessions, he would curl up with his head touching my leg, purr loudly, and no longer try to bite me. Well, not often.

"Iggy," I said after a particularly intense mothering session, "we've survived your teenage years, and you have indeed turned into a fine young man. But you're still not getting the car keys."

Iggy just kept on purring.

~Harriet Cooper

The Kindest Cut

*I learned a long time ago that minor surgery is when
they do the operation on someone else, not you.*
~Bill Walton

The night before Garfield's neutering operation, he stared at me with wide green eyes from my daughter Janette's arms, mirroring her sadness although he had no idea why. He just knew his water and food dishes had disappeared. Doctor's orders—nothing to eat or drink the night before surgery. Suddenly he caught her off guard and successfully jumped away from Janette, running off into the next room.

"I love Garfield the way he is! Don't take him to the doctor!" Janette cried.

"We can't risk adding to an already overcrowded world cat population," I insisted. Then I glanced at a few scratches on her hands. "The doctor also says it will calm Garfield down a bit."

"I'll miss him!" she cried.

"You need to get some sleep, sweetie. Garfield will be fine," I assured her with a hug and a kiss.

Later, I couldn't fall asleep myself. Garfield was getting fixed in the morning. He was going to be hospitalized overnight. Who would lie on top of my feet the following night to keep them warm? What if he never forgave us for submitting him to such torture? What if something went wrong at the vet? It's a mystery to me how my husband, our four children and I became so attached to this cat in four

The Kindest Cut : Who's the Boss? 117

short months. Yet, the next morning I was standing in the vet's office, my heart breaking as the competent nurse started to walk away with him to perform a very necessary surgery.

"Do you need me to stay?" I asked, as Garfield tried to wrestle the kind nurse, oblivious to her substantial size advantage. She shook her head as she disappeared into the operating room where I'm sure she had backup. I knew it had to be done, even though no one wants to see a loved one go through pain. Forget about keeping down the kitten population—I had watched tigers spraying their territory on the Discovery Channel and had no desire to see that happen to my sofa. Bringing home a calmer cat wouldn't hurt either.

I could hardly see to drive home through the tears filling my eyes. I opened the door to the house and for the first time in four months I could open it wide—there was no Garfield attempting to make his weekly break from his housecat existence. I walked down the basement stairs without tripping over him, as he would usually run around my feet trying to get my attention. I sat at my computer without his warm body on my lap trying to catch the pointer on the screen. How had life existed without him? We should never have named him Garfield. There was nothing fat or lazy about our cat, unlike Jim Davis' cartoon cat Garfield. Our Garfield was more like Bill Watterson's Hobbes of *Calvin and Hobbes*. He was originally a barn cat, and he never forgot his first few months of hunting wild barn mice. He was constantly leaping from nowhere to pounce on our unsuspecting and usually bare feet. The vet suggested that if he had the procedure, he might be a little less wild.

The kids came home from school that day with sad faces, missing their little pet that always ran to the door. They knew he was running to try to escape, but they always pretended he was running to see them. At their insistence, I called the vet to check on Garfield, and was informed that he was sleeping soundly post-surgery and all was well. Must be nice, I thought later, as it was taking me forever to fall asleep without my feline footwarmer. The next morning, as I turned on the tap to brush my teeth, there was no furry face to push aside and fight with over the stream of water in the sink. How boring. As soon as I got the kids off to school I was back at the animal hospital, signing the credit card receipt to repossess our cat. I waited expectantly for him to be brought out but after a few minutes the nurse appeared empty-handed. What went wrong? I panicked. They had told me it was a simple, routine surgery to neuter a male cat! But every surgery involves risk....

"Could you please come get Garfield yourself?" the nurse asked. "He doesn't want to cooperate with me."

What a relief. Nothing went wrong—he was just being Garfield. I dragged him out of his cage as he tried to scratch and bite, and took him home so he could attempt to bite the waiting arms of my children. He made me want to rethink my stand against declawing, as I half-heartedly considered another visit to the vet. Then I reminded myself that I wouldn't like my fingernails yanked off, so how could I do it to Garfield, the youngest member of our family?

Garfield did appear calmer by that evening, but it was obviously just a result of the anesthesia, since on day two of recovery he was back to his old self with a vengeance. He was on a rampage against anyone who had a part in letting him suffer at the hands of the evil vet. He seemed to want to inflict scars on us to match the scars he bore. If a barn mouse had gotten lost and ended up in our house he would have been dead meat. Ferociously defending yourself and your territory all day takes its toll on a cat. Garfield's a lover and a fighter, but he knows when to give it all up at the end of the day. He docilely reassumed his role of my nightly footwarmer and everything was fixed, permanently.

~Jayne Thurber-Smith

Tapped for Service

*Those who bring sunshine to the lives of others
cannot keep it from themselves.*
~James Matthew Barrie

When I walked into the pet superstore that Saturday, all I wanted to do was buy cat litter. I just made a tiny detour to visit the adoptable shelter animals on display. That's when Laser — a five-month-old Siamese kitten — reached out of his cage and tapped me on the shoulder. Little did I know that he was going to change my life.

I took Laser home, and he continued to be extraordinarily outgoing and friendly. When I learned about a local animal-assisted therapy volunteer group, I knew it was for us. What could be better than doing volunteer work with your pet? Although cats are a minority of the pets involved in animal-assisted therapy — the vast majority are dogs — Laser turned out to be perfectly suited for that line of work.

People often ask me what Laser actually does during his therapy visits. His job consists mostly of cuddling. We regularly visit a children's hospital, the university psychiatric geriatric unit, and a local nursing home. Whenever my schedule permits, we also go to the palliative care unit at the university and other facilities. Even after volunteering for twelve years, I am still astounded by the small miracles that animals can work for people who are suffering or in pain.

Once a severely burned teenager with much of his body wrapped in gauze was sitting in a wheelchair in the lobby of the children's hospital. Laser sat on his lap, but was not satisfied with sitting just on top of the blanket — he tunneled underneath it. That was unusual for Laser, and the young man gave a big grin. His nurses later said that it was the first time he had smiled since he had been in the hospital.

Another time a hospice patient asked for a cat visitor. Laser visited her every week for three months, and even as she grew progressively weaker, the woman always perked up when Laser arrived. She loved it when he curled up on her bed so she could pet him and talk to him. We visited her for the last time just two days before she died. Even though she was in and out of consciousness, she smiled when I put her hand on Laser's back, and when we left, she whispered, "Thank you."

One woman we visit at the nursing home eagerly looks forward to Laser's visits. She always tells the same story about how Laser visited her for the first time right after her shoulder surgery, and how she made an effort to use that arm to pet him. Every time we visit her she holds Laser on her lap, rocking him and speaking softly in his ear so that only he can hear.

Along with cuddling, Laser likes to wrap his front paws around the neck of anyone who holds him. So while visiting teenagers on the psychiatric unit of the children's hospital one day, I told them that Laser's specialty was giving hugs. To my surprise, they all lined up wanting hugs and Laser willingly obliged. Afterward, one young lady told me, "That felt so good. It's been so long since I've had a hug."

I am grateful every day for the privilege I have of seeing Laser touch lives and make people happy. And I think how different — and less fulfilling — my life would be if Laser had never tapped me on the shoulder that fateful day.

~Nancy Kucik

The Miraculous Mr. Whiskers

God helps those who persevere.
~The Qur'an

The newspaper ad read "Free Kittens" and gave a number. The lady who responded to my call said she only had one left, a tabby, and it had been the runt of the litter. When I offered to come by to take a look, she said that she would rather meet me somewhere, like in a parking lot. We agreed on a spot on the outskirts of town, in the parking lot of a small store. Shortly after I pulled in, a white Ford Escort pulled up with a harried woman at the wheel and three kids rolling around in the back seat. A toddler grabbed a white-footed tabby kitten, squeezed it a bit too hard, and shoved it out the window to me.

"The neighbor's kid cut off his whiskers, and he's got some fleas," she stated. Then she rolled up her window and they were gone before I could open my mouth.

I placed the kitten in my car and ran into the store for some cat food and kitty litter. When I came back the only sign of my new passenger was a tiny piece of cat poop on the driver's side floor mat. The cat was supposed to be a present for my daughter Rose's fifth birthday. What had I gotten myself into?

The big day arrived and Rose was smitten with her new kitten.

What he lacked in whiskers, he made up in attitude. Scratched and beaming, Rose named her new pal Mr. Whiskers.

Mr. Whiskers had a prickly personality. He seldom relaxed, and had more fight than purr in him, but Rose doted on him and endured his moodiness like an overindulgent parent. We kept Mr. Whiskers inside because we lived in a wooded area and heard coyotes howl nearly every night.

One night, a friend came to help tear down a shed and there was a lot of going in and out the front door. Mr. Whiskers slipped out and didn't return. That night before bedtime, Rose stood on the porch in her bare feet calling for her kitten, but Mr. Whiskers didn't come. I told her we would try again in the morning, but I was worried that Mr. Whiskers would not make it back.

First thing the next morning, Rose went out on the porch again to call for her kitten. Nothing. I knew that the coyotes had gotten him. I walked the property while she was in school, looking for tell-tale scraps of fur or drops of blood, but I found nothing. The coyotes did their job well. Rose came home, called for her cat again, and tried hard not to cry when he didn't come. I, too, tried hard not to cry when I heard my daughter standing on the porch, calling "Heeeere Kittykittykittykitty" over and over and over again.

Over the next few days, Rose tried magic to get Mr. Whiskers back. She tore a piece of paper in half, wrote something on each piece, slipped one piece under her pillow and went out on the porch with the other piece. She closed her eyes, mouthed some words that I couldn't hear, and threw that other piece of paper into the air. When the piece of paper landed on the walk, she asked me not to pick it up, because it was a spell to bring the kitty back. She also mixed up a concoction of stuff from the bathroom cupboard and the spice drawer and asked me to not throw the potion away, because "it's to help find kitty." I stashed the bowl of magic glop atop the refrigerator, feeling like a complete enabler. I had no hope that Mr. Whiskers would return, and I felt awful, like I had betrayed the trust of both the kitten and my daughter. I pictured Mr. Whiskers, thrilled to be out on his nighttime adventure, suddenly feeling the hot jaws of a coyote closing around the back of his neck.

After about a week, and after bracing myself for her tears, I told Rose that I didn't think Mr. Whiskers was coming back. But Rose wasn't ready to start mourning. She had plans to implement phase two of Operation Find Mr. Whiskers.

"Mom, I've seen people put up posters when they lose a pet," she said. "I think we should make some posters."

I said to myself, "I would have done that a week ago if I thought the cat was still alive," but I took a deep breath, and said to Rose, "Okay, we'll do it. But don't get your hopes up." I wondered if this was a mistake, letting her pursue what was clearly a lost cause.

We found a photo of Mr. Whiskers in a rare state of repose, sacked out on Rose's pink poncho, and made posters. We walked the neighborhood; I tacked some onto telephone poles while Rose carefully folded hers and slid them into newspaper boxes. Each time she put another poster into someone's box, my heart crumbled a bit more. How much longer could I let the front-porch-calling, magic and posters go on when I knew that all the hope in the world wouldn't bring her kitten back to her?

Two days later, the phone rang while Rose was in school. "I got one of your posters, and I think I had your kitten. It was pretty banged up. I took it to the animal clinic," he said.

I called the clinic and they told me that they had an adolescent tabby female dropped off from our part of town. I dashed out of the house, still telling myself "female." It was probably the wrong cat. But my heart was soaring, and I couldn't stop smiling. I finally felt hope.

At the vet's, a skittish, skinny tabby with a scraped chin and scabby front paws was carried out to me. It had been two weeks, and I wasn't positive that this beat-up kitten was even ours. The vet said that the animal's injuries were probably sustained by jumping out of a moving vehicle. I recalled that our friend had driven an open-topped jeep the night that he had come to help us with the shed. Maybe Mr. Whiskers had stowed away, and then panicked.

I gently rolled him over to look for the spot on his inner rear haunch that I remembered. An electric charge shot through the animal as it tensed, expelled a hiss and swiped furrows in my forearm. It was Mr. Whiskers alright. And the vet had one more bit of information for me: Mr. Whiskers was a Miss.

I couldn't wait to break the good news to Rose when I picked her up from school. The big reunion went down in typical Mr. Whiskers fashion: Rose was ecstatic and tenderly scooped up her kitten. She was promptly rewarded for her undying faith with a scratch on the cheek.

"Ow," she said, as she lovingly deposited the cat back onto the couch. "Mom, I knew he was out there somewhere. I knew he would come home if we kept looking. I knew we could bring him back."

"Honey, I've got to tell you something," I said, looking into her eyes. "You are the one who brought your cat back. I thought the coyotes had gotten him. I didn't think those posters would work at all, because I thought he was already gone. If you hadn't pushed for those posters, we might have never found your cat."

"That's okay, Mom," she said. "I know you didn't think Mr. Whiskers was okay. But I did. I believed enough for both of us."

In the excitement of finding the cat, I had forgotten to tell my daughter that He was actually a She. "Honey, guess what? When I went to get the cat, the vet told me that Mr. Whiskers is actually a female cat."

"That's alright," said Rose, nonplussed. "We'll still call her Mr. Whiskers. And when Mr. Whiskers grows up, she can have kittens! When Mr. Whiskers has kittens, can we keep one, Mom?"

Fortunately I stopped the "Absolutely Not" before it came out of my mouth. Because if that ornery kitten could vanish and teach me to have a little faith, I had better be open to what Mr. Whiskers' future kittens might have in store for me. Also, I had better stock up on Band-Aids.

~Anne Erickson

The Felonious Feline

It's always darkest before the dawn.
So if you're going to steal your neighbor's newspaper, that's the time to do it.
~Author Unknown

Several years ago, my husband and I visited the local animal shelter to adopt a new feline friend. We had recently bought a house and moved into a new neighborhood. We shuffled past several rows of orphaned meowing cats ranging from kittens to seniors. A Siamese-mixed kitten, about six months old, leaned his front paws against the wire cage and released a piercing yowl and grabbed my attention. I stopped to admire him and peered into two pleading sapphire blue eyes.

"Would you like to see this one?" the attendant asked.

"Yes, please," I answered. He had beautiful eyes that seemed to say, "Please pick me."

The man released the lock. When the cage door swung open, the furry ivory-colored feline leaped into my arms and wrapped his front paws around my neck, giving me a big hug. My heart melted, and as I stroked him he began to purr.

"I'll take him," I said, and smiled at my husband. He winked back.

We signed the papers, paid the fees, and rescued the milky white male creature. On the drive home I named our new mysterious friend Sherlock, for Sherlock Holmes, unaware of the episodes that would follow.

Sherlock bonded quickly to us and his new home, or so I thought. At about two o'clock in the morning a week later, a strange scraping woke me. The noise sounded like a metal object being dragged across the linoleum. My husband grabbed his flashlight and we both crept down the stairs to investigate. We entered the kitchen, flipped on the light and discovered Sherlock. He froze, my heavy metal keychain hanging from his tiny mouth. I always placed my keys on the hall table when I arrived home from work.

"Sherlock, I'll get you some toys tomorrow. You can't play with my keys," I said, and made a mental note to stop at the pet store on my way home the next day. Sherlock dropped the keys, and using his feline wiles, he produced a thunderous vibrating purr before padding over to me. I scooped up my new four-legged companion, scolded him, and returned to bed.

The next night Sherlock rummaged noisily through the house, waking us again. My husband shrugged, turned over and returned to sleep. I did the same. In the morning, I noticed my hairbrush and wedding ring were missing from the bathroom.

"Sherlock, did you take my wedding ring and brush?" I asked. He looked into my eyes and then rotated his head side to side as if to answer, but purred instead. He trailed behind me and rubbed against my legs as I searched the kitchen. A thorough hunt finally revealed my things hidden under the kitchen table.

"Bad Sherlock," I scolded. He purred even louder and circled my legs.

Since Sherlock displayed high nighttime energy, I decided that I could either shut each room's door or put him outside after dark to prowl. That first evening when I opened the front door Sherlock eagerly raced outside.

The following morning, I cringed when Sherlock crept in. A child's sneaker, an old rubber glove, two used batteries and a baseball mitt were scattered on our porch.

"Sherlock. Why did you take these things? They don't belong to us," I said. He face wore a puzzled look. I waggled my finger at him. "Don't steal anymore. Do you hear me?" He flashed a mischievous grin, turned and walked toward the kitchen for his morning meal. I packed the stolen goods in a box and placed them in the garage.

As the days wore on I had to face the facts. Sherlock was the neighborhood thief and his nightly loot was mounting up. Red-faced, I informed the neighbors of Sherlock's scavenging ways. As Sherlock's sordid reputation spread, the neighbors would come to visit us when something of value had disappeared. Sherlock would offer hugs to the people he had stolen from. I convinced myself that Sherlock was compensating me with treasure in exchange for adopting him.

I will always be grateful to Sherlock for introducing us to our new neighbors in his unique way! And because of his nightly forays, he was loved and missed by them all. In the end, I forgave his thieving ways, because the first thing Sherlock Holmes had stolen was my heart.

~Suzanne Baginskie

The Force Was with Him

The Force will be with you, always.
~Ben Obi-Wan Kenobi

"The kitties don't love me anymore," said our five-year-old son, Robbie. My wife, Vicky, and I heard his plaintive cry from the kitchen where we were finishing our breakfast.

"How do you know?" I called out. Robbie approached the table.

"When Lukey or Princess see me coming, they run away. They hide under the sofa," he said. "I just want to hold them."

Robbie led me into the living room and pointed to the hiding place. Getting down on my hands and knees, I peered under the sofa. Sure enough, two pairs of beady eyes were watching me intently.

"Well, Robbie," I said, "your mother and I have told you before that Lukey and Princess are no longer babies and sometimes they like to be left alone. They are getting older now and don't need all the attention they once did. They still love you because you saved them and you named them."

"No, they don't," Robbie said angrily, and stomped from the room.

Robbie's dissatisfaction with the felines' behavior had been growing steadily for the past few weeks. Lukey and Princess, two foundlings, had been a part of our family for four months. The next door neighbor had found four kittens in a cardboard box at the dump and brought them home. When Robbie saw the tiny, longhair tiger cat, and then the cat started to purr when Robbie picked her up and hugged her, Vicky and I knew the family had a new addition.

For the next three days, Robbie fed her in the garage, cleaned up after her, played string tag with her, and had her sleep in his lap. Because Robbie loved tales of adventure and fantasy he dubbed his cohort Princess Leia. Four days later, as Robbie was feeding Princess, another abandoned kitten wandered into our garage, much to Robbie's delight. He gave the shorthaired gray tabby some food and rushed in to give us the news.

"Guess what? Princess has a brother!" Robbie said. "Come see the new kitty!"

Princess did get a new brother, and his name was Luke Skywalker.

For the next couple of months, Robbie and the cats were devoted to one another, especially around meal time, string tag time, and rest time. Then, as the cats gained the freedom of the house, spent more of the day outside, and became more independent, Lukey and Princess decided that Robbie's constant lavishing of affection should be avoided. Not that all was lost, however, because the two cats allowed him to pet and hug them when they were asleep on our bed and Robbie could sneak up on them, feed them, open and close doors for them, and clean their boxes. Over the next ten years, all three of them grew up and matured.

After Robbie graduated from high school, he went to college, and only came home for certain weekends or vacations. He missed his "kitties" and, when at home, he would make a special point of reminding Lukey and Princess what the two of them owed him. He would hold one or the other and say something like, "Remember that I'm the one who has made all this rest, relaxation, luxury, recreation, and support staff possible. Please don't forget that."

However, the best laid plans of cats and men often go awry, and all three lives changed when Robbie was diagnosed with leukemia in the fall of his junior year. After many weeks in the hospital undergoing chemo and other treatments, Robbie came home for the Christmas holidays. Because he was so weak and tired, he spent much of the time in his bed. Lukey and Princess, who had never shared his bed previously, except under duress, suddenly determined it was the place to be.

Once again the three of them were inseparable. Whether Robbie was reading, watching TV, or sleeping, his friends were there. Lukey would be either on his back with his paws up in the air nestled between Robbie's side and arm or on top of Robbie's chest. In either position, he would often be purring. Princess resided on a pillow beside Robbie's head.

Just before New Year's Day, Vicky and I went into the bedroom and saw the trio engaged in their usual companionship. With Lukey on his chest and purring, and Princess by his head, Robbie smiled at us and said, "The kitties love me. I think they have always loved me."

Four days later, Robbie returned to the hospital in Atlanta, but the insidious disease did not allow him to leave it. Shortly thereafter, Lukey and Princess succumbed to old age. Vicky and I were left with little solace but the wonderful memories of our son and his two cats. Now, Robbie, Luke Skywalker, and Princess Leia all reside together in that galaxy far, far away.

~Leigh B. MacKay

My Cat's Life

I Am Cat, Hear Me Roar

38

Escorting a Cat

After a day's walk everything has twice its usual value.
~George Macauley Trevelyan

I looked down at her and she looked up at me. The year before my wife and I had picked her out from the animal shelter. "Do you want to go for a walk?" I asked.

"Meow!"

It was a cute, furry face — black, white and yellow — and her tail was wagging.

"Just don't run away, okay?" I said.

"Meow!"

I opened the front door and she slid out, brushing against my leg. I set the timer on my wristwatch and I followed her. I was hoping for a pleasant thirty-minute walk. She stepped off the porch, hopped down the rock ledge, trotted along the side of our house and ran across the backyard. Then she ran up the hill toward the cypress bush and crept inside. She sat on a soft bed of leaves and calmly peeked out through the branches into the nearby woods. As a younger man, I would never have had the patience to walk a cat, or wait for it to emerge from under a bush. But now I enjoy the solitude it brings. I enjoy being alone with my cat.

My wife wants to keep our cat safe inside the house, with soft pillows and plush carpeting. But I think that's cruel. I say, a cat should be a cat. A cat should sniff, explore and experience the world. My wife insists I walk our cat on a leash. But me walking a cat on a leash is not going to happen. Our compromise is that I escort the cat. Wherever the cat goes, I go. So, essentially, the cat walks me. I've been escorting Kiwi each day after work and, recently, have realized that I am bonding more with my cat than with my wife. I am learning so much about this beautiful little creature. She loves climbing high into trees, eating insects, and sniffing deer poop in the grass. This summer she was stung on her pink nose by an angry yellow jacket while sniffing a poisonous mushroom. If my wife knew any of this, she would have a coronary.

I enjoy getting out of the house to walk the cat. I enjoy watching Kiwi crouch down and wiggle her little butt before she attacks a tree. I enjoy watching her tentatively paw green grass, spiders and soft moss. I laugh at her wide-eyed, befuddled expression when she contemplates the acrobatic squirrels jumping from tree to tree, or the birds pirouetting in the blue sky. Someone once said, "A dog is prose; a cat is poetry." I agree. Our cat is a poem with fur.

It's peaceful walking my cat. A cat does not argue with me or yell. It simply goes about its own business. I merely follow. There is no friction or difference of opinion with my cat. Sometimes I step out of myself and watch myself watching Kiwi. My neighbors must think me eccentric—an odd middle-aged man, always alone, wearing a red hat, smiling at something in a bush or a tree. Watching my cat, I've discovered that she is a graceful and agile hunter who thinks falling leaves are animals. She enjoys rubbing against thorny pricker bushes. I've also noticed she's becoming more confident and, with a rolling gait, is venturing deeper into the woods behind our home.

As a younger man, I didn't observe things much, or appreciate simple pleasures, like walking a cat. But I do now. Consequently, I'm happier. I'm content being alone with my thoughts and my funny pet. Sometimes I take along the word jumble from the local newspaper, or an unread section from the Sunday news. Periodically, I look up, not wanting to miss anything special, like Kiwi pawing at a worm or chasing a chipmunk.

Our young daughter adores our cat, too. Since she is our only child, my wife and I figured a cat could be an excellent companion—like the little sister she never had. After school, our daughter enjoys putting Kiwi in grocery bags, playing fetch with her, or dressing her up in dainty outfits. A cat isn't a sister, but it's better than nothing.

"Zoe," I sometimes ask, "do you want to come with me to walk Kiwi?"

"No, Dad," she usually says. Zoe has just turned thirteen and prefers the computer, texting, or going to the mall with friends. I guess a teenager needs to be a teenager, just like a cat needs to be a cat. But a father needs to be a father, so I end up walking her little sister alone. The other day I was looking down at the word jumble, trying to unscramble the letters—hitbr. When I looked up, Kiwi was gone.

"Kiwi?" I called.

I looked everywhere, but her camouflaged fur blended well into nature. I couldn't find her anywhere. She had vanished. I searched around our home a third time. "Why weren't you more careful?" cried my wife in my mind. I searched for Kiwi in all of her favorite spots, under the porch, under our car, behind flowerpots, and up the hill under the arborvitae bush. But the only thing I saw was my wife's imaginary worried face. I began to think about "Lost Cat" posters stapled onto telephone poles. I thought of Zoe, and "Lost Child" photos on milk cartons. I kept searching.

"Kiwi?" I called out. Where was she? It was getting dark.

"A cat has to be a cat," I practiced saying, which I would soon have to repeat to my wife.

"We lost her!" she would sob. I zipped up my jacket and kept searching, but my heart was beginning to sink.

"Kiwi!" I tried again. It was getting darker and colder. I thought about the dogs in the area. I thought about the stray cats in the neighborhood. Strays are filthy. Would Kiwi, our little poem with fur, become pals with them? Would she pick up bad habits, and go wild? Would Zoe's little sister prefer independence and freedom instead of our soft pillows and plush carpeting? Kiwi was an important part of our family. Did she know we loved her? Did she love us?

"Kiwi?" I called again. I looked at my watch. Our quick thirty-minute walk was turning into a horrible nightmare. I walked up the hill to the cypress bush and peered into the woods. "Kiwi?"

I stepped into the woods. Dead brown leaves crunched under foot. "We lost her!" my wife's voice repeated in my head. As I walked deeper into the woods, I remembered an event eleven years earlier. My wife was sitting in a white hospital room and a kind doctor was sitting beside her. He told us that the child growing within her wasn't viable. I looked up into the trees blowing in the cold night breeze and I began to understand her better.

I continued to search the woods and suddenly felt a sob coming on. It came out long and hard, but it was dark and I was alone, so it was okay. All I could see was my wife's sad face as the doctor consoled her. Her sadness was rubbing off on me because, I realized, her sadness was my sadness.

Then I thought of Zoe, our other piece of poetry. Earlier this morning she was arguing with her mother about going to the mall with her friends. Each day, Zoe is growing more independent and confident. A teenager has to be a teenager.

That's when I heard something rustle in the leaves, and I felt something rub against my ankle. I looked down and staring up at me were green eyes glowing in the dark. It was Kiwi. I bent down, picked her up, and cradled her in my arms. I held her against my leather jacket and kissed the back of her head. Then we started walking home. A cat has to be a cat, I guess. But sometimes it's a baby.

~Peter Wood

39

Tunnel of Love

The manner of giving is worth more than the gift.
~Pierre Corneille

Thunkity-thunk. The sound made my heart drop since it meant that our teenaged white ring-tailed cat, Quare, was on the move and he was not alone. The noises grew louder as my cat neared our den from the far end of our home. The pounding sounds did not come from the hall however, but rather they reverberated from under the trailer—the return vent had been turned into a tunnel. Quare was dragging in his latest catch for our reluctant approval.

These thundering noises put into question the reason we selected this remote, rural location. We needed a peaceful place where Rob could study and I could write lesson plans, so we parked our trailer next to the Bosque River. It felt ideal. When Quare discovered that he had open access to the den via the return vent, we thought it was terrific. No more getting up and down to let the cat in and out. He'd pop up from behind the couch where I sat grading papers and we would cuddle. Rob and I were sure this cat tunnel would aid in our quest for peace, but we were quick to learn that when night fell, peace became elusive. That was when our nocturnal teenaged pet, in the prime of his life, roamed the woods and brought Mother Nature into our house.

Call me calloused, but knowing my cat offered his gruesome prizes because he loved us did not impress me. Pouting, I said, "Well, we certainly named him right. Quare Closum Fragot means trespasser, and right now he's trespassing into my personal space."

Nevertheless, Quare, my own hunter-intruder, was oh so worth loving.

"Should we close up the hole?" I asked Robert.

"What and miss all the excitement?" he replied.

Not happy, I took a self-taught course called Tunnel Sounds 101. A gentle whoosh meant Quare was zipping home alone. When the noise changed, I knew I was in for R.E.M. or Rapid Evacuation Mode. If the tunnel sounds became magnified, it meant he bore a souvenir from his night out on the river. I knew I only had seconds to escape a face-to-face introduction to his limp gift. In a flash I would jump up seeking a safe zone, the papers I had been grading floating to the ground behind me. Since a "safe" area in a confined mobile home is contradictory, I would settle for dashing into the tiny kitchen.

On one occasion Quare emerged into the den with a long black snake. Fighting for its life, the snake wrapped its body around Quare's white tummy, neck, and front legs. It looked like Quare was wearing a snakeskin tuxedo. Proud of his accomplishment, he strutted, but not for long since he kept tripping on his squirmy catch. Robert, having heard Quare's clunking followed by my scream, hurried to the den. Distracted by Robert's arrival, I took my eyes off the coiled couple. Quare made a beeline for me. Something touched my leg and my feet did not stay planted for more than a split second. I took a mighty leap, and clamped onto Robert—knocking his glasses sideways. Once he peeled me off him, and reset his glasses, Robert slipped to the door, opened it wide and pointed.

Quare looked at him, then me, and something inside him shifted. Under his snakeskin tuxedo he crouched into a protective stance. He would defend us from the snake. A low sound came from his throat, and for a second, the snake stopped twisting. In a tactical move, Quare slipped his front legs free from the writhing mass, and maneuvered to the door. He bore his squirmy burden like a backpack, and marched his prisoner out into the dark of the night. We were safe—for now. Little did we know that the worst was yet to come.

It was late afternoon, and I heard crashing thuds in the vent. The sounds hammered and echoed. A greater fear settled in me since Robert was at school and I was home alone. My instinct was to run out the door, so before my papers had a chance to float to the floor, my hand had already opened the door. But something sounded strange. The bumping sounds banged separately. Was Quare being chased? Startled at the thought, I froze in place. I realized that if my cat needed help, I was it. Quare popped up from the vent, scrambled to me, clawed his way up my leg, and into my arms. Intense vent sounds continued. Green cat eyes and my own brown ones were riveted to the place we knew an intruder would surface.

We heard the creature at the entrance, but it did not immediately emerge. Instead there was a weird high pitched screech-wail accompanied by banging sounds. Finally, yellow eyes, and an enormous body infiltrated our home. It crouched on the top of the couch, and it seemed as stunned as me. The panting cat was twice as big as Quare and had black markings on his tufted ears and legs. A bobcat. His hackles were spiked and I prayed that he would simply dash out the open door. Instead he hissed, and screamed long and loudly. Quare had dissolved into a trembling mess. Frantically, he dug his claws into my arm. I pried him off me and sat him between me and the wild creature.

"You got us into this. Now get us out," I told him.

Quare squatted and shook. Since he was being no help I forced myself to move. I inched slowly to Quare's food bowl, scooped out a handful of dry cat food, and cautiously tossed it toward the open door. The bobcat sat down. I picked up my quaking cat, claws facing out, and walked farther away into the hall. I peeked around the corner into the den to watch the growling complainer. Hunger won. The yellow-eyed brute ate his way to the door.

At the threshold he paused and studied the woods, his bobbed tail rigid. His muscles tensed, then suddenly, in one bound, he leapt over both steps. I dropped Quare, ran to the door, and pulled it shut. Then, I rushed to Robert's study, grabbed his thick law dictionary, and dropped it on top of the tunnel-hole. Now we were protected by the law.

Shaken, I plopped onto the couch. Within seconds, Quare came and curled up on my lap. As I nestled him, I realized that there were times my little teeny-bopper protected me from intruders, and other times, I protected him. We had become quite a team. Still, I wished he had purred, "Don't worry, I won't bring you any more trophies."

But alas, his gift-giving didn't stop.

~Sandy Lackey Wright

Welcoming Audrey

There are two means of refuge from the misery of life—music and cats.
~Albert Schweitzer

Twelve years ago my husband and I were living a pretty good life in a small southern Tennessee town when our world was shaken to the core. Our middle child, Donnie, was suddenly taken from us in an auto accident in North Carolina. Four-year-old Audrey had been Donnie's cat for three years. Donnie had gotten her at a shelter, and she was a true joy in his life. After Donnie's death, since we had a very rambunctious dog, we made the choice to let his stepsister, Charlene, take Audrey into her home. Audrey was happy there for five years, and then Charlene and her family decided to move. Since our dog had developed inoperable tumors and had to be put to sleep, we offered to take Audrey, and we were anxious to shower Donnie's cat with our love.

I knew that there would be an adjustment period for Audrey because after our dog's death we had adopted a large cat named MoJo from a local shelter. He was a lover and a sweetheart, but he was also domineering in his size and stature. Audrey would have to learn to get along with her new companion.

Poor Audrey came into our home and cowered under MoJo's watchful eye. When she came out of hiding to eat her food, he would try to get close to her and she would hiss and retreat at the very sight of him. He began to enjoy stalking her and watching her reaction. Audrey would check to see if he was around, and if he was, she would run into a room to hide under a bed or a piece of furniture. Then MoJo would stand guard at the doorway to keep Audrey imprisoned in the room. I tried chasing him away so that she could come out and feel safe, but MoJo was making it extremely difficult—and enjoying it a little too much.

About that time I heard from my friend Suzy whose dog had passed away. Suzy lived in Alabama and enjoyed the company of her small dog, and I knew how much she was going to miss him. She had also visited me a few months before and become attached to MoJo. He would follow her everywhere, jump in her lap, and even slept on the bed with her. Suzy told me during her visit that if we ever needed to find a home for MoJo, she would take him. I knew that MoJo was just the healing companion that Suzy needed, and I also knew that with MoJo in another loving home, Audrey would have a chance to be loved by us and to adapt to her new environment. So the transaction occurred. Suzy adored MoJo, and we began the task of winning over our late son's cat. Little by little Audrey came out from hiding. She would eat, bask in a spot of sun by the back door, and occasionally let us pet her, but only when she felt like it. I could not get her to come close to me or sit with me, and I knew that that is what a cat enjoys best—sitting on a lap and being petted and loved.

One afternoon I played a CD of my son's guitar recital. It did not occur to me that Audrey was accustomed to hearing guitar music, even though she had lived with Donnie, who was a classical guitarist. He undoubtedly practiced and played on a daily basis. As soon as Audrey heard the music, she came running to me. She was purring and rubbing against my legs. I reached down to pet her and put her on my lap, and that is where she stayed, purring and responding to my every touch. It was my son's music, finally, that soothed the frightened cat, and assured her that this was a safe and loving place. All I could say to her was, "Welcome Home, Audrey."

~Beverly F. Walker

My Name Is Tabitha

Are we really sure the purring is coming from the kitty
and not from our very own hearts?
~Emme Woodhull-Bäche

Sometimes little inconveniences can be a godsend. Such was the case one wintry morning as I walked to the local newsagent to collect the Sunday paper. When I got there, I was disappointed to find that the doors were still locked, on the coldest day of the year so far! While huddling under the awning to avoid the wind, I began reading all the ads posted on the storefront window. One stood out from all the rest with a caption that was irresistible. It read:

"My name is Tabitha. I am very sad because my owner has had to be taken to a nursing home and I am not allowed to come! I need to be an only pet as I have not been known to get along with others. I need to be loved and spoilt. My guesstimate age is about nine years old. However, that is a matter of opinion, wouldn't you say? All I want for Christmas is a home and a loving lap to sit upon."

When I looked at the three pictures attached I fell in love. There was a telephone number to call. Since I did not have a pen and paper handy, I kept repeating the number over and over until I reached home. As soon as I walked in the door I wrote the number down. The timing had to be just right before I let my husband, Jack, know about the ad. Since we had lost our cat five years before we had sometimes talked about getting another pet, but that was as far as it had gone.

Lately, every time I brought up the subject Jack's reply was always the same, "Let's think about it with our heads and not with our hearts."

The next day at work all I could think about was Tabitha. Once I got home, I got up the nerve to tell Jack about the ad I had seen.

"Here's the number," I said, handing him the piece of paper.

My husband agreed on one condition. "We will take her on the basis that we can return her after a week, if either party is in disagreement," he said.

"Oh, all right," I said. "But you are making her sound more like a piece of merchandise than a cute, cuddly cat."

To my surprise, he handed me back the paper and said, "So, make the call."

I was thrilled but apprehensive too. I called and Julie, the previous owner's daughter, said she could bring Tabby over the following evening. I was both elated and hopeful that Tabitha would choose us as her new caregivers. I rushed home from work Wednesday evening to ensure that our home was neat and tidy as we waited nervously for our visitors. When the doorbell rang, I sprang to my feet. As I welcomed them, Tabitha greeted us with a shrill "meowwwww." Once she was free to roam, she rubbed against every nook and cranny she could find, making it her territory. I watched Jack's expression change from ambiguity to acceptance in minutes. I could see that we were in agreement about making her ours.

It has been two weeks since Tabby has been with us. I wonder what she is thinking behind those curious green eyes as she watches us. While we are both trying to adapt to her cat behavior, I am sure she is trying to adjust to our human ways. We notice she purrs to Frank Sinatra. It turns out that Tabitha's former owner loved his singing too. One chapter has closed and a new one has begun.

~Terri Meehan

Cat Season

The cat is domestic only as far as suits its own ends.
~Saki

One morning in early March a scrawny gray-and-white cat wandered into our front yard just as my husband had predicted. That winter we had lost our elderly calico, the last of a lineage that graced our home for two decades. I wanted to fill our empty nest with a cat from the local shelter but he insisted we wait. "Spring is just around the corner," he said. "It won't be long till some stray shows up."

We still had several cans of stinky salmon-flavored cat food in the cupboard so I filled a bowl and left it on the porch for our visitor. From that day on, the feline we nicknamed "Snooty," because of her aloof behavior, had a free meal ticket. I had hoped for something friendlier than this homely homeless creature that kept her distance and only showed up at dinner time, but she was obviously starving and needed us.

It didn't take long to notice Snooty's low-slung belly and enlarged teats. Then one afternoon I saw her in front of the vacant house across the street with three young kittens. When we tried to approach, they all scurried under the house. We continued to feed Mama Snooty and soon her timid babies arrived to join in our back porch feast. More bowls of food went out but we had to watch through the window. They all scattered if we came too close. It was clear this feline family was afraid of people. I began to research feral cats and found an animal shelter that would loan us a trap to catch the kittens. If we hoped to raise them, they had to be taken from their mother by the time they were five weeks old. Otherwise they would never adapt — they would always be feral.

By early April, Snooty had disappeared but her children still showed up regularly at mealtime. We set the wire-framed trap on the back porch and placed their dinner inside. I felt heartless capturing them like wild game but the shelter convinced us that it was the right thing to do. Feral cats live short and difficult lives, and Snooty was proof that they would only produce more feral cats. We watched and waited, out of sight, as the curious little ones sniffed around the cage. My husband rigged a string under the kitchen door that attached to the latch on the trap. After a day or so, hunger took over and one by one the kittens cautiously entered the cage. I cringed each time I pulled the string and opened the kitchen door to see the desperate fear on their furry little faces. Although they clawed and tried to squeeze from our grip, they never let out a cry. Feral cats learn early that silence is important for survival. Within a day we captured the female and the male who looked the most like his mother. But the third kitten, a fluffy male tabby, avoided his fate for a few more days. On one attempt to grab a meal, the trap caught him in the rear end as he fled. He still wears the battle scar — a permanent kink in his tail.

When all three of our adoptees were finally safe indoors, they huddled together silently in a small box, inside a large wire cage on our living room floor. There were none of the usual mewling kitten noises, and although we left the cage door open all the time, they only ventured out at night after we went to bed.

Through the summer months our new family slowly adjusted to us. We lured them out of hiding with food and feathers on strings and catnip-stuffed mice. My husband built a wooden scratching tower and wrapped it with rope. Soon they were playing "King of the Mountain," climbing up and pushing each other off.

By the time fall arrived, we were ready to take down their cage. With unlimited entertainment, cuddling and plenty of food to fill their round little bellies, they finally preferred to crawl in our laps to sleep.

The following spring, when we opened our doors, I was concerned our brood might return to their feral ways. I held my breath, watching as our three feline teenagers cautiously stepped out onto the porch. Soon they were slinking across the lawn, their heads darting in all directions, exploring the outdoor sights and smells they hadn't seen for months. I worried all day they wouldn't return. But several hours later, all three wandered home. They'd learned where to come for food, shelter and love. It only took one season to refill our empty nest. And three more to turn a litter of terrified feral kittens into well adjusted, happy cats. On any given evening, you'll find them curled up and purring in our laps.

~Maureen Rogers

Warning, He Bites!

When a cat chooses to be friendly, it's a big deal, because a cat is picky.
~Mike Deupree

I entered the cat section of the shelter, looking at the pairs of eyes peering back at me, observing all the ears turning as my footsteps echoed down the hall. I had come for Homer, a smallish black cat with a gentle disposition, but then I was told that he would not like our new puppy. So I had to leave Homer and see if there was another cat that wanted to come home with me.

Midway down the hall I was drawn to a cage with a large message written in red marker on the information card: "Warning, He Bites!" The slim, buff-colored cat was asleep in the back of the cage, but as I peered inside he opened an eye and smiled — sort of — showing two tiny white fangs.

A young cat, less than a year old, he swiftly got up and came to the front of his cage. Loud purring spilled out through the bars as he nuzzled the metal grid. I wanted to touch his long, soft fur but I remembered the sign and hesitated. I had always had a way with cats, even strange ones, and had never been bitten or clawed, but then again I had never encountered a cat with a warning label before.

He turned around and bent his head against the cage. I had a clear path to give him a scratch behind his ear, which most cats enjoyed. He continued purring as I carefully stuck my index finger between the bars and touched the soft fur behind his ear. Then he froze. The purring stopped.

I didn't move my finger for fear he'd move faster than I could. I waited to see what he would do. One paw was lifting slowly as if to hold my arm in place—I assumed so he could give me a good bite. Then the paw halted and a few seconds of purring began. But then it stopped. Bravely, I gave his ear another scratch. The paw moved again and I saw a fang. I braced myself for the stinging pain of a bite but then the purring began again.

For half an hour I stood at his cage letting him get used to me petting him. In the end he did not bite me, much to the shelter manager's surprise. She had watched the whole thing and exclaimed that I must for sure be his special person because no one else had been able to touch him without being nipped.

Despite his warning label, I took this wonderful cat home and for seventeen years he stood by my side—biting when necessary, but purring much, much more often. If I had listened to that warning and passed him by I'd never have known one of the best friends of my life.

~Shawn Marie Mann

Big Bang Bailey

Most of us rather like our cats to have a streak of wickedness.
I should not feel quite easy in the company of any cat that
walked about the house with a saintly expression.
~Beverly Nichols

Little did my fiancé, Rich, know that when he agreed to take home a cute little abused and abandoned kitten that he was really getting a lot more than he bargained for. Our running, jumping, climbing trees cat, Bailey, had a personality the size of a Great Dane and the attitude to match.

There were no problems at first, other than the typical antics of living with a kitten. He liked to climb, and therefore was on the counters, tables, couches, the CD tower, etc. Once he knocked over the CD tower while attempting to jump from it onto the top of the wall unit. Down crashed five hundred of Rich's over-a-thousand-strong music collection, waking us up from a dead sleep on Saturday morning. I thought Bailey was history. Luckily for him, no CDs were harmed in the execution of this feat. He had character and no trick was too great for him. He was a blast, and he made our first house a home.

Remember when I said he had the personality of a Great Dane? He had the voice of one, too. On our first Halloween as a family, the neighborhood kids started to arrive and ring the doorbell as is customary. On the first chime of the doorbell, Bailey ran for the door and began barking. Rich looked at me, and I looked at him, and in unison we asked: "Did Bailey just bark?" Yes, it seemed that our lovable little man didn't want to run and hide like most cats; he wanted to greet the costumed kids as much as we did.

His voice was never too far away. Bailey would have a running commentary as he walked around the house, as if informing us of the current situation. If we were in another room and he wanted us to come out, he would cry out in a tone of voice that sounded as if he were saying "Helloooo?" and wondering where we were.

However, as Bailey grew into adulthood, he began having crazy tirades where his pupils would dilate, his hair would stand up, and he would run spastically around the house crying and talking more than usual. I thought they were normal occurrences, and we knew that during these episodes we couldn't touch him and just had to let him be. But out of these spells came an increased aggressiveness towards Rich. At first I didn't see it. Since I was the one who found him, we bonded instantly. Rich, on the other hand, was the "other man," or so Bailey thought.

One morning, as Rich was getting ready for work and I was in the kitchen preparing breakfast, I heard a loud crash, boom, and a very loud scream. Wondering if Rich was okay, I called out and ran into the bedroom to see what happened. There was my fiancé, fresh out of the shower and looking rather perturbed. He informed me that "my" cat had tripped him.

"Don't be ridiculous," I told him. "Bailey can't trip you."

"Yes," he assured me, "he did." He was coming around the corner of the bed and Bailey stuck out his little beige-and-white paw and tripped him. He fell into the nightstand on the way to his final destination, the wall. Trying not to laugh, I suggested Bailey was probably trying to crawl out from under the bed at the same time Rich was walking by. Rich thought otherwise.

A while later, Rich told me that Bailey also tried to scare him by jumping out from behind walls, furniture, and other hiding places. I thought the game was cute and told Rich that Bailey was just trying to bond. Again, Rich felt otherwise. Several days later, Rich called me into the family room. Having spotted Bailey coyly hiding around the corner of the recliner, he decided this would be an opportune time to demonstrate Bailey's evil ways. Sure enough, as Rich approached the end of the chair, Bailey jumped out, standing on his hind legs, and began boxing like a kangaroo. It was adorable, but, I had to admit Rich was right; Bailey was acting overly aggressive toward him. It wasn't that Bailey completely despised Rich — he would knead Rich, and he slept on Rich's side of the bed. However, when Bailey got annoyed or agitated, Rich bore the brunt of it.

Bailey's episodes became more regular and I began experiencing some of his aggression as well. I began to wonder if something was really wrong. I dreaded the thought of having to give him up. I decided that was not an option. He was a family member and we would work through this. The vet suggested behavior modification classes, but that seemed ridiculous and it was out of our price range. I sought a second opinion. It turns out that Bailey's behavior was common and occurs in cats that are weaned too early or abandoned. Anti-anxiety drugs usually help. Relieved I went home and told Rich the good news.

"Great!" he replied. "Now we have to pay for drugs for the cat too."

The drugs worked, and although it was a bit tedious to give Bailey the liquid cocktail each morning, it was worth it since we got our lovable character-filled cat back.

When our lives began to settle down, we adopted Jazmine, a white German Shepherd/Yellow Lab mix. Usually when you add a large dog to the family, you worry about how the dog will treat the cat. Well, not us. We were more fearful of how Bailey would treat Jazmine. Could Jazmine handle him? Bailey really didn't think he was small and his bravado rivaled that of a Doberman when prompted. Thankfully, Jazmine was just what the doctor ordered... literally. Jazmine and Bailey became best friends. Within a month of Jazmine's arrival, Bailey was completely off the medication and he hasn't needed it since.

Bailey has brought life into our home. His lively personality, crazy antics, abandonment issues, and unceasing zest for life have kept us rolling in laughter and sometimes crying. But most of all, Bailey has taught us what family is truly about. Family can drive you crazy, make you laugh till you cry, and push the limits. But, in the end, regardless of all its foibles and flaws, headaches and heartaches, we never give up on them — they are family. We fight till the end to keep our loved ones no matter how much of a bang they make.

~Francesca Lang

Loving a Mean Cat

One must love a cat on its own terms.
~Paul Gray

Sometimes, our cats love us more than we love them. Sometimes, we love our cats more than they love us. Rasputin was a cat in the latter category. As her name suggests, she was more than a bit prickly. She was my very first kitten, and she came with the name from her original family, who had named her after the famously unstable Russian monk. "We should have known that we weren't getting a sweet, little kitty," my mom said. The first night we had her, while I was gently holding Rasputin in my lap, this not-so-sweet kitty launched her first strike. Rasputin attacked me with her fangs and claws, hissing up a storm and drawing blood in the process. Having grown up around cats, I knew how to treat them, and little Rasputin's unprovoked aggression left me stunned and sore.

At the time, we thought it was because Rasputin was scared, being in a new environment. Later, we realized, it was just Rasputin's nature. An attractive, gray cat with bright eyes, Rasputin looked like she should be cuddled up on a lap, purring contently. Her cute looks, however, were deceiving. Rasputin was more likely to hiss than purr, and she would hiss just because you walked into the room or because you looked at her funny. Rasputin didn't like visitors, but she also didn't seem to particularly care for us. But that didn't stop us from trying to win over Rasputin's heart. We plied her with love and attention. That didn't work. We gave her special treats and catnip. That also didn't work. I even took her to the parish priest to be blessed on St. Francis of Assisi Day, and he tried renaming Rasputin "Frances," in the gentle saint's honor. But it didn't help. She was still mean.

Eventually, we realized that Rasputin was more of a "look, don't touch" kind of cat, and we learned to ignore her hissing, unless it looked like she was going in for a bite. Rasputin even began seeking our attention, but always on her own terms. Even then, you always had to watch out. If she approached you with a purr, she would still bite you when she got tired of being with you, or she might bite you for no apparent reason.

By this time, Rasputin came to be known as "devil kitty," especially to my friends. Even though devil kitty eventually came to tolerate my family, she never, ever accepted visitors. Still, that never stopped visitors from trying to gain Rasputin's acceptance. "Oh, cats love me," visitors would say, as they tried to coax the hissing ball of fur over to them. "Well, Rasputin's not like most cats," I would tell them, as Rasputin went in for a bite. "She won't like you, and it has nothing to do with you or how much other cats like you." Even if visitors didn't interact with Rasputin, they still usually had unpleasant encounters with her. "Why is your cat hissing at me?" was a common question, especially because many times Rasputin would simply come into the room to hiss at them for the entire length of their visit. Neither I, nor my family, ever had an adequate answer to that question.

Despite the biting and the hissing, we loved Rasputin for eighteen years. When she was gone, we even missed her hissing. She may not have been sweet, but she was our cat, and she was a part of our family. "We loved that cat even though she was horrible to us," my mom said. Eventually, though, I decided to get a new cat that I named Mr. McKitty, and Mr. McKitty is as sweet as they come. He purrs and cuddles, and he even greets visitors at the door with a friendly "Meow." Mr. McKitty doesn't even know how to hiss. As my mom says, he's my reward for having first loved such a mean cat.

~Julie Neubauer as told to Jeanette Hurt

"NO, IT'S NO MISTAKE, ALL BAD CATS GO TO DOGGIE HEAVEN."

How to Warm a Heart

A meow massages the heart.
~Stuart McMillan

When people ask me how I came to own my cat I say, "Oh, Mau and I? We met online." A week before I saw her online, I received a phone call—the kind of call no one ever wants to receive. It was my brother calling to tell me that his wife's younger brother had been killed in a car accident the night before. Suddenly everything in my life dropped away. My schedule for the day disappeared. What had felt like priorities moments ago now made no sense.

I felt isolated from my brother and his wife, who live states away. I regretted not knowing my sister-in-law's brother better. I felt unimaginable sorrow at the loss. I also felt confused about my own life, and I had no one in my small one-bedroom apartment with whom to share my grief. I spent that weekend alone, mostly shuffling around my apartment. I would stand at my chilly living room window for long stretches of time and watch the snow fall, then I would move to the couch, and then I would go back to the window. My apartment felt so empty, and I felt so empty. I had wanted a cat for ten years, but the reason I had never gotten one was because I was afraid of eliminating a dog person from my dating pool. Yes, I had no cat because of an imaginary boyfriend, one who did not like cats. Death revealed to me how ridiculous this withholding of love was.

On that Sunday morning, I sat down with a cup of coffee at my laptop and perused pet websites, a process reminiscent of the online dating that I had done. And just like many online dating profiles, Mau's profile looked too good to be true. Her gray fur splotched with light orange and white was varied enough to assuage an indecisive person like myself. Her face was adorable and her personality looked to be a fit, too. The next day, I followed the directions that I had scribbled on a scrap of paper to the cat rescue on the outskirts of town. The rescue was connected to a cat daycare, so along three shop windows, cats sprawled across ledges, swatted toys, and jumped from carpeted cathouse to cage, and back again to carpeted cathouse. Like many an Internet date, I second-guessed my decision to be here. Surely I was in over my head. But a cat could not lie about her age, height, or marital history, right?

I had heard couples describe their love as "love at first sight." I never could have believed it until I met Mau. My love for her was immediate. Curled up in the back of her cage, Mau moved only to extend one of her tiny white paws at me when I pulled my hand away from petting her, as if to say, "No, wait. Don't leave me." And I didn't.

I hope to love a man as much as I love Mau, because then I will get married. That probably sounds pitiful but it's true. What is also true is that my cat keeps my heart open to the possibility of a lasting romantic love, which had become increasingly difficult to fathom as time has passed. But now, each night, Mau sleeps sprawled across my chest, keeping my heart warm.

~Lauren Gullion

My Cat's Life

It's the Cat's Meow

Laughter Is the Purrfect Medicine

Laughter is a tranquilizer with no side effects.
~Arnold Glasow

About three weeks ago, I noticed something unusual in our cat's litter box. Yes, more unusual than the heart-shaped urine clump Jasmine lovingly created for us on Valentine's Day. And stranger than the time she swallowed the string from a Christmas ornament and made us a new and improved ornament the next day in her box. It was blood. After a wrestling match, the likes of which World Wrestling Entertainment has yet to witness, I managed to shove Jasmine into her carrier and drive her to our veterinarian's office. The vet told me that Jasmine had an infection. I could handle that. The vet told me that Jasmine needed a change in diet, and that the new food would be much more expensive. My bank account could handle that. The vet told me that I would have to give Jasmine a dropper full of antibiotic liquid twice a day for two weeks.

"Are you nuts?!" I bellowed. "I'd rather hand-feed piranhas."

The vet thought I was overreacting. He grabbed the office cat. "Here, I'll demonstrate," he said condescendingly. The sweet, furry creature lay docile. She willingly opened her mouth when prodded for the demonstration. It seemed to me the vet could have inserted hot pokers into this cat's eyes and she would have purred. Jasmine, on the other hand, turns into Catzilla if we even try to pick her up for a quick cuddle. How would I ever hold her, open her mouth and insert the required dose of antibiotics? On the drive home from the vet, I prepared for the ordeal. "How hard can it be?" I asked myself out loud. "She's small. I'm tall. She weighs about twelve pounds. I weigh, um, slightly more than that." At home, I got hold of Jasmine without losing a limb, but I couldn't grip her and open her mouth at the same time. I needed two more hands or…

"Sweetheart!" I called my husband. When I told Dan what we needed to do, he looked at me as though I had asked him to jump into a pit of slithering snakes. I assured him this was far worse.

"Okay," he said. "She needs the medicine to get better. I'll hold her and you squeeze the antibiotics into her mouth."

The first morning we tried, Dan held her and I worked furiously to get her to open her mouth. When she tried to bite me, I squirted. A surprising fifty percent of the liquid ended up inside her mouth. The rest spilled on her chin, but she quickly licked it off. Success! We felt as though we had won the Olympic event of Feline Medication Administration, and since Dan and I still had our fingers and hands, we high-fived each other.

The next night, Jasmine used her back paw to scratch Dan's palm. He bled so much I thought he would need a transfusion. He bandaged his hand and his ego and tried again. He eventually held Jasmine still. This time, I managed to get a surprising eighty percent of the liquid inside her mouth. The other twenty percent fell into the carpet fibers along with crushed Cheerios, a half-eaten raisin and a set of lost Legos. I was feeling confident now. Dan was feeling woozy from lack of blood.

The next morning, Dan donned his business suit. He had an early meeting at the office. "Come on," he said. "Let's get this over with. I'm running late." He grabbed Jasmine with amazing finesse. More sure of my ability, I opened her mouth and squirted the full eye dropper of thick white liquid… all over my husband's slacks.

Over the next two weeks, my husband's slacks were well medi-cated. We, on the other hand, were sick of wrestling with our feisty feline. We reached under every piece of furniture in the house to retrieve her, but unfortunately, the only things we snagged were impressively large dust bunnies. And they looked too robust to need antibiotics. Once, when we held Jasmine securely, she slugged the eyedropper across the room with her front paw. We signed her with the Phillies. We would have given up, but our cat's health was too important. So we struggled twice each day to get the medicine from the bottle to the inside of Jasmine. We have a few scratches to show for the effort, but mostly a lot of laughs from our attempts. And laughter must be the best medicine because despite our hilarious misses with the medicine dropper, Jasmine got a clean bill of health from the vet. Thank goodness. Because if he had told us that we needed to give Jasmine any more medicine, my husband and I would have ended up in the hospital. The kind with padded walls, barred windows and white jackets.

~Donna Gephart

48

Vacation Cat

*The cat is the only animal which accepts the comforts
but rejects the bondage of domesticity.*
~Georges-Louis Leclerc de Buffon

A few years ago, my husband Jeff and I decided to take a trip to the Queen Charlotte Islands off the coast of British Columbia. It was going to be an adventure—complete with a seven-hour road trip, an eight-hour ferry ride, and a stay in a no-frills cabin once we got there. Our two cats would have to sit this one out, as their idea of roughing it meant not being allowed on the bed. It was always difficult to leave Minnie and Spookie behind, although we knew they would be well looked after.

On our first day, Jeff was outside our cabin chopping wood for the first morning fire, and as I sat on the step, I saw a blur of orange out of the corner of my eye. Under the stairs, two yellow eyes peered up at me. I called out, but once the cat knew that he had been seen, he scurried back underneath where he had appeared. I was intrigued, since we had been told that there were a number of stray cats in the woods nearby. We brought in the wood and decided to leave the sliding doors open to see if the orange shadow might return. It wasn't long before he walked in and made his way gingerly to a warm spot in front of the woodstove. While grooming himself, he kept one eye on both of us, but once he was content with his appearance, he wandered over to the couch where we were sitting and jumped up. We froze. Carefully he found his way between us and lay down. He was a shorthaired cat and when he moved we saw the outlines of his muscles in his sleek body.

That first evening, when I attempted to pick him up, he bit my finger. Not enough to draw blood, but a gentle warning. It was then that we decided he would be known as Bitey.

Bitey was a hunter and a fierce one. And yet, though his claws were sharp, his affection for us was overwhelming. He would climb up to my chest until he was eye level with me and stare deep into my eyes. We fed him, but soon found out that he did not need us for his meals. Disappearing for a short time, he would return with a small bird in his mouth, dropping it on the floor at our feet. When neither of us accepted his treat, he picked it back up and took it outside to eat it under the steps.

Bitey followed us everywhere. When we hiked the beach, he trailed behind, vocal the entire time. Why come along, we thought, only to make such noise? Did he think we were leaving? On the way back, he would run ahead and be there to meet us back at the cabin. That first night, he found a space on the bed and slept there through the night. At first I feared that he might have fleas, or even worse, but his purring won me over.

From then on, we had a constant companion at our feet. He would leave the warmth of the bed early in the morning to hunt and then return when we were about to have our breakfast. He groomed himself by the fire while we planned our day. In the evenings we built fires amongst the dunes and watched the sun go down. Bitey would lie just out of the light from the fire, his tail flicking back and forth. The week passed quickly and our hearts were heavy knowing that we would soon have to return to the working grind. Of course we were excited to get back home and see our own two cats, but it was going to be difficult to part ways with our new friend.

On our last night, as he was nestled on our bed we whispered about how we could take him home with us. He would settle in, learn to be an indoor cat. We decided that we couldn't leave him. The last day arrived and we began to pack and load the truck. Bitey sat on the steps for a while and then disappeared. When it was finally time to go, Bitey had made his own decision. He was gone.

The following year, we decided to head back to the island for our holidays. This time, we planned to stay for two weeks and were eager to get to our destination. We both wondered aloud what the chances were of seeing Bitey again. It was a harsh life for a cat on the wet island. There were many dangers.

This time we took a small container of cat food with us just in case. We spent the first day chopping kindling, unpacking our supplies and making plans for the next day's activities. We watched for Bitey but there was no sign of him. Later in the evening, as the fire crackled and the wind howled outside, a glimpse of orange passed in front of the doors. We had left them open just a little, hoping for company. He hung back until we called to him. Then, as if he knew the routine by heart, he followed us inside the open door and settled down beside the fire. He didn't leave us to go and hunt that night.

Bitey stayed with us for the next two weeks, only leaving for his morning hunt. He brought many gifts for us, always leaving them outside on the steps. On the second-to-last day we were horrified to discover that he had brought us a squirrel. Not wanting to upset him, we stifled our screams of disgust until he took it back outside with him and proceeded to devour it under the stairs. Once again the time was upon us to say our goodbyes. Bitey watched for a moment, and then, without a backwards glance, he was gone. My heart was heavy as we pulled away, but I knew Bitey was not ours to take home. He would not be happy away from this life he had. It was perfect for him.

~Ava Siemens

49

Cleopatra
and the Cookies

Even if you have just destroyed a Ming Vase, purr.
Usually all will be forgiven.
~Lenny Rubenstein

For years, whenever something in my home has been lost, broken, mangled, chewed on, spilled, or otherwise changed in some way, the members of my family have always blamed our cats. I've done it myself, although with a tiny bit of guilt, since I know my cats are perfect in every way. If I sent an article to a publisher with a typo, the reason was, "Samson must have walked on the keyboard right before I hit 'Print.'" Then I would give Samson extra pets because he was innocently sitting on top of the printer at the time, and I had awakened him from his slumber when the printer started issuing each page. If something I cooked didn't taste as I wanted it to, I would say, "Peaches was on the counter. She must have distracted me while I was adding the flour." Then I would go find Peaches and give her a gazillion kisses because she is the one cat who never goes up on the counter because she is too plump to jump.

When you have five cats, it's easy to find someone to blame. That's not to say my cats don't get into mischief. Buttercup has a nasty habit of knocking over the bathroom trashcan to inspect the daily loot that has collected in it. I have caught her in the act. Usually she scoots off too fast because I guess she knows that eating dirty tissue isn't civilized, but when I catch her, I always tell her, "It's okay. I know it's hard not to be curious. I know it's hard not to do disgusting things. I know you were abandoned at birth and have no role models. I know you still want to be Queen of the Jungle."

On one occasion, Zorro was fast asleep in a homemade, one-of-a-kind, matched-the-room-perfectly, irreplaceable bowl. A loud noise outside my house spooked him and his body jerked in fear. As his body suddenly lifted a foot above the table and he turned in midair to flee to his safe spot under a bed, the bowl went flying onto the floor. It shattered into forty-two unfixable pieces. After cleaning up the dangerous shards, I found Zorro and held him close to my heart. "Poor, Zorro," I said. "I'll bet that loud noise really scared you, Mr. Pudding Brain. Don't you worry about it for one little second. I'll just have to make you a new perfect dish."

All of my cats have moments like this—except Cleopatra. Cleopatra is the most perfect cat in the universe. We tell her that quietly so the other cats won't feel bad. Cleopatra is the ruler of her domain and never does anything wrong. She sets the example for the younger cats. She is the queen. She was here first and she knows the rules. She takes her job quite seriously.

One morning a few weeks before Christmas, I got up early to make many dozens of cookies for my husband to take to work for his company holiday party. When I heard a strange, crinkling, crunchy noise in another room, I went to investigate. When a person works alone in a home office typing all day, strange noises are a good reason to take a cookie break. I often have visions of me sitting at my computer oblivious to the fact that my house has burned to the ground around me while I was off in Never-Never Land. On this particular morning, I went from room to room looking for the source of the crinkling, crunchy noise that managed to break my concentration.

Buttercup was curled up in a ball on the ottoman in the family room. Her leg was twitching, a sign that she was dreaming about running after jackrabbits. Zorro was curled up in his new favorite bowl on the table where the old favorite bowl used to be. This bowl is made of copper. Samson was asleep on his back in the empty bathtub.

And Peaches was walking between my legs, probably also aware of the strange sound but too afraid to do anything about it on her own. And yet, the sound continued.

As I neared the kitchen, I realized what the sound was. All of the cookies I had made were spread out on the table and the floor around the table. They were crumbled and crunched beyond recognition. The foil paper I used to separate each layer of cookies was shredded. And lying on her back, covered in cookie crumbs, was Madame Cleopatra, Queen of Cookie Land. There were no crumbs around her mouth and when I sniffed her mouth, there wasn't even the faintest hint of cookie breath.

I pulled my cell phone from my jeans pocket—the jeans that are slightly tighter now that I had to sample at least one of each cookie as I baked them, and I took a picture of Cleo rolling in the crumbs. Then I sent the picture to my husband and both of my sons. Several minutes later, I got three replies in a row. Each message said, "Don't be mad at Cleo. I did it."

~Felice Prager

Naughty and Nice

The opportunity for doing mischief is found a hundred times a day,
and of doing good once in a year.
~Voltaire

The mischievous look on his face was enough to tell you he was trouble. His golden eyes could look so innocent, even while he plotted his next mission of destruction. His beautiful thick coat of bold gray-and-black stripes showed he came from a champion bloodline. This was no ordinary cat. He was a cat of great affection, playfulness and deviousness. He would have made a great mouser, and he knew it. Geordi came into our life, along with his brother, Asher, one year after we were married. We had no children and my husband had never owned a pet. When I met him, I had a five-year-old Siamese, Chloe. She was set in her ways and distant from my husband, who wanted a pet that would love him back. We did our research and met wonderful breeders of American Shorthair cats. They had Silver Tabby Classics, and before we knew it, our adoption of one cat turned into two.

Asher and Geordi provided us with endless fun and love. Although they looked identical to outsiders, we could easily tell them apart, not only by markings, but by behavior. Asher was a fun loving teddy bear of a cat. He loved to be petted, played with, and adored. Geordi was a different story. He was a true, mischievous "nine lives" kind of cat. The kind of cat that gives cats a bad name. If you told him not to scratch on the couch, he would. If you gave him a scratching

Naughty and Nice : It's the Cat's Meow   177

post to scratch on, he wouldn't touch it. Any kind of mischief he could find, he found. He loved to sneak up on Chloe, my Siamese, and scare her. He loved to pounce on his brother, Asher, when he was asleep. Whatever his mind could think up to irritate someone, he would do.

Then came the happy day that we found out I was pregnant. My husband and I were overjoyed, but we weren't quite prepared for what came next. By the end of the first trimester, I was unusually warm. My doctor discovered my blood pressure was elevated. He decided to put me on high blood pressure medication, but because I was pregnant, he put me on an ineffective, older drug that would not hurt my developing baby. He warned that the first day of medication would be difficult, as I might get a severe headache. I went to the pharmacy to fill the prescription, and again, was warned of the impending headache. I went home, took the medication and waited.

It happened just as they warned. An intense headache had begun. There was nothing I could do, so I went to bed, lay on top of the covers, and tried to sleep. I woke on my side, but I felt something peculiar. There was Geordi, sleeping next to me, with his head on my knee. I was taken aback, not only because Geordi preferred to sleep with Asher, but because my husband had carefully trained the cats not to sleep on the bed with us. But this was not just another case of Geordi being disobedient. This was different. Geordi knew something was wrong, and was trying to comfort me. From that day on, he was a different cat.

As time wore on, my blood pressure continued to soar, despite my taking increasing amounts of medication. Soon a second drug was added, an attempt to keep me from having a stroke. I was miserable and worried. The medications made me drowsy, and I felt like I was in a fog. The doctor put me on partial bed rest, which made me feel more isolated. But I was not alone. Geordi became my faithful companion. He followed me everywhere, seeming to understand that when my husband was at work, I was alone and needed him. The two other cats acted normally, like nothing was wrong. Only Geordi seemed to understand.

I tried to stay as close to home as I could. In order to pass the time, I would read. The large amount of medications made me drowsy. One afternoon, as I was sitting on the couch reading a book, I fell fast asleep. My head went back and to one side, a very uncomfortable position. Geordi came, looked at me, and decided I needed help. He climbed on the back of the couch, and placed his paws on my left shoulder, pressing as hard as he could. It was enough to wake me. I lifted and turned my head, only to feel his thick fur and warm body on my face. He had wakened me out of concern. He knew humans didn't sleep like that, and saved me from some very sore neck muscles. The days continued on as we became more and more concerned about my health. Eventually I went into toxemia, and had to go to the hospital for non-stress tests twice a week to make sure my baby was still healthy. During all of this, Geordi never left my side.

At last we were in the final weeks of the pregnancy. One night, as my husband and I were about to fall asleep, we realized we weren't alone. I looked up, and there, at my feet, was Geordi. He curled up next to me. Our cats knew my husband's rule and they hadn't tried to sleep with us for a long time. I was deeply touched when I realized Geordi was breaking the rules, just to be by my side. My husband recognized Geordi's defiance was, for once, out of love for me, and allowed him to stay. And stay he did. Until the night, some weeks later, I had a splitting headache, and realized I was in deep trouble with my blood pressure. The doctor sent me to the hospital immediately.

After a difficult delivery, we finally brought our daughter home. My blood pressure was still elevated slightly, but I was out of harm's way. Geordi seemed to sense that my return from the hospital with another human, albeit a small one, signaled the end of my need to be protected. He no longer followed me around, or tried to sleep with me. His desire to be with me was diminished by my newborn daughter's earsplitting cries. But I was so distracted by caring for my newborn that I hardly had noticed anything was different. Until one day, Geordi reminded me of the way things used to be.

I had fed and put my daughter to sleep in my arms. It was time to put her down for a nap, so I went to the nursery. I looked in the bassinet. There inside, was Geordi, trying to look like he was asleep. He had rolled all over the sheets and baby blanket. Everything was covered in thick, gray-and-black fur. The thought of placing my newborn daughter in all that cat hair made me wince. He looked up at me, with an all too familiar smirk on his face. Geordi, the mischievous cat, was back.

~Joanna G. Wright

My Study Partner

I have studied many philosophers and many cats.
The wisdom of cats is infinitely superior.
~Hippolyte Taine

Sassafras, Sassy for short, is the color of root beer, hence her name. She has the rich dark brown color of root beer and the lighter caramel color of root beer foam. She is a longhaired domestic with a big fluffy tail. Sassy adopted me the day I moved into her apartment. Actually, the apartment belonged to Susan, Sassy's "mom" and my new roommate. Nevertheless, anyone who lives with cats knows that the cat rules the home. Doors are opened, meals are served, and laps are made available upon request. Sassy jumped on my bed the morning it was moved in, and she made it her own. She would be curled up there when I returned from work in the evenings and would stay there throughout the night. Sassy had adopted me whether I wanted to be adopted or not.

A year after we got Sassy, Susan became very ill and was required to move in with her daughter. Her daughter is allergic to cats so Sassy could not move with Susan to her daughter's home. We looked at Sassy sleeping soundly on my bed. The decision had already been made by Sassy. Who was I to say no? Sassy and I settled into a nice routine. I would feed her in the morning and then head off to work. She would be in charge of the apartment while I was away. One of her favorite positions was on a living room chair in front of a window where she

My Study Partner : It's the Cat's Meow 181

sat sentry, basking in the warm sunshine while watching the birds flying and the hummingbirds feeding on our porch feeders.

When I returned in the evenings, we would sit on the porch and watch the sunset together while the hummingbirds buzzed around us and the neighbors stopped by for a chat. I would enjoy hot or iced tea depending on the weather, and Sassy would enjoy her pre-dinner treats. After the sunset, we would move inside and settle into our evening routines. I would work on my studies for my doctoral coursework. If I was on the couch reading books or papers, Sassy would curl up on my lap or beside me leaning on my hip. She would sleep through the study hours, quietly purring. If I was typing at the computer, she would settle on the back of the desk chair. Sometimes I would forget that Sassy was back there and I would get up too quickly. I would be rewarded with a set of cat nails digging into my shoulders and a large wail in my ears to let me know she was not happy about having her sleep disturbed.

As my courses continued, my study hours grew longer. I would study later and later into the evenings. In addition, I was spending more and more time at the computer desk rather than sitting on the couch reading reference books. Sassy would always curl up in her spot on the couch and look longingly over at me, waiting for me to leave the computer desk and join her on the couch. Some nights I never made it over there.

We also had a standard time for bed each night. Sassy would get up at midnight and stretch long and languidly while heading for the bedroom for the evening's sleep. She would stop at the door of the bedroom and look back at me as if to ask, "You coming?" She would then sit at the entry of the door and wait. Usually, I would smile, call it a night, turn off the computer, and follow her. After a few relaxing exercises, I would stretch, get into bed, and settle in for a good night's sleep. Sassy would jump onto the bed, stretch once, and then settle down next to me. She would be purring softly before I had yawned three times.

However, as my studies progressed, my time at the computer often stretched beyond bedtime. Sassy would wait at the bedroom door until she tired of waiting. Then I would hear her jump softly on the bed. Yet, within a few minutes she would be by my side again, looking up at me as if demanding I stop what I was doing and head for bed too. I would smile at her, pick her up, hug her, and chat with her for a while. Then I would put her back down so I could finish my work.

Despite my best efforts, my hugs and mindless chatter did not appease Sassy. She would sit glaring at me and wait. Finally one night, Sassy developed a plan. She jumped onto the desk, stretched out across the keyboard, and lay down. This simple act did four things: It put Sassy directly in front of me, almost at eye level. She covered what she determined was taking me away from her, and by her action, she stopped me from moving forward with my studies, forcing me to pay attention to her. Finally, she made me laugh. I swooped her up, gave her a hug, turned the computer off, and headed to bed. Sassy repeated this action often, and that internal clock of hers was never wrong. She only stopped my work when it was well after midnight and well past our bedtime. Sassafras, my study cat, helped me maintain a healthy balance of work, school, sleep, and play.

~Sheila Embry

"May I have the mouse back, please."

King of the Wild

*God made the cat in order that humankind might have
the pleasure of caressing the tiger.*
~Fernand Mery

Amid the sounds of the crickets and peepers, his plaintive meows wafted through the windows on the warm summer breeze. I first became aware of the large black tomcat as he serenaded his way through our yard one evening. The bruiser had distinguished white markings on his chest and face, and it looked like he was wearing an elegant tuxedo with tails. I named him "Tennessee Tuxedo," after an old, similarly-dressed cartoon character.

Tennessee must have crossed over several miles of woodland and farmland that bordered our home. He was arrogant and brawny and listened to no one. He slept wherever he grew tired, hunted whenever the mood struck him, and ate whatever he caught. Tennessee claimed no one and no one claimed him. Aloof and independent, he kept his distance. If he saw or heard people coming, he disappeared into the woods in a flash.

I began leaving tempting morsels on our porch. Eventually, he accepted the food, which appeared to be the one exception to his rule of total independence. When hunger dictated, Tennessee would come onto our porch to eat, but only if we were inside the house with the door shut. Tennessee preferred that we leave scraps at the edge of the yard, but that arrangement had some drawbacks since raccoons, opossums and red foxes inhabited an abandoned apple orchard bordering our property. Whoever got there first staunchly defended his right to the meal. After a while Tennessee began arriving early, waiting patiently, just in view. When I went out, he would disappear into the trees just long enough for me to get back in the house and then come out and eat.

For several years Tennessee patrolled our neighborhood, loudly announcing his arrival everywhere he went. Long before we could see him, we could hear him as he roamed the woods. At times he merely proclaimed his presence. But at other times his cries warned and challenged any other creatures in the area. From time to time, as I studied Tennessee from my kitchen window, I would notice telltale signs of recent combat—an ear that sported a ragged tear, a scratch across his nose, or a missing patch of fur. Though I would have loved to take him to the veterinarian for immunizations and treatment, he wouldn't let me near him.

As Tennessee aged, I noticed that it took longer and longer for him to recover from his battle wounds. Damage to his eye eventually caused permanent scarring and he limped from an old injury to his front leg. Over time he didn't run as far, or stay away as long, but he still scrambled off into the woods when anyone opened the door to go outside. He was suspicious of anything out of the ordinary. Merely putting the summer lawn furniture on the porch would keep him away for days.

One day a young, black cat appeared at the edge of the woods. Tennessee gave him the usual vocal warning about trespassing, but the younger cat did not back off. He left only after he had thoroughly checked out everything that interested him. Tennessee's authority had visibly waned.

With the coming of autumn and the defoliating of the trees and bushes, the old cat could easily be seen hunched in the leaves about ten feet into the woods, paws tucked under his body and his eyes closed. He began spending time in an old shed on our property, so I put the food and water there for him over the winter. I enjoyed watching this eccentric character, always hoping to see some sign that he would welcome my friendship. Though he still kept his distance, I sensed that he was beginning to feel that someone cared for him. His casual, aloof attitude only thinly veiled a lonely, fearful old cat that had never trusted anyone.

One evening the following spring, Tennessee didn't show up at suppertime. I wasn't too concerned at first, for he still occasionally roamed off to parts unknown for a couple of days. He usually came back from these crusades with a few new scrapes and bruises. After four days, however, I decided to ask around if anyone had seen him. Tennessee's black-and-white markings, ever-present limp and cruisin'-for-a-bruisin' personality were unforgettable, even legendary in our area. Though the neighbors instantly knew which cat I meant, no one had even caught a glimpse of him recently. True to his elusive character, my lonely, standoffish friend simply vanished.

A few weeks later a stray mother cat chose our shed to birth her kittens. In Tennessee's former digs, nestled among two marmalades and a calico, lay a miniature likeness of the black-and-white feline. The old fellow may have disappeared, but he had left a gift—an offering of friendship—in his tiny tuxedoed legacy.

~Pam Williams

Drools' Fool

The smart cat doesn't let on that he is.
~H.G. Frommer

Two years ago we moved into one of the sprawling subdivisions that have mushroomed all over the desert valleys of Arizona. The neighborhood is a nice mix of younger and older couples with their assorted pets. In our little cul-de-sac, the pets of choice seem to be dogs. The couple with the three kids has a Shepherd-Hound mix, the people two doors down have three dogs, the single mother with her little girl has some fluffy midsize dog, and in our house lives my daughter's miniature Dachshund. When the new couple moved in a year ago with their Pug and Poodle they were a perfect fit in our dog-loving little circle.

I am in the habit of sitting outside on the front porch with a book. I can keep an eye on my granddaughter while she plays with the neighbor kids on their bikes or scooters. In the 100-degree-plus summer days, this activity doesn't last much longer than half an hour before we make our way into air-conditioned comfort.

It was on one of these scorching days that I first spotted the cat. He came up from the drainage ditch under the sidewalk and just sat there for a moment watching the kids before he ambled his way over to my porch meowing all the while. I felt that the least I could do was to give him some water, so I ran into the house and filled up an extra dog dish with some cool water. The cat, a longhaired tabby with a gold nose and green eyes, was appreciative and drank half the bowl before coming up for air.

After that I kept a bowl of water on the porch. As time went on I added a bowl of dried cat food. In a month the cat was living on our porch. Every time I went outside to sit on the porch and read while the kids played, he jumped into my lap for some attention. I began calling him Drools because he dripped drool and shook it everywhere when he was being scratched behind the ears. I began to consider him my cat. My neighbor with the Pit Bull let me know when the cat wandered into his yard and irritated his dog. The neighbor with the three kids told me how he sat in front of their sliding glass doors and tormented their dog at 6 o'clock in the morning. So, on days when the heat was particularly oppressive, I began sneaking him into my bedroom to sleep in the cool room. I hoped that if he stayed in my room it would not affect the members in my family who have allergies to cats and he would quit bothering the neighbors.

As summer turned to fall and then winter, Drools occupied a space at the foot of my bed any time it got too hot or too cold. He filled the void left in my lonely heart since the loss of my own dog to heart disease three years earlier.

Then, the next spring, on one of those beautiful desert mornings when everyone is outside washing their cars or doing yard work, I finally had a chance to chat with my next door neighbors Dan and Stephanie. Up until then we had just exchanged friendly waves as we left for work in the mornings.

"So how do you like living out here?" I asked, after learning that they had moved from a big city.

"Oh we like it fine. It's great having a big yard for the dogs," Dan replied. "They love that they can go in and out through the doggie door. By the way, our cat isn't bothering you too much is he?"

My jaw dropped. "You have a cat?"

"Yeah, Jules, the tabby on your porch."

I choked out, "No, he doesn't bother me at all."

~Margaret Shaw

54

Honey and Her Teddy Bears

*[Teddy] Bears are like cats—they arrive disguised as nonentities.
Only time will reveal just who they really are.*
~Johnnie Hague

My lifelong affection for cats and teddy bears is obvious the moment you step into my house, and until recently, the furry critters co-existed quite peacefully. Then came Honey. Scrawny and free to a good home, the golden-colored young feline soon gained weight and became quite frisky. She would sleep at our feet each night, but in the wee hours of the morning she started prowling through the house.

One morning I awoke to find several teddy bears strewn about. It looked like a teddy bear picnic had happened in the middle of my living room. My husband Scott and I joked that the teddy bears were partying after we went to bed. Then one night, I woke up and heard talking. It took me a minute to shake off the sleep and recognize the voice was coming from my prized talking teddy bear. I stumbled to the living room and there was Honey staring curiously at the teddy bear. She had managed to knock it off the bookshelf, and the bear had landed right-side up. The fall had triggered the computer chip in the bear's ear so the bear began to talk.

"I like to play. What do you like to do? Do you have a best friend? Tell me a secret."

With each question, the teddy bear's mouth moved, his red heart flashed on and off as if beating, and his head tilted this way and that as if he was listening for a response. The intensity of Honey's scrutiny kept me from laughing out loud. She hardly noticed me as she listened and tentatively reached out her paw to see if he would bite.

For a while I encouraged her interest, giving her my second-string teddy bears that were already sad-looking, with clothes askew or fur loved off or missing an eye or two. She tolerated them while I watched, but played with them only briefly. Honey could sniff out the newer models. For instance, my largest stuffed animal, Sulley, an animated bear, didn't stand a chance against my feline predator. Grabbing Sulley's fuzzy turquoise tail, Honey pummeled his huge stuffed body with her hind legs. Her movements created the equivalent of Mr. Toad's Wild Ride as her front paws held tight to the cavorting stuffed animal's tail.

Somewhere inside my head a light bulb clicked on. I realized that she didn't know that kicking Sulley is what made him dance around. She thought he was alive and playing with her. Honey pounced repeatedly, then pulled him across the floor by one appendage or another. She clearly thought she was winning the battle.

Pretty soon, my bedtime ritual included closing doors to the guest room, to my office, to the living room, effectively cutting off her access to various stuffed friends. However, this didn't deter her. Knowing my routine, she began dragging one of her teddy bears down the hall to our bedroom sometime during the day. I never saw her do this, but every morning the evidence was at the foot of our bed. Honey and one or another of her beloved pet teddy bears would be curled up on the afghan, looking quite innocent.

~Sandi Tompkins

55

Maternity Ward

Becoming a mother makes you the mother of all children.
From now on each wounded, abandoned, frightened child is yours.
You live in the suffering mothers of every race and creed and weep with them.
You long to comfort all who are desolate.
~Charlotte Gray

I was exhausted after having climbed the two-kilometer hill from where my car had decided to go on strike. And to think that I still had two or three more kilometers to hike before I reached home. I sighed. I already envisioned myself flopping down in my La-Z-Boy chair, a large glass of ice water in my hand, kicking off my shoes, and closing my eyes. Thinking about it, my eyelids drooped. As I shuffled along the gravel road, I had a creepy feeling that someone was following me. My eyes popped open, I spun my head around, and froze. After looking in every direction and seeing no one, I continued to walk, but the feeling of being stalked increased. Again I spun my head around, slowing my pace. That's when I saw him, his size exaggerated by my fright. He crouched behind me in my shadow. My hand flew to my heart.

"Oh!" I said, taking a step toward a big gray cat, the object of my fright. "You scared me half to death!" As I walked slowly toward the cat he began to retreat. "Well, if that's the way you want it, fine."

My heart still pounding, I changed direction, heading once more toward home. Every once in a while I turned to see if the cat was still following me. He was, always just within my shadow. If I stopped, he stopped. If I turned around and walked toward him, he walked away from me. If I ran a few steps, he ran a few steps. It became a game. I decided that it was his intention to become my shadow. So, like one ignores a shadow, I ignored the cat.

It wasn't until the following morning when I went out to do the chores that I thought about the cat. But there he was, hiding in the shadow of the house. How had he managed to manoeuvre his way around the geese, the ducks, the turkeys, the chickens, the dog, and the two about-to-be-mother cats, Sugar and Cinnamon, to even enter our yard? And how had he been allowed by the menagerie to remain? Picking up a dish of cat food I crept toward the shadow. He tensed, slinking a few feet away. I set the food down and stood back to watch. As slowly as a shadow turns with the sun, the cat moved toward the food. Our big Malamute, Skipper, wagged his tail, as if approving my decision to let the shadow stay. I gave the big dog a pat on his head. Then and there he took it upon himself to become the cat's personal bodyguard.

Two weeks after the arrival of Shadow, as I had named him, Sugar and Cinnamon, on two consecutive days, presented the family with three kittens each. Then a strange thing happened. Shadow entered the house for the first time and began to explore. This time it was I who did the shadowing, and it was then, when I was following him around, that I discovered Shadow had not come alone, that "he" was a "she" and she was looking for a place to deposit her litter. An hour later she produced two kittens, one dead, and one as gray as herself.

At the same time as the cats were having their kittens, the hens were hatching their chicks. Fourteen lively, fluffy chicks followed behind their respective mothers. But one chick, not so lively, lagged behind, peeping at the top of its lungs for its mother to come back and get him. Mother hen had no time for an offspring who couldn't keep up, so she ignored him. The peeping grew louder.

Leaving her kitten in the safety of its box, Shadow trotted off in the direction of the distressed chick. Picking him up in her mouth, as gently as she would have if he had been her kitten, she carried him back to the house, deposited him in the box beside her own sightless baby, then nestled in beside them. For two days, until it died, she showered that chick with all the love and devotion that she had reserved for her own offspring. Every time she tried to wash him, he wobbled and tumbled over onto his back, peeping his protest, unresponsive to her love. Try as she might she could not make a kitten out of that fluffy yellow chick.

A devoted mother to an ungrateful chick, Shadow remained aloof and obscure, watching and following us in secret. One day, like a shadow on a cloudy day, she disappeared. But she left behind her one remaining kitten, who could often be found in the chicken pen, snoozing contentedly in one of the nesting boxes.

~Helen Splane-Dowd

My Cat's Life

A Purrfect Life

A Knock to the Head

Any conditioned cat-hater can be won over by any cat who chooses to make the effort.
~Paul Corey

"Isn't he crazy?" asked my wife, Catherine, with undisguised concern.

"He's not crazy," I assured her, "just misunderstood."

"He beat up a dog," she replied. I should never have told her that story.

"It was a small dog and that adoption wasn't the right fit. He's a shelter cat and shelter cats can be… a little unpredictable," I said.

The fact was that KittyHorse had been a shelter cat for a while. Officially he was the office cat for the SPCA Tampa Bay. Unofficially he had been declared a lost cause. Adopted on three different occasions, he'd been returned to the shelter each time because it wasn't the right fit.

"So, why do you want to adopt him?" Catherine prodded.

I hesitated but had to tell the truth. "He got into a fight with one of the other office cats and sent it to the infirmary. Nothing serious but the shelter director says he needs to go."

Now it was Catherine who hesitated. She knew that KittyHorse and I were buddies. On my first day at work the large orange Tabby had come into my office, looked me over, and once he was satisfied with what he saw, jumped onto my desk, took a running dash at me, and head-butted me straight between the eyes. When my vision finally cleared I found him sitting there waiting to see what I would do in response. So I did the only thing that made sense. I head-butted him back. From that day on we were the best of friends.

"He isn't going to try to murder us in our sleep, is he?" Catherine asked.

I couldn't blame her for being hesitant. She wasn't a cat person. She had never owned one. She had heard stories about KittyHorse but they hadn't made her want to get to know him. Now I was asking her to adopt him. Would it be the right fit? There was only one way to find out. I crossed my fingers and said, "You'll love him. I promise."

A week later, I placed the pet carrier containing our new family member on our bed. I opened the carrier's door and stepped back. Nothing happened.

"He's not coming out," Catherine pointed out. "Why isn't he coming out?"

"Cats like to be sure of their surroundings before they expose themselves," I offered. "Give him a couple of minutes." Catherine leaned down and peered into the carrier. Two large luminous green eyes peered back at her.

"Do you think he's afraid of us? I don't want him to be afraid of us," she said.

"No, he's probably just wondering why he's not at the office. He'll come out as soon as his curiosity gets the better of him," I said.

Sure enough KittyHorse slowly began to emerge from the carrier. He took in the room as he stepped out onto our bed and then he gave himself the long luxurious kind of stretch that only a cat can truly appreciate. KittyHorse then looked us over and, with the instincts of a born salesman, identified the person who needed the most reassurance. He trotted over to Catherine, brushed up against her, and began to purr loudly.

"See," I said, "he likes you. Pet his head."

Catherine reached out with a tentative hand. "He's not going to bite me, is he?"

"He's not dangerous," I replied.

"Tell that to the office cat he sent to the infirmary," she said.

KittyHorse could tell that she wasn't sold on him. The purring stopped and he gave me a look as if to say there was going to be a period of adjustment here. The next few weeks were quiet. KittyHorse retreated to the carrier whenever he felt like hiding and Catherine slept with one eye open — presumably watching for homicidal felines. But they were getting along well. KittyHorse continued to work his charms on her and she had taken to petting him, talking to him, and generally giving him some much needed attention. She was even beginning to anticipate his moods. If Catherine said the cat looked hungry, he was. If she said he wanted to play, he would chase some string around the room. If she said he looked tired he would retire to his carrier and take a nap. It got to the point that I wasn't sure if she was reading him or if he was reading her. In either case, they had come to an understanding — even if they weren't exactly friends. The day that I knew the deal was sealed though was when she came home from work with a large shopping bag.

"I got Mr. Horse a cat bed," she announced. She had taken to stopping by the pet store a lot over the last few weeks but we had never discussed buying a cat bed.

"Why?" I asked. "He doesn't need one. He sleeps in the carrier and when he doesn't sleep in the carrier he sleeps on our..."

As I had been talking KittyHorse arrived to greet Catherine, spotted the bag, and began pawing at it. Catherine, ignoring my assurances that the cat was perfectly happy sleeping on our bed, pulled out the lamb's wool cushion and presented it to him. KittyHorse immediately began to inspect his new mattress. He climbed onto it, flopped over, and declared it acceptable. The look on his face was one of pure joy.

"See," she told me, "he likes it. You like it, don't you Mr. Horse? I bet it's the first bed you've ever had and you like it, don't you?"

That's when it happened. Catherine leaned over to pet him and KittyHorse rose up to meet her. I could hear their heads collide from across the room.

"You okay?" I asked as I rushed over to her. Catherine had a dazed look on her face.

"He likes me," she said with a smile. "He actually likes me. I mean, that's what he did to you, wasn't it? He head-butted you to say you were friends."

That was true. The day we butted heads was the day we became friends. However, I didn't expect Catherine to be overjoyed by the same experience. But she was, and the cat was incredibly pleased with himself for having done it. It just goes to show that finding the right fit is like a knock to the head. You just know it when it happens.

~Arthur Sánchez

Eye of the Beholder

Beauty is not in the face; beauty is a light in the heart.
~Kahlil Gibran

O wning a purebred cat had always seemed pretentious. My cats were your ordinary, garden-variety felines, and I saw no reason to own any other kind. But all that changed the day I met a stunning Silver Persian named Shadrach. "A regal name," I thought. "I love it. It fits this cat." I was working as a veterinary assistant, and his owners brought him into our pet hospital after a run-in with a car. The right side of his face was badly damaged. The injuries he had sustained included a broken jaw, a lacerated bottom lip, a large gash on his nose, and a few missing teeth. He also had some nerve damage around his mouth. The most serious injury was to his right eye. It had taken the brunt of the impact, and the eyeball was hanging out of its socket. A few scrapes and bruises were the extent of the wounds to the rest of his body.

We knew the broken jaw, cuts, and bruises would heal. The missing teeth were insignificant. There was no way to tell at that time if the nerve damage would be permanent. But even if it were, we felt reasonably sure it wouldn't cause serious problems. We also didn't know whether or not the eyeball would have to be removed. Only time would tell. Either way, the eye would also eventually heal, though the eyesight would never be regained. The doctor assured the owners that, despite his considerable injuries, Shadrach should recover nicely. It would take a while, and lots of TLC, but he could live to a ripe old age without any problem. The owners talked it over.

"No, we'd just like you to put him to sleep," they said.

The doctor reiterated that he was certain Shadrach would have no continuing medical problems after the initial healing process. And he assured them that, if money presented a problem, we could work out a payment plan they could handle. But the owners insisted, "No, we don't want to see him this way. He looks like a freak. We just want you to put him to sleep."

I stood silently as they said their goodbyes. I wept as I carried Shadrach from the exam room and placed him in an empty cage, but not because he was going to die. I knew that wouldn't happen. I grieved for this precious creature who was being discarded because he was no longer beautiful. The people he had trusted to love and care for him were deserting him in his time of greatest need. When he was at his most vulnerable, he would be cared for by strangers.

Our hospital was a place of healing. No living being died there if we could prevent it. We euthanized when it was the humane thing to do and in the best interest of the animal, but never for expediency. Shadrach regained his strength and began to heal, just as we knew he would. The nerve damage was permanent but negligible. It was noticeable only because his tongue hung out of the right side of his mouth slightly, and his bottom lip drooped. It was of no consequence to him, nor were the missing teeth. For a while we thought his eyeball would have to be removed, but the eye finally healed, and the eyeball receded back into its socket.

He came to live with me after his recovery. Since I already had a one-eyed Beagle at home, adding a one-eyed cat to the family seemed logical.

Shadrach adapted rapidly to his new surroundings. The other felines appeared in awe of him. They sensed something peculiar and were hesitant to approach him. When their curiosity got the better of them, they would glance at him, but only on his left side. They never looked at the right side of his face. If he turned his face directly toward them, they would avert their eyes and slink away. He had an aloof manner that prevented them from playing together. But Shadrach seemed at ease, and content to wait until the others were ready to accept him into the fold.

The one member of our clan who readily accepted Shadrach was my Beagle, Buckwheat. Having lost his left eye as a baby, he already had a lifetime of one-eyed experiences under his belt. He seemed eager to share this knowledge with his new brother, teaching Shadrach to avoid obstacles on his blind side, and helping Shadrach adjust to a life of limited eyesight. They had one good pair of eyes between them, and they used it to their advantage.

Buckwheat also appeared to think this newcomer was no more peculiar than the other felines he lived with, all of whom were female. Perhaps a little male bonding was happening, too. Soon after Shadrach came to live with us, another orphaned cat joined our menagerie. Charley, like Shadrach, came burdened with physical and psychological scars. The hissing and spitting, which inevitably accompanies the introduction of any new feline into an established tribe, transpired as expected. But Shadrach refrained from participating. He seemed to sense that, like him before, this new addition needed compassion, not confrontation. He and Charley accepted each other unconditionally. Just as Buckwheat had befriended him, Shadrach befriended Charley. The three became good buddies, and a little more male bonding resulted.

When not hanging out with Buck and Chuck, as that pair came to be known, Shadrach spent his days gazing at the rainbow mollies swimming in the aquarium or batting at the fronds of my maidenhair ferns. Lying in the recliner while the sun shone through the window was a favorite pastime. Perhaps the warmth of the sun felt good on his healed but blemished body. He enjoyed the romping antics of his feline sisters but never seemed inclined to join. Maybe purebreds don't participate in such common folly.

All parties eventually got over their apprehension and were comfortable in one another's presence. At times Shadrach would sneak up beside a sibling and sit with his right side toward her, patiently waiting to be noticed. This usually elicited a lively response from the unsuspecting recipient of this prank, and roars of laughter from those who witnessed it. I sensed impish delight, but never malice. Shadrach was pleased with his life, and I think he rather enjoyed being the revered one. I preferred to call him Shad. I didn't want him to think me pretentious. But I always introduced him as Shadrach. It was an impressive name, and he was still an impressive cat. Viewed from the right side, his face did appear somewhat bizarre. But from the left, and in his soul, he was the same strikingly beautiful Silver Persian he had been before his accident.

Shad lived to a ripe old age and brought immeasurable joy into my life. He will always have a special place in my heart. And the adage "beauty is in the eye of the beholder" will forever remind me of this incredible cat.

~Marti Hawes

A Special Cat

Be what you are. This is the first step toward becoming better than you are.
~Julius Charles Hare

"**M**ichael, there's something special about that kitten," I said, as four-year-old Michael looked into the box of kittens. They had been born late the previous night while he slept.

"He's pretty," he said, stroking the tiny, orange-striped kitten.

"But look," I said as I gently pulled him away from his litter mates. Tears spilled out of his green eyes when he saw that the kitten was missing his right front leg.

"He'll need some special care," I said. "We have to help his mother make sure he gets enough to eat."

"I'll name him Special, and he'll be my special kitty," he replied.

As the days passed, Michael and I made sure that Special had feeding time with his mother after the rest of the litter was finished.

"All those bad kittens are pigs," exclaimed Michael.

"They aren't bad, they're just hungry," I said.

"They keep pushing Special away," he continued.

"They're stronger than him," I said.

"They're naughty," he replied.

"Their eyes aren't open yet. They can't see that their brother has only one front leg," I said, putting my little boy on my lap. "Remember we have to help him until he gets strong."

When the kittens started walking, Special didn't. He pushed

himself around the box on his belly. When the other kittens began to climb out of the box, Special didn't. He walked around in the box, and fell down a lot. He spent extra time with his mother, getting extra feedings while the others scampered around the house. One day our neighbor was visiting.

"Why didn't you have him put to sleep?" she asked when our children were out of earshot.

"I figured we could take care of him," I said. "He's not in any pain. He was born that way, and he walks almost as well as the other kittens now."

As the months went by, Special played with his siblings. The others chased each other up our sweet bay tree. Special didn't stay behind. He climbed up behind his brothers and sisters, pulling himself up with his front paw. He let go, moved his paw upward and attached again with speed and agility. Michael laughed and cheered.

"If it hadn't been for you, he wouldn't have lived," I said. Michael beamed.

As the kittens got older, I decided to have Special neutered so he wouldn't fight. I didn't think he'd have a fair chance against four-legged cats. I shouldn't have worried. Climbing trees with one front leg strengthened him beyond any four-legged cat. He chased neighbor cats out of our yard, and if a dog dared enter our yard, one swipe of Special's paw on his nose sent him home, yelping.

One day a mouse came out from under the refrigerator and ran across the kitchen floor. Special caught it easily. It was under his front paw. He held it there. Every time he began to lift his paw, the mouse tried to escape. He caught the mouse several times and played with it until the poor mouse finally died. Special caught birds too. I didn't have the heart to put a bell on his collar to warn them. It didn't seem fair.

Our veterinarian had fun with Special too.

"Okay, bring the cat to the examining table, and we'll see about his shot," he told his new assistant. She didn't look as she reached into the pet carrier. She reached around in the carrier, until finally, looking in with a puzzled expression, she got him with both hands.

"Oh," she exclaimed. "Usually I hold them straddled on my arm." I smiled and tried to look understanding.

"Read the name on the carrier," said the vet with a snicker.

"My four-year-old son named him that," I said.

"I see why," she said, smiling. The vet caught my eye, and laughed.

"I love it when you bring Special in here. I always get my newest assistant to help with him," he said.

As the years passed, my little towhead grew into a dark-haired teen, and Special got old. When Special climbed trees, he always jumped down, because he couldn't climb down like the other cats did. When he was ten, he jumped too far, and hurt his shoulder. He never healed from it, and his limp became more pronounced.

Early one morning last spring, Michael found Special dead, curled up in the grass under the clothesline. We wrapped him in his blanket, put him in a nice box and buried him. A special stone marks his grave.

But Special lives on. Michael has grown into a conscientious, considerate young man. He's twenty years old, volunteers in a nursing home, and is in college, in Basic Law Enforcement Training. I think taking care of Special helped him to become aware of and concerned with other people's problems. That poor little helpless kitten he helped has taught him to help the world.

~Sharon Palmerton Grumbein

The Disappearing Cat

It is impossible to find a place in which a cat can't hide.
~Bill Carraro

With a mostly white body and a few orange spots scattered on his back, Kiki was ordinary in appearance. As for his behavior, well, that's a different story. He was a frisky, cute kitten and a sweet, loving adolescent cat, but midlife hit him hard. He wasn't content with his surroundings, and he took on a new identity. He became a magician—and he was the star of his own disappearing act.

Often when my husband, Dwayne, cleaned out the shed attached to our house, Kiki sneaked inside and climbed up to the attic. He couldn't get down on his own, so he would pace above the kitchen, meowing loudly. We lost count of the number of trips Dwayne made to the attic to rescue Kiki. Surely, we thought he would learn that no good could come from these disappearances. But, unfortunately, those were just the first of our rescue missions. One summer day, our family was playing in the backyard when we heard a plaintive cry. We didn't recognize the sound at first, but when Dwayne walked to the edge of our property to investigate, he realized it was Kiki.

"Which one do you think he's in?" Dwayne asked, gesturing to our neighbors' two storage sheds. One belonged to a friend from church who had several cats herself. But the other was owned by an unfriendly woman who instructed her sons to chase Kiki and shoot him with a water gun whenever he set foot on their property. We walked from one shed to the next, calling his name until, with a sigh of relief, we determined he was inside our friend's shed. Thankfully, she was home and more than happy to free him.

Kiki's most frightening—and eventually funniest—disappearance happened during an ice storm. The roads were in terrible shape so we hadn't left the house in three days.

"I'm really worried about the cat," my husband quietly confided one evening. "When was the last time you saw him?"

I couldn't answer. With three children under age six, I had been pretty busy, and much to my shame, I hadn't noticed Kiki's absence. We immediately started looking for him. We searched under beds, inside closets, and even ventured into the dark, forbidden basement, all to no avail. Out of options, I finally tried the garage.

"Kiki?" I called.

"Meow, meow," he replied. It was a beautiful sound. I was anxious to see my feline friend and worried about his health. But where was he? He wasn't in the tool cubby or on top of the car. He wasn't sitting on the window ledge, either. I was stumped until I walked alongside our minivan. "Meow!" I glanced inside, and there, sitting in my daughter's car seat with his white front paws pressed against the window, was Kiki.

I was thrilled to see him and quickly pulled open the door. Kiki jumped down with a happy chirp and rushed toward his food and water. I gave him a big hug then carefully climbed inside, expecting the worst. After all, this had been Kiki's home for three days. I looked around. Amazingly, the cloth seats and armrests were intact. I sniffed the air. Somehow, the minivan didn't smell like a litter box, but Kiki surely would have needed one. I opened the cargo area and saw where Kiki did his duty—on an old, crumpled newspaper. The only price we'd pay for Kiki's recent magic trick was frayed nerves.

Like Kiki, I haven't always been content with my situation. Sometimes I've daydreamed about fancy clothes I can't afford or wished I lived in a bustling suburb instead of a sleepy town. But the grass isn't always greener—or the cat food tastier—on the other side of the fence. I'm happy to report Kiki has emerged unscathed from his midlife crisis. After his adventure in the minivan, he hung up his magician's cape and finally seems to realize the best place of all is to be surrounded by people who love him.

~Melissa Zifzal

Peaches Goes on Catkins

Dieting is wishful shrinking.
~Author Unknown

e never call her fat—at least not when she is in the room or when she is within earshot. And when we discuss her extreme appreciation of food we whisper. Even when she is asleep, Peaches has exceptional hearing and can hear a bag of cat food from any corner of the house. So to preserve her fragile self-esteem, we refer to her as "extra medium" and never refer to her need for excessive amounts of food as "gluttony." She is merely more enthusiastic about eating than the other cats. Actually, the truth is that Peaches has a weight issue. She is, well, kind of round.

We adopted Peaches as an adult. Her mother died in childbirth and she had been bottle-fed by my son and daughter-in-law. She was brought home to a small two-room apartment which she shared with a male tuxedo cat named Samson, a rabbit, and a small dog. From what they told me, there was always a small ruckus over food. The older cat and the dog pushed tiny Peaches out of the way when they were hungry and fighting for dominance. Peaches, afraid of missing a chance to eat, began to sleep near the food bowls to ensure her fair share. When we used to visit, Peaches was playful and happy, and indeed she spent all of her downtime resting by the food bowls.

My daughter-in-law developed a problem with her immune system and became very ill. Her doctors said her environment had to be cleaned up in order to help her, and she and my son were forced to give up their pets. They found a home for the dog, and by that time the rabbit had died. They asked us to take the cats. I already had four cats and didn't really want two more, but it came down to the pound or us. When we finally said we would adopt Samson and Peaches, my son drove fifteen hours to deliver them, and, despite being an adult, he cried when he left them to drive back home alone.

Samson came into the house and, being a dominant male, began to let my existing cats know that he was their new boss. None of them took Samson seriously, and even though Samson hissed and swatted everyone, no blood was drawn, and he blended into the pack rather quickly. Peaches, on the other hand, ran under a chair at the farthest end of the house and wouldn't come out. My husband, other son, and I took turns down on the floor talking to her and petting her, but she was totally freaked out by her new environment.

Eventually, I tricked her. I put the food bowl in the hallway where she could see it and made a cat food trail to the bowl. With five other cats, it was hard to know which one was eating the trail, but it kept disappearing. I kept moving the bowl farther out until it was in the kitchen where it belonged—at the other end of the house. In time, Peaches was waiting with her new brothers and sisters as I filled their bowls each morning. As usual, I left all the cats' food down on the floor so no one missed an opportunity to eat. The problem was that Peaches ate all the time, regardless of her level of hungriness. If someone came into the room, Peaches ran and ate. If we had company, Peaches ran to her bowl. If we changed the channel on the TV, Peaches needed a snack. If I moved a magazine on the table, Peaches had to eat. She was eating all the time, except after 10 p.m. when she put herself to bed. And the bed was getting too small for Peaches, but instead of seeing it as a dietary issue, I bought her a bigger bed.

Recently, I held Peaches and weighed the two of us together. Then I weighed myself and subtracted that from the combined weight. Peaches weighed seventeen pounds—heavy for a cat like her. I, too, was not happy with my weight. Having always dealt with extra weight myself, I knew there was only one answer. It was time for Peaches and me to go on diets.

My diet was easy. I know I am not punishing myself, and I know that eliminating calories and high-carb food is the way I lose weight the fastest. And I know that if I exercise, the weight will come off faster and hopefully stay off. I am motivated by new clothes and compliments.

But weight and health cannot be explained to Peaches. I bought cat food for weight control, and I only leave the food on the floor for an hour in the morning and at dinnertime. After that I lift up the bowl and put it on the kitchen counter where the healthier, thinner cats can still get to it, but Peaches can't. I figured that if she gets thin enough that she can jump up onto a counter again, she will be able to have between-meal snacks, too.

Peaches sits forlornly in the kitchen next to where her food bowl was. She waits for hours for us to put the food down. Occasionally if she looks very sad, I take a small handful of her diet food and put it down in a small bowl for her. We continue to pay attention to each cat, but since Peaches is dieting, and I can commiserate, I tend to stay down on the floor with her longer. Her favorite game involves running after a flashlight beam. Each cat gets a turn to run around like crazy, but Peaches gets the longest turn. And, as if they know something is going on, the other cats let her run around and pretend she's skinny.

~Felice Prager

Reprinted by permission of Off the Mark
and Mark Parisi ©1991.

Cat vs. Girl

I can't decide if I have a cat or a cat has me.
~Esther Marton

My cat and I have always had a special relationship. As a child, I remember thinking that we had mutual respect for each other, and that we each held an equal amount of power in our relationship. Now that I am older and wiser, I realize that I never had any power. She had a way of making me feel like I was in control when I really wasn't. Our interactions were always of this nature, beginning from the first day we met when my mother brought her home from an animal rescue shelter.

My mother delegated the job of naming her to me since I had named our previous cats, brilliantly calling them Miss Kitty, Gato (Spanish for cat) and Little Girl. This time around, however, I was determined to come up with the most incredible and original name for my new black-and-white tuxedo friend. I sat in the bathroom with her and watched her scoot around as she explored her surroundings. I was waiting to find the name that would reflect her personality. Nothing was coming to mind, so I decided to throw out some names to see if she would react.

"Sheba?" I said. She stopped her exploration and looked at me, her face expressionless. Then she turned and walked away from me.

"Spike?" I tried again. She didn't even bother turning and looking, she just twitched her tail. I should have known better. Spike is clearly a dog's name. Speaking of which:

"Dog?"

She definitely wasn't interested. I wrinkled my nose and gave in. "Socks?"

She turned and padded lightly over to me as my heart sank. Did she like my least favorite name? She stepped onto my lap and stretched up her body so we were eye level, her front feet on my chest. Then she smacked me across the face with her paw.

"Okay Kitty, not Socks," I said, and she started to purr. I look down at her and cautiously patted her on the head. "Good Kitty," I said, using the name again. She purred louder and snuggled into my arm.

"Kitty?" I said one last time. The now curled-up ball of purr settled in. "Okay, Kitty it is!"

The name "Kitty" actually worked well, because she usually came when we called her. The key word being "usually," because whenever we called her, you could actually see her weighing the amount of effort required. Her eyes would blink slowly and deliberately whenever we made kissy noises at her or patted our laps enticingly. She knew that after a while if she didn't come to us sooner or later we would get up and come to her.

The last time I ever challenged her authority was my sophomore year in high school. I was convinced that if I put my mind to it, I would be able to take control. She walked into the bathroom where her food bowl was kept, and paused when she realized that I had put her least favorite flavor of cat food in her bowl. I was standing at the sink, pretending to focus on brushing my teeth so I could watch what she did without her noticing. She turned and looked up at me, her tail twitching with warning. Quickly I turned my eyes back to the mirror and leaned forward, pretending to check my teeth for spots I had missed. She gave one short warning meow. I pretended not to hear her. She tried again, louder this time, and I felt her paw bat me lightly on the back of my calf. I turned and looked at her innocently and waited. I could see her debating whether or not to hit me again, but I remained firm. She turned around and walked out of the bathroom without another sound. I released the breath I hadn't realized that I had been holding.

I leaned against the sink, savoring my victory in my quest for power over my cat. This was going to be the first of many. Then I heard it: the unmistakable sound of a large amount of liquid splashing onto the floor. I ran into my room just in time to watch Kitty delicately step out of my closet, shake her back paws off, and trot by me back to her food bowl, tail held high.

~Rebecca Davis

Not a Regular Cat

*When I play with my cat, who knows if I am not a pastime to her
more than she is to me?*
~Michel de Montaigne

The wind-blown rain splashed in the puddles around me, fracturing the reflection of the lights from the gas pumps. I shivered in the Michigan chill as I filled the tank of my old Ford. Tired of watching the pump tick off the gallons, I looked around at the gloomy March night. I saw something move underneath a parked pickup truck. After I capped the gas tank I walked over to see what living thing might be out in this weather. Two cats, wet and dirty, with white fur showing through grease and mud, gazed steadily at me. I went into the station office to pay for the gas.

"Are those your cats under that truck?" I pointed outside.

"No. Somebody must have dumped them yesterday. I didn't feed them. I hoped they'd go away, find a house someplace, but they're still here."

Something made me ask, "Can I take them?"

"Sure, if you want," he said, sealing the deal by offering me a cardboard carton.

Back at my apartment in a farmhouse, I opened my heavy package. After soapy washcloths, towels, and combs were applied to the sorry creatures, the inventory consisted of a longhaired, pure white, green-eyed, adult female and a half-grown, shorthaired white male, presumably her son. In honor of the place we met, I dubbed them Premium and Regular.

The next day, Regular had the symptoms of severe respiratory and eye infections, refused food, and curled up in a miserable ball by the radiator. When I got home from work that evening, he was a very sick cat.

"Feline distemper. Usually fatal because of dehydration," the vet said. He thought Premium would have symptoms by now if they were exposed at the same time, but she might be spared if she had been immunized as a kitten. The vet knew I worked in a hospital and that I could manage an intravenous feeding tube at home. He suggested an IV to combat the dehydration, but he had limited hope that it would save Regular.

"You can try it," he said. "I'll set it up and you can take him home and sit with him. If it works, he'll be improving by this time tomorrow. I'll give him an injection of antibiotics before you leave. That is, if you're going to take a shot at this."

Regular lay on the bathmat, and I was on a pile of quilts nearby, watching the IV fluid feed from the bottle hanging off the shower curtain rod, counting the drops per minute, and dozing. The next afternoon, Regular looked brighter. I scrounged up jar lids and saucers, placed tiny dabs of a variety of foods, and lined them up like a cat buffet. Through his still-clogged nose, he sniffed and refused tuna, cottage cheese, cat food, and scrambled egg, but settled on the strawberry ice cream. He was on the way to recovery.

Regular grew into a beautiful, athletic adolescent cat with a sleek coat and eyes the color of new leaves. Premium reclined on my bed pillows while Regular prowled the apartment and the yard, never going far, but always busy pursuing bugs or batting dandelions. When my neighbor's grandfather came from Ohio to visit for a few weeks in June, he took notice of the lithe white cat and coaxed him to spend time on his lap when he rocked on the downstairs porch. He also gave Regular a surname. Cat.

Mr. Klick was eighty-one years old with a history of training horses. He told me stories of the last days of the United States

Cavalry, and how he was contracted to retrain "spoiled" horses whose riders allowed the animals to have their way a few times too often. Cavalry remounts, they were called, when Mr. Klick and others like him made the horses fit for duty again. We would sit in the shade while he regaled me with tales of the old days. He would call Regular Cat to his lap and sit stroking him, often tracing the cat's prominent muscles with his finger. Maybe it was the shortness of the coat, or the solid white color, but Regular Cat had easily discernible shoulder and thigh muscles. I wondered if Mr. Klick was thinking of thoroughbred horses, the strength of their build, and how he had controlled that power. Now, still wiry in body, but walking with a cane, did he mourn the loss of the work he loved? He sometimes dragged a long wisp of hay along the floor while he talked. Regular Cat ran and pounced. The old man found some scraps of lumber to use as small hurdles and enticed the cat to jump over two or three in succession.

"Look at him! Look how high he went that time! He's fast!" he said proudly.

Regular Cat sought the old gentleman's company. He waited under the rocker or near the door, and attacked his elderly companion's ankle as he walked by. Mr. Klick left on July 5, but returned just before Labor Day for a last visit. His granddaughter, Jenny, had found a job elsewhere. She would be leaving the farm and the old man wanted to come to Michigan one more time. I was picking the last of the tomatoes in my little patch when Jenny approached.

"Grandpa is leaving in few days," she said.

"I know," I replied. "I'm sorry I won't be seeing him again. I'm sure he's just scratched the surface of horse stories."

"That's for sure, but I came out to give you a heads-up," she said. "He's going to ask you if he can take Regular Cat with him when he goes."

She assured me that he would understand if I refused, but she wanted to give me a few days to think about it.

"I don't need a few days," I said. "I'll get a copy of his health records and you can use my cat carrier. Only one thing. I thought your grandfather lived part-time in Ohio and went to Florida for the winter."

Jenny laughed. "Regular will go with him. He'll be an indoor cat so he won't get lost no matter where he goes. And if you're wondering what will happen if Regular outlasts Grandpa, I promised to take him. Of course Grandpa plans on being around another twenty years and probably will be."

And so it happened that the old horseman and the uniquely muscular cat became a pair, living in Ohio during the milder months, and wintering in Florida. Abandoned and rescued, then adopted again, the white waif was far from being a Regular Cat.

~Ann E. Vitale

My First Cat

Does the father figure in your cat's life ever clean the litter box?
My husband claims that men lack the scooping gene.
~Barbara L. Diamond

Throughout my life, the cat was always an intruder, a thief in the night that slowly wiped out my exotic birds. After years of thievery, I gave up my aviary, determined never to own another bird until the world was cleansed of cats. My wife, however, had owned a cat all her life up until we started dating. She omitted to disclose this fact until five years into the marriage when she arrived home with "it."

"What is that thing?" I asked.

She continued to smile and proudly showed the black fur ball in every possible profile.

"I found him under the car when I went to the bakery," she proclaimed. "Jasper was all alone. I couldn't leave him there."

"You already named him?"

She smiled at me and nodded, holding him before me one more time.

"Take him back. The bakery can put him in tomorrow's pot pies," I said.

"No," she squealed, cuddling him closer, the daughters moving in to swoon over him.

"He's black like Darth Vader," the younger one giggled with delight, having never asked for a cat, but realizing that the glasses she wore for two years had kittens on the side of the rims. In one afternoon, I had lost my position as the man of the house to a four-week-old street cat. As expected, the daughters were done with Jasper inside of a month, and all of their assigned chores suddenly reverted to me. While cleaning out his litter box late one night after a sixteen-hour day, I did notice that the cat was putting a move on my wife.

"He's cuddling me," my wife proclaimed as she continued to stroke him behind his head. His beady eyes stared at me and he flicked me off with his tail.

One afternoon I returned home to discover that he had entangled himself in four different balls of yarn. With hard evidence of wool tampering, which would have gotten me scolded, Jasper got cuddles. When he pulled the curtains down, leaving me to waste a Saturday at Home Depot trying to coordinate drapes, Jasper was rewarded with gourmet cat food. I was lucky to be allowed to buy myself a Snickers bar. At Christmas, Jasper got a $200 kitty condominium. I got a $20 Borders gift card, for which I contributed $10. On New Year's Eve, he got a tuxedo costume and I had to chauffeur him to seven different parties that he had received an invitation to. I was stopped from entering at every single door.

I had enough. I sat down to write an advertisement to give him away. The first draft was rubbish. I tore that page off the notebook, balled it up and threw it across the room. The cat took off, and brought back the paper ball. I picked it up again, and threw it the other way. Jasper went the other way, and brought it back. The cat was playing fetch. Could the cat be taught manners, tricks and maybe even obedience? I threw the paper ball away repeatedly, and each time, Jasper brought it back.

For the next week, we played fetch. I called in sick one day just so we could play fetch. My wife yelled at me at 3 a.m. for staying up and playing fetch. Jasper was even on YouTube, playing fetch. He went from personal adversary to a million hits in under a week. Jasper never played catch with the daughters, not even with my wife. They all tried but he never responded to them as he did to me. Jasper and I had found a game.

"Cats don't play fetch," one of our friends quipped.

"My cat does," I said, stroking Jasper behind the head.

Then Jasper flicked him off too.

~Grant Madden

The Truce

One is never sure, watching two cats washing each other,
whether it's affection, the taste, or a trial run for the jugular.
~Helen Thomson

Catfights. Those hormone-charged, highly emotional rumbles between two females intent on tearing each other limb from limb. Nails flashing, hair flying, screams of anger pierce the air. The causes of catfights can be as varied as the participants. Until marrying a farmer and moving to the country, the only catfights I had ever witnessed were in the restrooms and hallways of my high school. But when we bought our first house, it came complete with three cats—a momma and her two babies. Over the years, we have sheltered countless cats in our barns, and in the spring and summer, with our windows open to the cool night breeze, we are often jolted awake by the sounds of a late-night catfight. Usually the fight was between a male tomcat on the prowl and a rival male defending his territory—but that was before Holly arrived.

Since we live on a busy road and have a soft spot for animals, our home is often a refuge for unwanted cats. They arrive in the spring or fall, past the fun kitten stage and just on the brink of being able to produce their own babies—and tame enough for us to know they spent the first half of their life around people.

One cold fall morning, my son stepped out the door to wait for the bus and there she sat, a beautiful, black, white, and orange calico with large golden eyes. She wove around my ankles and gently butted her head against the kids' hands when they petted her. They named her Holly (short for Halloween Cat), led her to the food dish in the barn, and introduced her to the other cats. Holly kept her distance, but tolerated the other barn cats. All of them, that is, except Darla.

Darla, acquired when she walked out of the cornfield one summer day as a kitten, sported a gorgeous washed-out calico pattern of white, gray, and pale orange. Accustomed to the kids handling her, Darla was laidback and social with cats and people alike. Everyone, that is, except Holly.

From day one, they shared an inexplicable animosity. They lived in peace with the other cats, but if they passed within ten feet of each other, a raucous catfight broke out. Nails flashed, hair flew, and screams of anger pierced the air. Their hatred continued through the winter and all of the next year.

The following spring, Holly delivered her second litter of kittens: an orange tiger, a black-and-white spotted one, and two white-and-orange combinations. She kept them in the hayloft, separated from the other cats, and she rarely left the wooden crate she called home.

Two weeks later, Darla claimed an old wooden box on the ground floor of the barn and rested there all day, her bulging stomach stretched to capacity. Then an amazing thing happened. Holly moved in to share the box with Darla. No more animosity; no more fighting; no more hatred. They shared a peaceful co-existence, and pregnant Darla seemed comforted by Holly's presence. Holly licked Darla's ears, face, and neck, while Darla rested, eyes closed while purrs resonated from her throat. Several times I moved Holly back to her own box so she could nurse her babies. Each time her kittens finished Holly descended the stairs and crawled back into Darla's box, curling her body protectively around her new friend.

Within the day, Darla's labor started and Holly continued her ministrations. As each of Darla's tiny new kittens arrived—first two miniature calico versions of their mom, followed by an orange tiger and then a smoky gray one—Holly took over, cleaning each baby and then nursing it as Darla struggled to birth the next one. Darla seemed to grow weaker with each new arrival, and it appeared she lacked the strength to care for them. Fearful that Holly would claim Darla's babies as her own, and then not have enough milk for all of her eight kittens, I moved Holly several times back to her own box and encouraged Darla to nurse her own kittens. But again, Holly fed her own family, and then returned to take over the care of Darla's kittens.

Finally, maybe in an effort to appease me, Holly moved her entire brood down the wooden stairs and into Darla's bed with the tired momma and her newborn babies. Within a few days, Darla regained her strength. Now able to nurse and care for her own babies, Darla no longer needed Holly's assistance. I moved Holly and her gang back up the stairs to the loft and this time she stayed. When the cold winds of winter arrived, and all the kittens were old enough to care for themselves, Darla and Holly went back to disliking one another. However, I will always remember the amazing compassion and mercy our cats showed that spring in our barn.

~Nikki Studebaker Barcus

First Love

Our perfect companions never have fewer than four feet.
~Colette

"**I** want to marry Comet," I announced to my family when I was nine years old.

"You want to marry someone fat, unemployed, and hairy?" my dad replied sarcastically.

Yes, that was exactly what I wanted. Comet, my white, and slightly overweight tabby cat, was all I could ever hope for in a happy marriage. His character was impeccable, and I couldn't imagine any human male meeting the high standards he had set.

I grew up a sickly child, and due to my complex medical condition, my parents had to drive me to an elementary school almost half an hour away from our house that had a full-time nurse on staff in case of an emergency. After school, the summer months were a little lonely since most of my friends lived thirty to forty-five minutes away.

Early in the summer of my eighth birthday, our cat had her first litter of kittens. I stared in rapture as each small body came into the world, took a gulp of air, and let out the first squeals of life. One by one they came. The first three of the four kittens were dark calicos with small patches of gold across their backs. Then the last kitten came rolling out, covered in snow white fur with large patches of orange that looked like my three-year-old sister had finger painted them. I saw his small pink mouth open, swallow a breath of air, then unleash a sneeze that shook his entire newborn body.

I watched as his eyes opened for the first time, revealing gold-colored eyes. I stared into them intently, wishing for telepathy to connect us. It was love.

"Your name is Comet," I wanted to tell him, "because your spots look like stars."

I saw him walk and experiment with his first bites of solid food. Completely devoted, I felt as proud of my kitten as though I had given birth to him myself. Weeks of begging my parents to let me keep him proved successful and we became inseparable. He followed me everywhere, even to church. He learned how to climb my bunk bed to sleep on my pillow, and would, on rare occasions, leave me "presents" like dead mice or small birds.

As I grew older, my condition worsened. Nights spent in the hospital weren't uncommon, but after a successful surgery, I was sent home. My exhausted parents fell into their first peaceful sleep in weeks, believing the worst was over. It may have been an hour or two before I awoke, my temperature spiking and the sheets clinging to my wet limbs. I wrestled away the fabric and gingerly climbed from my bed to the floor, only to convulse from heaves coursing through my body. I stumbled into the bathroom, clutching my stomach, hoping for what was inside to stay there. It was to no avail, and as I felt the thrust of my stomach again, I whispered into the dark, "Mom, Dad, help," and then I blacked out.

Hours later, I awoke in the hospital, hooked up to highways of tubes and wires. I heard the words "infection," "dehydrated," and "it's a miracle." As my vision became sharper, I looked into the eyes of my mom, holding my hand, telling me that I would be fixed up in no time.

"What's wrong? What happened?" I croaked.

"You were very sick, sweetheart. Your dad and I wouldn't have known if Comet hadn't woken us up. He was throwing a huge fit, and wouldn't leave us alone. When I got up to throw him out of our room,

I heard you and we got you here as fast as we could." Mom looked so tired, but I saw relief in her face.

Comet rarely let me sit in a room alone after that night. I called him my knight in shining fur, made plans for when we would be married, and ignored my dad's comments about him being unemployed. As I have grown older and learned that interspecies marriage is frowned upon, I know I am well on the path to becoming the crazy cat lady on the corner. Love is blind, and a little crazy, but I believe it is worth it with a cat like Comet.

~Nan Johnson

My Cat's Life

Are You Stalking to Me?

Cats Are Like Potato Chips

Psychologists now recognize that the need in some people to have a dozen
cats is really a sublimated desire to have two dozen cats.
~Robert Brault, robertbrault.com

I guess word must travel far and wide when there's a house full of suckers, because in addition to our legitimate barn cats we had a steady stream of freeloaders. If they made it into our barn with any regularity our mission was to tame and socialize. Then as soon as said freeloaders were tame enough to get a hold of, we would whisk them off for appointments with their reproductive destinies.

One of these consistent freeloaders was a wild short-haired, plain-brown tabby that looked like Puck, one of our legitimate barn cats. For lack of any other reference, we referred to this feral free-loader as The Puck Look-Alike, a moniker that morphed to simply Puck-alike. For several years, Puck-alike used the barn as a sort of halfway house for litters of half-grown, more-than-half-wild kittens. I resigned myself to the fact that as timid as she might be, Puck-alike wasn't going to abandon our barn, and that she would continue to drop off her kittens with us. I sweet-talked and cooed to her when I saw her near the food, and slowly she stopped bolting at the first sign of people, and gradually became less wild. And none too soon, because it was becoming clear that Puck-alike was in a kitten way once again.

"Here's the plan," I informed my husband, Arnold. "I want to bring her up to the house, keep her in the spare bedroom, and she can have her kittens there. Then, we can get her fixed, socialize the kittens, and find them all good homes."

Arnold has a marshmallow for a heart, especially where cats are concerned, and he readily agreed. We closed off the spare bedroom and brought in Puck-alike. We didn't know how soon she was going to have her kittens, but I didn't think it could be long. I told Arnold that I expected it to be within a week—two at the most. But Puck-alike did not have her kittens in one week, or two, or three. Instead, she simply grew and expanded, apparently quite content to gestate. After a month, she looked as if she had swallowed a football. The short tabby hair on her sides poked out, refusing to lie flat anymore. She was all eyes and belly, waddling around on four teeny-tiny paws.

"I can't believe she'll last more than another day or two," I said.

"That's what you said three weeks ago," Arnold pointed out, unnecessarily.

A week later, Arnold called me from home with an important observation.

"There's something sticking out of Puck-alike's butt," he said.

"Sounds like she's going to have her kittens," I said.

"I think it's coming out backwards. I see a tail."

"Is it moving?" I asked.

A pause while he checked. "Yep, it's wiggling around."

"Good," I said. "Is Puck-alike still pushing?"

"She's pushing, but I'm not sure it's moving," he replied.

My veterinarian had given some cat-birthing advice to me since I had been in the same situation in which Arnold now found himself—playing midwife to a cat giving birth to a breach kitten. I relayed the same instructions to Arnold.

"Grasp however much of the kitten you can get hold of, and very gently pull when she pushes. Watch that Puck-alike doesn't bite you. And if all you have a grip on is the tail, don't pull too hard, or you'll have a Manx cat."

Arnold calmly followed directions. I listened to him coaching Puck-alike.

"Push, push!" he said. "There ya go! What a good girl! Push!"

He came back to the phone and told me there was progress — the kitten was emerging. He asked if he shouldn't be dabbing Puck-alike's brow as he coached her.

"I feel like I should be boiling water or tearing up bed sheets or something," he said. Soon, Arnold reported that Puck-alike had delivered the kitten.

"What's it look like?" I asked.

"It's sort of a blob."

"That's not very helpful," I said.

"Okay, it's sort of a dark gray blob."

I predicted that several more blobs were pending. Many hours later, when I got home, Puck-alike had clearly completed delivering her litter of not six, seven, or even eight, but rather, a grand total of three kittens, again proving me a poor prognosticator. On point of principal, we did not name the kittens. Why name a kitten you know you're not going to keep? I took pictures and prepared to bombard my friends, associates, and acquaintances with images of irresistible fluffy precious fur balls. Presented cleverly, kittens practically sell themselves, especially when they're free.

When the babies were about a week old, Arnold said, "Which one are we going to keep?"

"We're not keeping any of them," I replied.

A week or so later, Arnold said, "We should keep two of them instead of just one."

"No," I said. "We're not keeping any of them!"

"Well, we need to keep two, because then they'll have each other to play with," Arnold said, as if we were actually having this conversation.

"Arnold, we already have six cats in the house," I said. "We can't take any more. We're not keeping any of the kittens."

Arnold sighed.

The days went by, the kittens grew and thrived, and learned to eat cat food and use the kitty litter. It was time for all of the parts of our well-laid plan to come together. I made an appointment with the vet for Puck-alike to get spayed. The kittens were old enough to be weaned and were very well socialized. It was time to organize their departures from the nest.

"I think we need to keep all of them, not just two of them," Arnold said.

"We're not..."

"Well, if we only keep two of them, the one we don't keep will feel abandoned," said Arnold. "So we need to keep all of them."

"We are not keeping any of the kittens."

"Besides," Arnold said, ignoring me, "people hate gray cats."

"People do not hate gray cats. And we're not keeping any of the kittens."

Arnold sighed. Again.

The next week, in a simple, uncomplicated procedure, Puck-alike's kitten-bearing days came to an end. Stage one of the plan was accomplished. The kittens were healthy, cute as the dickens, and very well socialized. Stage two of the plan was accomplished.

But stage three—the critical stage where the kittens actually went to new homes—well, that stage failed to launch. Puck-alike never had any more kittens and her last litter was healthy and friendly, but they never did leave our home. I guess that part of the plan crashed and burned when Arnold sat in the maternity ward, dabbing Puck-alike's brow and telling her to push.

~Karen Donley-Hayes

67

Boris & Bluebell

True love stories never have endings.
~Richard Bach

He invited himself onto our patio late one summer evening as we braved the 100-degree heat to grill steaks. Short body, boxy head, scars and oil slicks marked his back. We called him Boris, and he purred his approval by rubbing our hands. He courted us, perching atop the picnic table, tabby tail curled politely, blinking golden-green eyes. We melted. Bites of steak and water were offered, and he graciously accepted them with purrs of thanks. His social skills extended through dinner and we started altering our schedule to meet his, eating on the patio in anticipation of his nightly visits.

Inside our apartment lived three pampered felines who jealously watched. After a Boris visit they would come sniffing, mouths open, ears flat, and breathe in information. They would rub where he had rubbed, reclaiming us with their own familiar scent.

One day Boris followed us in, neatly sidestepping the gawking, hissing creatures confounded by his brazen trespassing. We watched, wondering, waiting. His movements seemed planned, as if he knew what he was doing and the trouble it might cause. The housecats fled to places of safety—the open closet, the bookcase headboard, and as far back on the bathroom vanity as possible. There, they hunkered and snarled. He ignored them. He was on a mission, padding grandly from room to room, sniffing, seeking, his golden-green eyes taking in everything before returning to the glass door where he asked in a high-pitched mew to go back out. Amused by the improbable sound from this streetwise tom and by his inspection of our home, we wondered how we measured up.

Not long after his tour of our home he returned with a friend. She sailed with him, side by side, over the patio wall, landing with as much grace as her swollen belly allowed. Blue-green eyes watched warily, but he took his place beside her, rubbing against her, then rubbing against us. It's okay, he seemed to say, blinking at her. Obviously, this was his lady.

We hastily responded, offering food to the mother-to-be. We called her Bluebell. There was something beautifully sad about this homely white cat with gray tabby patches. He allowed her to eat before finishing the offered treat. She didn't welcome our touch. She lowered her body to avoid our hands. Boris, however, was grateful for a bit of love. Then a rub, a tiny mew, and they were off, over the fence, leaving us speechless and the inside cats furious.

They came over the patio fence daily, with Bluebell struggling as her body grew, and they always ignored our open door. The patio was the only acceptable entry, so we prepared a birthing box there, not sure if she would use it.

We were surprised one evening when Boris scratched at the glass door. He had only been inside once and had never asked again. We opened the door and he trotted in, Bluebell wobbling beside him. He led her to the food dish, water bowl, and litter box. We watched, openmouthed, shushing our indoor kitties that backed into corners and hissed their anger at this new intruder. Bluebell sat plump in the middle of the living room with Boris beside her, his golden-green eyes finding ours and holding them steadily. We brought the birthing box inside.

Blinking approval, rubbing our legs, Boris went to the door, but Bluebell remained, turning her head toward him as if saying goodbye. We let him out and stood by the door to see if she would follow. She stood and looked hard toward the door before waddling to the box, ignoring our cats' protests. Boris leapt the patio fence, leaving his beloved behind.

Four tiny kittens were born the next day. Bluebell suckled them, bathed each in turn, and left them only to eat, drink, or use the litter box. She was a protective mother, snarling her threats when our cats wandered near. She was tolerant of us, and allowed us to cuddle and hold the squirming balls of fur. She accepted our affection, food, and shelter, but her heart wasn't in mothering. Her blue-green orbs lit up only in the evenings when Boris sailed clear of the fence and landed smartly on the patio table. She would abandon her babies and race to the door, insisting with a shrill meow to be let out. At first we were afraid that she would leave, but her distress and agitation at seeing Boris and being unable to get to him was evident. We opened the door and were treated to the sight of lovers reunited. They touched noses, rubbed against each other, bathed one another, and shared the dish of food. After a while, he cleanly leapt the fence and she sat beside the door looking in. We opened it and she returned to her kittens.

Bluebell was a firm mother, yet never mean to her growing, rowdy children despite their sharp teeth that bit her nipples and their claws that dug into the soft flesh of her belly. She played with them, showed them how to lap the baby food oatmeal mixed with water and milk that we set out for them to try. Little curtain climbers, they were strong, healthy, beautiful, and, unlike their mother, affection-ate. They would seek us out for a romp or to fall asleep nestled in our laps. When she wanted them, she would mmmrrrruuuppph or gently carry them by the scruff to the box.

Boris and Bluebell continued their nightly trysts and when the kittens were three weeks old, she began to go with him when he left, returning shortly to be let in. We knew it wasn't our affection that brought her back, though we had fallen in love with her. She was there for her kittens.

Eyes open, eating kitten chow and spending more time away from their mom, the kittens prospered, blending with our cats, even enticing them into play at times. Bluebell observed while maintaining her aloofness. She spent more time with Boris, both staying away longer. We would rub his chin and he would purr his gratitude. Sometimes he would even squeak a word of thanks. Bluebell once or twice offered up a brief rub, but her heart belonged to Boris. Certain she would never desert her babies, we let her go and waited for her return, but then it happened.

We scoured the apartment complex, put out food, and asked everyone if they had seen "our" strays. Some recalled seeing them heading towards an empty field but couldn't remember when. We checked the animal shelters, the pound, and even the dead animal pickup to no avail. As the weeks passed, we realized the truth. Boris and Bluebell had left the kittens to us. We found homes for all of them except Pumpkin, who remained with us as a precious reminder of her parents, with a loving, gentle spirit housed in a homely package.

~Patti Wade Zint

The Gift of Lily

Too often we underestimate the power of a touch, a smile,
a kind word, a listening ear, an honest compliment, or the smallest act of caring,
all of which have the potential to turn a life around.
~Leo Buscaglia

"You know, you talk about your cat like she's a baby," my friend interrupted me. The comment came through the phone like a hand slapping my face. Perhaps she thought I was wasting her time by sharing stories of my life with my cat, Lily. A waste because she didn't deem my stories on a par with her stories about her baby. Her words silenced me. She was right that I treated Lily like my baby. Her behavior and milestones helped me feel joy and optimism after I lost two babies of my own.

When I had visited the SPCA, Lily, an ordinary tabby cat, had sidled up to the mesh of her cage. On tiptoe, she had pressed her body against the cool metal bars, begging for some petting. Her nose bobbed against my fingertips and she purred. I had adopted pets before, but this time there was no question. Lily was the one. We had just moved into a house flanked by tiger lilies just like my childhood home. To me they were a promise of new and beautiful things after some hardships. In bringing this cat home, it seemed right to name her Lily, pronouncing her a symbol of a new beginning and good promises. Lily proved to be very easy and generous. She was the first lap cat that I had ever had. And she was my cat. My husband didn't seem to mind her, but there was no great love between them.

When I had found myself pregnant for the first time, my husband and I started building our dreams. When I miscarried in less than a week, I crawled into bed after my husband left for work, pulling Lily under the sheet with me. We took long morning naps for a few days, her furry form snuggled into a curl at my belly as I lay in the fetal position, while blinking lights from the Christmas tree in the living room sprinkled pastel red and green on my bedroom wall. She stuck to me in those days, or any days when I was sad, depressed or struggling. While I cooked, she preened her head against my ankles.

When I found myself pregnant again, anxiety held back my joy until I passed the week when I had lost the last one. Then as I passed the seventh and eighth weeks, my husband and I built our dreams again. This time it was real. The last time had been a fluke. The doctor said it looked liked I would have an easy time of it—not even a lick of morning sickness. But in my third month, loss visited again. I curled into the fetal position as the pains ebbed through my lower back. Before he left for work, my husband brought me Lily, and placed her warm, yawning body against mine in a silent but meaningful way to say he was sorry. I curled around her body, and from time to time felt her scratchy steel wool tongue on my forearms as she bathed herself, and I tolerated her extended hind leg pushing into my cheek, toes splayed. As she slept, I hugged her damp fur to me as I cried. When the pains turned to contractions and I tried to alleviate them with stretching, doing backbends over my exercise ball, and then finally succumbed to them, pinned down just as surely as if my pelvis has been stapled to the carpet, Lily was always near.

After I returned from the hospital, Lily was my companion. She stayed with me through my anger and tears. She mewed for her food, forcing me up to feed myself. She let me massage her head absentmindedly as I peered, eyes closed, through the wall of the bedroom and imagined I could see the field of tiger lilies outside, where I wish we had buried our baby girl, but I had not had the presence of mind to do. I looked at the underside of Lily's paw one day, pink and milky white, as she stretched and relaxed it under the pressure of my index finger, like a flower blooming and closing for the night. Like a newborn baby opening its fist to the air, then gripping his mother's trusted finger.

As I mourned, Lily's mews grew even sweeter, and every expression, sign of affection and new activity from her swelled my heart and pushed grateful and sorrowful tears to my eyelashes. I doted on her. I bought her things that I, a farm girl who once had dozens of cats, had always thought silly. I bought cat-scratch posts, a jungle gym and catnip—all for the pleasure of seeing Lily's pleasure. And in the evenings, we lingered on the porch swing, watching the night fall on the cow pastures, pond and the grove of trees sheltering geese. I carried her, because she let me. I coddled her, because she let me. I met her needs, kept her safe, and made her a life full of all good things I could offer.

My husband even forged his own relationship with her. In one of my favorite pictures of him, he's sleeping with Lily roosting on his chest, her sleepy head cocked back under his chin. And as long as she lived, her place at night was my side of the bed—whether at my shoulders where her fur sometimes wafted up my nostrils, or at my feet where she chortled her lawnmower-rant when I wiggled my toes.

One evening, I sat on the porch swing by myself. As night fell, her spot on the bed was empty. No Lily. The next morning, my husband found her on the side of the road, near a telltale layer of rubber on the road from an eighteen-wheeler. My husband buried her out by the tiger lilies, where I wish my two babies were buried, too. For a long time, I often believed, when waking in the night, that I felt her warm spot. I'll always remember that as the year when I lost three babies. Sure, the implications of losing my pregnancies were certainly different, but I'm not sure I mourned Lily any less than I grieved for them. I talked about Lily like she was my child, I missed her like she was my child, and I will always be grateful that I was granted the privilege to "mother" Lily.

~Renee Lannan

Cat in Mourning

T he sun beat down on the sidewalk as I walked up to the house. Before I reached the door, I saw a mother cat and her three newborn kittens. The striped gray mama cat lay panting in the heat with her tongue hanging out. The kittens straddled her boney side in the Texas heat.

"Dad, look!" I called over my shoulder.

"Who would abandon a cat on a day like this?" he questioned. "I don't know if they will survive."

We quickly scooped up the mama and her babies and took them into the air-conditioned house. The place we lived was small and there was barely enough room for our family, much less a house full of cats.

"We can't keep them. We just don't have room," I said as I cuddled a little soft ball of fur. But we took them in to help them recover from the heat and grow stronger. It didn't take long before the cute kittens found loving homes, but no one wanted the mama cat. So mama cat was allowed to stay, and soon we dropped the "mama" and just referred to her as Cat.

Every morning my dad would give Cat a pat and rub as he walked out the door on his way to work. In the evening when he got home there was Cat waiting for his return. After dinner Dad would give Cat a treat from his plate and sit under the shade tree with her on his lap. We teased Dad about his pet. She would follow Dad around like a watchful friend and always seemed to know where he was going. Like clockwork she climbed onto the porch railing and waited for his pat and rub as he left for work. When Dad was working on the car or working in the yard Cat was right there by his side. She would walk beside him and rub his legs when he stood still. Sometimes in the evening Dad stood on the porch watching the planes from the nearby airport fly over. I would look out the window and see my dad with his bright blue eyes and blond hair and there would be Cat sitting next to him on the porch railing, as they watched the planes together.

As far as I know they never said much to each other. Yet, there seemed to be a bond between them. Could it be that Cat sensed that Dad was ill and was living on borrowed time?

Not long after that Dad's weakened heart failed. The paramedics came and tried to revive him but he died. In the wee hours of the morning, after friends and neighbors had left, I lay in my bed trying to comprehend that Dad was really gone. I was too stunned to even cry. Then I heard a heartrending wail outside the porch door. Pulling the curtain open I saw Cat. Her mournful cries rose and fell as she stretched her face to the dark night sky. She voiced my unspoken sorrow and loss. For days she paced back and forth crying and looking for her master and friend. The day Dad was buried I noticed that Cat's wails and searching stopped. She just sat on the porch railing with her gray head on her paws. The next day Cat was gone. We never saw her again.

Did God send Cat to Dad to comfort him and prepare him? Were they contemplating heaven as they looked up at the stars? I don't know the answers, but I know that Cat's wails gave voice to my anguish and pain. The memory of Dad and Cat sitting together on the porch steps in companionable silence is mine to relish and gives me comfort.

~Lynn Cole

Here Kitty...
Go Fetch!

Cats do not have to be shown how to have a good time,
for they are unfailingly ingenious in that respect.
~James Mason

I adopted her on a cold day in January. She reminded me of the cat who owned me as a child and the moment I set eyes on this orange tabby kitten, I knew Cassidy was coming home to live with me. From the beginning her personality was different than any cat I had ever known. She purred continuously. Her tail was always up in the air. Beginning with her first night in my home, she slept with me. Now, most nights she sleeps on me. As she grew out of kittenhood and became a mature cat she started conversing with me in her own language, and we understand each other perfectly.

As she closed in on her first Christmas in our home, she was part of the house decorating committee, removing ornaments from our Christmas tree and then strategically placing them in just the right corner for an extra bit of "bling."

Wrapping Christmas presents with my daughter Beth one evening, Beth pulled out a decorated pipe cleaner that was used to tie a decoration on a bow the previous Christmas.

"Are you going to use this, Mom?" Beth asked as she waved it at me.

"No, you might as well toss it in the trash," I replied.

With a flick of her wrist Beth tossed the fuzzy pipe cleaner toward the trash, but it missed and fell to the floor. Cassidy, not missing a beat, charged full speed and pounced full force on the pipe cleaner. She pushed it with her left paw and then tapped it twice with her right paw. She picked it up in her mouth and danced with it.

"Beth, please take that away from her. I'm afraid she'll swallow pieces of it."

Beth picked it up and tossed it into the garbage. Cassidy followed it as it flew through the air and she, too, landed in the garbage to retrieve her "toy."

Later that evening when it was time for bed, Cassidy followed me upstairs with the pipe cleaner dangling from her mouth. She jumped on the bed, dropped the pipe cleaner, and with her tail in the air gave me a pleading "meow?"

"What?" I asked, foolishly.

"Meow?" She sat next to her "toy" and stared into my eyes, then pawed the air as if to say, "C'mon—play with me!"

It was clear what she wanted so I took the pipe cleaner and tossed it onto the floor. To my great surprise, Cassidy sailed off the bed, picked up the pipe cleaner, brought it back to the bed, dropped it in front of me and said "Meow?"

"Cassidy, you're a cat, not a dog!"

"Meow?" was her only response.

"Okay." Cassidy had won.

We repeated the exercise for forty minutes. She was having a blast and I could not believe I had a cat that played "fetch." With Christmas a few days away, I asked Beth what we should get Cassidy for Christmas.

"Oh Mom, c'mon—you know... pipe cleaners!"

How foolish of me to think that my cat would want a squeaky toy or catnip! A package of pipe cleaners from the craft store cost less than two dollars. On Christmas night, I made a circle out of a new pipe cleaner and threw it like a flying saucer. Cassidy bolted after her new toy. That night we played for an hour and she finally lay down on the bed exhausted and dropped off to sleep.

Nowadays I find that when Cassidy is ready to play fetch she finds her toy, sits beside it and stares into my face. With her head cocked slightly to the right, she waits patiently and meows occasionally just to remind me that she is there, waiting to play. If I don't respond right away she will paw the air until I give in. Admittedly, she is hard to resist, but she knows that. People laugh when I tell them I have a cat that plays fetch. They often ask if she's a "dog wannabe." Granted, she is unique, she is special, and she has "cattitude." But then again, don't they all?

~Elisa Yager

The Miracle Kitty

Kittens are angels with whiskers.
~Author Unknown

The funeral home was packed with mourners. Our family had been grieving for days, but when my sister-in-law, Cari, entered the foyer, she looked even more bereft than we felt already. "It's Tigger," she told me, her voice trembling. "He's been hit by a car."

"Oh no," I said, shocked.

"The vet doesn't expect him to make it through the night," said Cari.

I moved to tell my husband, Jeff, who, equally shocked, went with Cari to find their brother, Greg. Huddling together, they waited for their oldest sister, Kathy, and youngest sister, Marci, to arrive with my mother-in-law. We knew that Mom would be heartbroken, since Tigger was my father-in-law's beloved cat, and Dad had passed away three days before, on Easter Sunday.

As mourners continued to arrive, I tried to wrap my mind around this new turn of events. I'm a firm believer in synchronicity, in "everything happening for a reason," and I love observing all the "meaningful coincidences" that enhance our lives. But on that dismal April evening of my father-in-law's memorial service, I didn't see anything meaningful—or enhancing—about this. Tigger's fateful accident so soon after Dad's death felt nothing short of cruel.

The lovable yellow kitten with the feather-duster tail had come into Mom and Dad's life by happenstance. Mom had been the first one to see the abandoned longhaired calico lounging beneath their deck two summers before. By removing one of the blocks of deck flooring, Dad had previously contrived a shelter of sorts for their longtime cat, Bojangles, thus providing protection from bad weather when Bojangles had to go outside. It was to this secluded spot that the calico had gravitated. Mom and Dad knew that once Bojangles discovered the calico, he would want to fight, so they tried to run the stubborn stray off—but to no avail. What my in-laws didn't know, however, was that the calico had just become a mother, and that Mama had chosen that sheltering deck nook as the perfect nursery for her tiny new kittens.

The kittens made their presence known in late June—four littermates in all. One was a tiger-striped shorthair; another, a pretty calico just like her mom; the last two were yellow longhairs that my mother-in-law felt sure had Maine Coon cat genes. The kittens' arrival was the very definition of love at first sight, but, although Mom and Dad adored their new little feline family, they were also resigned to the fact that once the kittens got old enough, they would have to call the animal shelter. They couldn't begin to care for five additional pets, particularly since the calico and her little ones would most likely remain feral. And then there was the issue of Bojangles. The persnickety black cat had ruled their household with an iron paw for many years, and at age seventeen, he wasn't big on sharing.

Tigger, of course, changed everything.

He was one of the yellow longhairs—the kitten with the sunshine eyes and comical personality who became a fast favorite. Dad especially loved him, naming him Tigger because even as a wobbly baby he could jump as high as a door handle. But what truly defined him was his beautiful, expressive tail. Fuzzy as a dandelion, fluffy as Daniel Boone's cap, it swished when he walked, giving him a swagger he used to his best advantage.

The idea of keeping him soon started to surface in our family. The calico was quite protective, though, and her youngsters terribly afraid of people, so catching Tigger wouldn't be easy. My niece tried for several days to do so, and when she finally did, Mom shut him in the bathroom to keep him safe. When Mom fed him the first time, she picked up this hyper little ball of golden fur, and immediately he curled under her chin and began to purr, going from "wild cat" to "family cat" in an instant. Once Tigger was "tame," the calico moved on with the rest of her litter, as if her sole reason for visiting had been to deliver her baby into Mom and Dad's open arms.

From that moment on, all fates were sealed—Dad's most of all. He got vast pleasure from the angel kitten with the devil-may-care attitude, and the two were all but inseparable. As Dad's health continued to decline, Tigger entertained him, providing humor and purpose to Dad's days. Together, they basked in the sun. Dad laughed when Tigger flashed his cat-who-ate-the-last-fish-biscuit grin, chased squirrels and played in the rain. Even Bojangles relented. You could almost see the resignation in the old cat's eyes. Tigger was, after all, a frivolous little thing, too insignificant to be taken seriously.

"Very serious," Mom's vet told her the morning after the memorial. We were going to Dad's funeral that day, but Mom had called the vet first thing. "If he lives, it'll be a miracle."

That "miracle" would include removing Tigger's tail—the beautiful Coon cat tail that so defined him—all the way to the coccyx, as well as resetting his dislocated right hip and leg bone, leaving him with a splint and a sling afterward to hold everything in place. For us at the funeral that day, mourning Dad felt twice as painful knowing Tigger was undergoing surgery at the same time. It suddenly seemed that the possibility of losing the orphan kitten was more than any of us could bear.

It's been more than a year since Tigger's accident. He pulled through the surgery just fine and although he stayed for a month at the vet's and was in a sling for another month at home, he's made a complete recovery. Minus his tail, he still basks in the sun and plays in the rain, and yes, while he does look funny without that lovely swish-and-swagger, the loss of it somehow merely adds to his droll demeanor.

Mom's vet still calls him the "miracle kitty," and I believe that it's true. I'm not sure if cats have nine lives, as the old cliché suggests, but I am sure that I am grateful for the one precious life of Tigger, for his resilience and courage. He fought a good fight and survived, and was by Mom's side in those first anguishing months without Dad. When Bojangles passed several months later, Mom and Tigger grieved again.

"I should have let him go with Daddy," Mom said to my husband and me that first week Tigger was back home. "He's suffered so much, but I just couldn't face losing him too."

"You and Tig needed each other, Mom," said my husband. "It's good he's here."

"He's right where he should be," I agreed.

For angels and miracles go hand in hand, and I'm certain that Tigger, Mom's little angel and miracle kitty, is in exactly the right place, at exactly the right time. I'm convinced that Dad made sure of it.

~Theresa Sanders

72

Family Man

When a Cat adopts you there is nothing to be done about it except to put up
with it until the wind changes.
~T. S. Eliot

My husband, BJ, and I knew our cat, Willow, was beautiful but we didn't realize she had attracted a suitor until the day there was an orange cat sitting on our patio staring in. He just sat there content to watch Willow lounging on the couch. Day after day, he was there. After about a week, BJ decided it was time to have a talk with this feline Casanova. He opened the patio door and the cat strolled in and curled up with Willow on the couch.

We were surprised and amused by his nerve. Every day, the cat would show up, spend the day with us, and then meow by the door to be let out at night. We obliged since, after all, he wasn't our cat. He was nobody's cat as far as we could tell. He had no collar or tag. I don't remember how long we waited before we admitted to ourselves that he was our cat and bought him a collar and tagged him as "Buster." The very next day, we received a call from our neighbor. We weren't home so she left a message.

"Hi Darlene. I think you have my daughter's cat. Call me when you get this message."

I didn't even know her daughter had a cat. I'd never seen it before.

I was crushed when I heard the message, and BJ and I agreed that it had been too good to be true. When I called her back, the story of Buster the cat was so funny that I forgot how upset I was. Buster, or

Pepin, had been adopted as a kitten by a neighbor, but that neighbor had to move and couldn't take the cat. They tried to find him a home, but weren't able to so they left him, hoping someone would take him in. Another neighbor did, the one who called us. She let her daughter keep him, but the cat had to stay in the girl's bedroom because they had dogs. During the day, he was let out to roam around the neighborhood, and this was when he would come to our apartment to be with Willow, eat her food, play with her toys and charm her mommy and daddy. Then he would leave us, go back home, eat his own food, play with his own toys and spend the night with his mommy.

When the neighbor's young daughter came over to collect her cat, I faked a smile as I watched my beloved Buster being carried away. He had brought so much joy to our little family in just a short time. I thought about Willow and how she would miss him. About half an hour after Buster/Pepin left us, the young girl called and asked if she could come over. She brought her cat back and bravely stated that she felt he would be happier with us, where he could have the run of the house without fear of being mauled by her family's dogs. She made me so happy that I wished I could do something for her. I told her how grateful I was, but that must have been little consolation. We told her that she could come by anytime to see Buster—which she did a couple of times, but then she stopped coming.

A year later we moved into a new house. Willow had passed on, but we still had Buster, and he loved his new digs. Sometimes we wouldn't see him all day.

"Where do you go all day, pal?" BJ would ask him.

We got our answer one day when we opened up the paper and there was Buster, posing for a picture with another family—the caption labeled him as "the family cat." Buster was back to his old tricks again. We had a good laugh about that, but kept a shorter "leash" on him from that time on.

These days, Buster stays pretty close to home. He's older now and his days of family hopping are over, but we will always remember how Buster gave a whole new meaning to "nine lives."

~Darlene Prickett

73

From Feral to Friendly

You will always be lucky if you know how to make friends with strange cats.
~Proverb

My first glimpse of Rocky's raccoon-striped tail and brindle spotted head and back occurred as he rolled my yellow cat Abe onto his back. I was horrified at the sight of my cat being pinned under Rocky's striking white paws. From that day on, Abe became an indoor cat, and Rocky continued to show up for free meals. When my friend, a vet, saw him at my door, she urged me to get him neutered. She insisted it would cut down on his fighting and risk of disease. Using a humane trap, he was easily enticed into captivity by a plate of tuna. Neutering and initial shots went off without a hitch and I was advised to keep him inside for a day or two.

Although Rocky had been feasting at my house on a daily basis for several months, he had never allowed me to get within five feet of him. He would dart off as soon as I approached. I kept him in my garage, sure that when I raised the garage door he'd run out.

Two days passed and Rocky had become a phantom. I would put his food out in the garage and look for him, but he was always hiding behind a box or on a shelf. The only evidence that he was there was when I returned minutes later and picked up the empty plate. The first time I raised the garage door, I watched the threshold to witness his escape. Time passed but I never saw him. Finally I closed the door, wondering if I could have blinked and missed his exit.

The next day I decided to place another meal in my garage.

Minutes later I returned to find it licked clean. Clearly he wanted to extend his stay a few days. Days turned into weeks, despite me opening the garage door every afternoon to allow him to check out. Six weeks after his surgery he was firmly entrenched and obviously enjoying the room service. Unfortunately, the weather was changing. As springtime took hold, I knew that the garage would soon be unbearably hot. As each day passed, I became more desperate for Rocky to leave. It was especially strange since he still did not allow me near him. I did, however, catch an occasional glimpse of him perched on a shelf or box watching me change his litter or water. I again tried the humane trap, but this time it didn't work. He had obviously lost his "every meal could be my last" mentality and let the tuna sit in the cage for three days. Frustrated, I went to retrieve the cage and just started talking to my elusive guest.

"What am I going to do with you? It's getting too hot for you in here! You have to go outside," I said. My voice cracked between words and I began to cry, wondering if he'd eventually die from the heat in my garage. Just then I felt something rubbing against my leg. I looked down and he paused. He didn't run away and I didn't move a muscle. Finally he looked up at me and I realized, for the first time, that he was blind in one eye. That did it. I couldn't put him back on the street. I slowly dropped my hand down and patted the top of his head. When I retracted my hand he stood on his hind legs leaning his front paws against my knee. His head now touched my fingertips. He wanted more attention. I continued rubbing between his ears and petting his back. It was a miraculous moment.

Each day after this, he ran up to me when I came out with food, litter, water, and we would repeat our bonding experience. I was able to pick him up and he'd rub his face against mine. Within a week, he was in my house sharing a room with his old rival, Abe. Now that there is plenty of food, the two have lost their need to fight. They often sit atop the hope chest that rests under my window ledge. There they form a neighborhood watch—between catnaps—until I return home from work.

~Marsha Porter

Three's Company

One cat just leads to another.

~Ernest Hemingway

"**M**om, I really want a pet," whined my daughter Meredith, then thirteen years old, as we walked to the mailbox. "I'm praying for one because miracles happen."

"It will take more than a miracle for your dad to agree to another animal in the house," I said, remembering the gloom that enveloped us after the death of our beloved cat, Tazzy. Even I didn't want to open my heart to another pet. It hurt too much. "Besides, I can't take on one more responsibility."

"I'll do everything," she said.

I arched a brow. "A pet is a lifetime commitment, and you'll be going away to college one day."

"Mom," she moaned and rolled her eyes. "Don't start that again."

Meredith stepped forward and opened the mailbox. She screamed. Mail scattered on the ground.

A dark blur passed before my eyes.

"A kitty," she said. "Well, I think it's a kitty."

We looked at the frail tabby cat that had pounced from the bushes. A skeletal cartoon character with long legs, an emaciated body, and a large head stared back with luminous eyes.

Meredith cooed at the straggly cat weaving around her legs.

"I'll call her Shadow Cat," she announced. "She's my miracle from the shadows." She leaned over and patted the top of Shadow's head.

"Be careful," I said and picked up the mail.

Meredith glowered at me and cuddled the cat to her chest. "Mom, she's helpless, and she's hurt."

I leaned closer. A recent wound circled her neck.

"We have to keep her," she said. "She's our gift from God."

Oh great, I thought. How do you not keep a gift from God? "We'll see if anyone claims her. But first, we need to get her to the vet."

The next day, the vet reported that Shadow was severely malnourished. As he examined her, he said, "It looks like someone tried to choke her." I cringed. Meredith frowned. He looked up at us. "But we'll hope that a collar caused the wound."

Whatever the cause, Shadow couldn't meow. But over the next two weeks, she proved that she could purr at full throttle. We couldn't imagine how anyone could hurt this loving cat.

Soon afterwards, Meredith and I were in the garage moving boxes.

Ka-plump.

I screamed.

"What?" Meredith cried.

We stared at a regal white cat with black and gold markings that had landed on the box from somewhere above. Enormous gold eyes stared back.

"Oh no," I said. "Someone cut off its tail." My immediate thoughts went to Shadow who couldn't meow because of someone's mean streak.

Meredith giggled. "Mom, it's a Manx. They don't have tails."

The cat's shrill meow made up for Shadow's lack of voice. Soft fur rubbed against my arm. She nuzzled my neck.

"It's another miracle from above... a gift," Meredith said.

How could I reject this beautiful cat? Another trip to the vet followed. Shadow's friend, Pyewacket, moved in.

Several weeks later, we were settling into a two-cat household.

Pye woke early and demanded attention with near-deafening volume. Shadow remained silent, but she blossomed.

One afternoon, Pye followed us to the garage to climb on boxes while Meredith and I worked in the yard. I reached into the corner to get my tools. An orange fur ball looked up with lazy eyes, and then stretched. Pye wandered over, but she dismissed the large male cat with a tilt of her head.

"She obviously knows him," Meredith said, and I had to agree. Otherwise, our finicky Pye would have pounced on the intruder.

I looked from the big Garfield-esque cat to Meredith and back and started shaking my head. "No more," I said. "I don't want to be the old lady with a house full of cats."

"They'll be company for you when I leave," she said with a wicked grin.

Abelard followed me outside. Every two steps I took, he plopped on the ground. I'd scratch under his chin, and he'd get up. Two more steps, he'd plop down again.

"I give," I said and gave him a good back scratching.

Abelard moved in and howled all the way to the vet's office. On the way, he urinated in the carrier. The vinegary stench permeated the car. I cracked my window. The wind roared. Abelard yowled, rolled onto his back, and pushed the wire door until it popped out of the frame. A wet, smelly Abelard stretched out on the leather back seat until I wrestled him back into the carrier when we arrived.

"Any more?" the vet asked with a raised brow.

"No," I said. "Three's definitely a crowd."

Truthfully, Abelard was no trouble. Preferring outdoor living, he wanted to live in the garage and be our guard cat. He'd come and go through the cat door. Every morning, he'd wait at the back door. Every afternoon, he'd meet me when I arrived home from work.

Over the years, the three cats with their own distinct personalities became a part of our daily lives. Birthdays and holidays passed. School years started and ended. The cats slept most of the time away. But during that time, I noticed that Meredith was doing more around the house. She'd kept her word about being responsible.

"You're growing up," I said and felt the familiar twinge. "You'll be heading to college soon."

"At least, you'll have the cats to keep you company," she said.

And they did keep me company as Meredith spent more time with friends and less time with me.

One afternoon, I pulled into the drive. Abelard spotted me. He dashed from his spot in the pine straw under the azaleas. I turned off the car and smiled, hearing his hearty meow. I opened the car door, ready to step outside until I saw him skid to a stop and back up. He hissed. The hair on his back stood up.

I paused with my foot dangling a few inches from the ground and then I saw the diamond triangles on the largest snake I'd ever seen. A five-foot timber rattler stretched alongside the border grass. In another second, I would have put my foot on the snake's back. The venomous bite could have killed me.

I eased my foot back inside the car, slammed the door, and called for help.

My husband and neighbors took care of the snake while Abelard and I watched from the sidelines.

"Aren't you glad we have three cats?" Meredith asked after the commotion. "Abelard, the last one to arrive, probably saved your life. I guess three's not really a crowd."

"No, it's more like three's company," I had to admit as I pulled the mail from our mailbox. College logos appeared on a half dozen envelopes. "I'll be okay being an old lady with cats," I teased, "because, if for no other reason, maybe you'll want to come home from college to see your three cats."

~Debra Ayers Brown

Chapter 9

My Cat's Life

For All Nine Lives

Stockpiling Memories

Memory is a way of holding onto the things you love,
the things you are, the things you never want to lose.
~From the television show The Wonder Years

S age, my domestic shorthair, stretches up and places his paws on my leg. I'm sitting in a chair on the deck watching the sunset. "Come on, sweet boy," I say, reaching down and lifting him into my lap. His silver-gray fur ripples beneath my fingers, and he stares at me with striking green eyes. Not that long ago he jumped into my lap with ease. Now, at sixteen, he's not as agile or as willing to make the leap. After he settles into a contented knot, my thumb automatically begins to rub the smooth pads on the bottom of his foot, each one like a tiny brown bean.

He came to me as one of several cats rescued through an animal group that I worked with. Sage charmed me with his calm nature and intelligence. Not to mention his gorgeous eyes, which have an uncanny way of seeing right into my soul. Ours was not a slow bonding but an immediate attachment to each other. Wherever I was, Sage was. He spent many hours sitting beside me on my desk as I worked. One afternoon we both needed a break from my writing, so I jiggled a bottle cap in my hands then made two fists. Sage watched with interest.

"Which hand is the bottle cap in?" I asked him.

He stared at my hands then reached out and tapped a fist.

Shocked that he seemed to actually understand what I said, I opened my fingers. The bottle cap lay in my palm.

"I'm impressed," I sputtered. "Let's see if that was a fluke." I shook the cap in my hands, made two fists, and held them out. He glanced at my fists but didn't move.

"Come on," I coaxed, shaking my hands. Suddenly, he touched a fist. Sure enough, the cap was inside.

"One more time? Please," I begged, though he was showing signs of restlessness. I had to know if he had made two lucky guesses. I held out my fists. Sage peered at me through hooded eyes. He glanced at the door. He yawned. Just when I thought he wouldn't do it, he flicked a paw at my hand. My mouth popped open. Three out of three times he had picked the hand with the bottle cap.

"Once more?" I asked, eagerly, like a small child who wants to play the same game over and over.

I thrust out my fists. Sage glanced at my hands, hopped off the desk, and disappeared through the door. I couldn't really be disappointed, well, maybe a little, but still, he had played longer than I had expected and left me amazed. I bragged to my friends and family about Sage's deducing ability. They rolled their eyes and humored me with comments like "Really," or "How interesting." Even if they couldn't appreciate how special he was, I could.

Sage and I developed many routines, and one was our bedtime ritual. After dinner, I would sit in the living room reading or watching TV. Sage lounged on my lap or on the footstool. With a snap, I would close my book, or click off the TV.

"Time for bed, Sage," I would say, standing and moving toward the doorway.

Sage followed me, leaped onto the bed and curled onto my pillow. When I lay down, he wrapped around my head like a fur hat. I would stroke his back and whisper, "You're my special boy."

Then one night he didn't lie on the footstool or curl in my lap. He didn't go to bed when I did. He stayed and slept on the back of the sofa. He began undergoing other changes: weight loss, drinking more water, lethargy. The vet did blood work and diagnosed Sage with hyperthyroidism, a common disorder in older cats. Liver tests indicated he was not a good candidate for surgery, so I started him on medication for the condition. I could live with that as long as Sage improved.

But he continues to change. Where he was once sharp and sure of himself, now he gets confused easily. When I open the door for him to go out on the deck he turns to see what I am going to do. If I don't follow, he comes right back inside.

Unlike in the past, when he followed me around with enthusiasm and independence, lately he moves like a puppet, unable to decide what to do, and relying on me to guide him. He also sometimes sits in the bay window with a vacant look in his eyes, staring at the wall or the windowsill.

"Sage?" I call to him.

My heart quickens and my breath catches when I have to repeat his name or lay my hand on his back to rouse him. Then he'll blink and his eyes will be bright and lucid when he gazes up at me, but I know he was gone for a while.

One day, Sage will leave me for good, but I don't dwell on that. Instead, I spend more time loving him. I never take him for granted. I seek him out the first thing in the morning and check on him the last thing at night. He craves attention more than ever, so I carry him around or sit and hold him, and let other things slide. I give him special canned food as often as he wants, and he's allowed to do things the other, younger cats are not, such as having free rein on the kitchen table. I kiss his face often. I hold him, sing to him, and sway with him cradled in my arms. I love him all that I can today, so he will never doubt how much he is loved and how much he'll be missed. I'm not mourning the loss of a constant companion and devoted friend, I'm stockpiling memories I can treasure forever.

~Teresa Hoy

76

Emily

There's a bit of magic in everything, and some loss to even things out.
~Lou Reed, "Magic and Loss"

A few months after our dog passed away, my son Jason begged me to go have a look at our local SPCA. Suffice it to say, the idea did not thrill me. I was still in mourning. I felt like a traitor just thinking about getting another dog.

"Come on Mom, we don't have to get anything. I just want to look. Please!" he begged.

"Oh alright!" I snapped. "We will go just to look." I could already feel my resistance starting to wane. When it comes to saying no to adopting an animal, I have the backbone of a slug and my son knew it. As we headed off towards the SPCA, I kept reminding him that we were just going there to look.

"Don't worry," he replied. "I know that we are not going to bring home another dog. I just want to visit some animals because I miss Sam so much."

Goodbye strong matriarch, hello slug woman. Once inside our local chapter, I was surprised to see my fair-haired son ignore the dogs and zero in on the cats. I started to feel a little bit at ease. He would never pick a cat. He has allergies. It was simply out of the question.

"Hey Mom, come look at these kittens, they are so cute! I know we can't have one but if we could, which one would you choose?" he asked.

I looked down into his sparkling blue eyes and knew that I was a goner.

"Jason," I said softly, "I would love to get you a kitten, but you know that you are allergic to cats."

"But that was a long time ago. We have been here for almost an hour and if I was going to have a reaction, it would have happened by now," he reasoned.

That was true. His allergies would usually kick in within minutes of being exposed. I was weakening. "You know it wouldn't be fair to the kitten if you suddenly became allergic to it," I said. It would be a disaster for all of us I thought.

"Mom, really I am fine. Please just give us a chance," he pleaded.

"Us? What us?" I asked.

He pointed to the lower cage. A little black paw had snaked its way through the bars and was clinging to the hem of Jason's T-shirt. I looked through the bars to see a very small and scrawny black-and-white kitten with a little pink nose. She had a Herculean grip on Jason's shirt. Every time I would get one paw free, another would take its place.

"It's no use Mom. She thinks she is coming home with us and I don't think that she can be told otherwise," he said.

Fifty dollars later, we were on our way home with Emily.

The little cat that I didn't want became a very special little friend and companion for the next twenty-one years. She was there through happy times and sad. She watched Jason grow into a man, and I think she was just as sad as I was when he left home.

A few years ago I had an operable form of cancer and had to be hospitalized for a few days. God was ever gracious, and they managed to get it all. I was told that I would be laid up for about two months. For the next little while I was not allowed to use stairs or drive my car.

Once I was home, that sweet little cat never left my side. She fretted over me when I groaned, and snuggled close when I cried. About three weeks into my recovery, I started to notice that Emily was not herself. Her arthritis was really causing her pain and her appetite was off. Now it was my turn to fret. I called my veterinarian and explained Emily's condition. He reminded me that she was an ancient cat and advised me to just make her as comfortable as possible. As long as she was still eating and drinking, that was as good as it was going to get.

I selfishly looked at her and pleaded, "Please Em, just wait until I'm on my feet and I promise I won't let you suffer."

Two weeks later on an early September morning, I kept my promise. I held her until she was no more. I gently kissed her goodbye and thanked God for this precious little gift called Emily. That funny little cat kissed my heart the day we met, and in my heart she will remain.

~Avril McIntyre

77

Arthur and His Opinions

The cat is above all things, a dramatist.
~Margaret Benson

Dog lovers would have described Arthur as "a cat who thought he was a dog." Those of us who knew Arthur, knew better. Arthur thought he was human. By feline standards, Arthur was a scrawny cat, a mere eight pounds of golden tabby. But those were eight magnificent pounds, and we're pretty sure that most of his weight resided in his voice box. You see, Arthur liked to talk—a lot. If he was awake and you were in the room, he would be yammering away, just to let you know that he was there, in the room, with you. Just in case you didn't hear him the first time, Arthur would throw himself at you, wind around your legs or strut across the coffee table, all the while interjecting himself into the conversation. "Mer-wow," Arthur said, as if to say, "I'm here. Now the real party can begin."

Arthur could expound on the weather, on his favorite brand of catnip, or why it just wasn't fair that he wasn't allowed to munch on the forsythia. "Yes," Arthur seemed to say. "I know the plant upsets my tummy, but it just tastes so good. A little vomit isn't too much to bear for such a good taste."

If Arthur really liked you, he would meow and purr at the same time. He also liked to talk on the phone. That really confused some telemarketers, but it endeared him to the rest of us. He liked to talk so much that I almost listed him in the phone book with me. I technically owned Arthur, but he really owned me. I rescued him after some neighbors in my apartment building had to move and couldn't take Arthur with them. I may have initially rescued Arthur, but he ended up saving me. Literally. Arthur rescued me not only from boredom, but he protected me. Once, in the middle of the night, someone tried to break into my apartment. Ever vigilant, Arthur began yowling and howling, meowing so loudly and kicking up such a fuss that I woke up with a start. But before I could even dial 911, Arthur had scared away the burglar.

Arthur also rescued me from gentlemen callers whom he deemed unworthy of my affections. Sometimes words, or meows, were not enough so Arthur conveyed his dislike in actions. In addition to talking, Arthur had another skill, which he put to use in such situations. Arthur could produce flatulence on cue, and on more than one occasion, he would toot his dislike. Arthur's skill was silent, but ever deadly, and he only aimed it with great purpose. On one particular occasion, when a suitor was in the process of breaking up with me, Arthur plopped himself right down between us, spread his legs really wide and began grooming himself, much to the dismay of the suitor. Then Arthur let a big one rip. Arthur said what I—and my friends and family—wanted to say, and he said it better than we ever could.

Arthur talked and tooted his whole life, even right up to the very end when a tumor had spread throughout his abdomen. Even though he may have been in quite a bit of pain, he still voiced his love and affection for me and others whom he loved. He also demonstrated for us his "other form of talking." In fact, when I took him for his last visit to the veterinarian, when I knew it was his time to leave us, Arthur let out one last vibrant toot, right there on the receptionist's desk. "I might be going," Arthur told us, with his last act of defiance, "but you're not ever going to forget me."

~Susan Ward as told to Jeanette Hurt

78

The Tail End of a Ninth Life

In the night of death, hope sees a star,
and listening love can hear the rustle of a wing.
~Robert Ingersoll

Twenty-five years old, suffering from kidney failure and senile dementia, my calico cat is lost in the house again. It happens a lot these days. "Meow!" she calls, a frightened cry begging me to come and fetch her, save her from whatever kitty-cat demons are dancing past her eyes.

"Meow!" Louder now and insistent, the pitch of the cry rises with her panic but makes my job of finding her that much easier in the too-big house she allows my husband and me to share with her.

"Delta," I say in my most soothing voice. "Where are you, little girl?"

She cries one more time and I find her, sitting at the top of the stairs looking like a waif from *Les Miserables*, but calmer when she sees me climbing up the steps. I gather her in my arms, crooning like a mother to a baby. Her white hair has the ruffled aspect of an angry hen and falls into my hand in clumps when I stroke her. It covers the floors and furniture, enough some days to look like a litter of kittens. I'll have to sweep twice before the day is done, but for now my cat and I are content to sit in an overstuffed chair, sharing a few quiet minutes together. Delta's loud purr tells me she is content to have her ears rubbed and her chin scratched. She elongates her neck, a clear sign that she likes her massage. When I stop, she pats my hand with her paw, indicating that I should continue. I smile and think back to our early days together.

Delta wandered into our lives a few months after my mother died. My husband, Terry, was in the third year of a four-year medical residency in a city where we didn't know many people. I was home alone most of the time, grieving and lonely. But all that changed one summer afternoon. I was weeding the front flowerbed when a pretty little calico trotted up our walk, acting like she owned the place. Thin as a needle and without any collar or identification, she arched her back and rubbed against my leg, then stretched out beside me, an overseer to my gardening. I figured that she belonged to one of the neighbors, but when I asked around, no one seemed to know anything about her. That was fine with us. Terry and I loved her from the start.

During our first year together, we learned that Delta was an accomplished huntress, liked to brawl with other cats in the neighborhood, and was fiercely loyal. Any dog foolish enough to set foot in our yard always came out on the losing end against Delta.

Then one day, a woman stopped on her stroll through the neighborhood and confessed that she was our cat's previous owner. With their only daughter graduating from high school and going off to college, they didn't want the responsibility of a pet. It didn't seem to bother her that Delta had run off. In fact, they had known Delta was with us for months and were glad that the twelve-year-old cat was happy and well.

We never expected Delta to last another dozen years, but she did. And she might have been sassy enough to thrive even longer if it hadn't been for a can of tainted cat food that killed her kidneys. These days, Delta knows that I am her caretaker, the one who runs when she calls. What she doesn't know is that her time on earth is short. She is at the tail end of her ninth life.

She doesn't know to be sad, but I do. Even with her white fur clinging in sheets to the seat of my black trousers, cleaning out two dirty litter boxes every day, and going through jar after jar of baby food until she settles on one she'll eat, and even when she cries in the night because she can't find her way, I value the short time we have together. It is why I am willing to hold her in my arms like an infant, listening to her cat motor run, smiling at the contented look on her face: eyes closed, nose up, chin at the proper angle for optimal scratching. Her tail swishes once. Twice. Then she rises from my lap, arches her back, and leaps to the floor, satisfied that I'm not going anywhere. She sits squarely in the middle of a Persian rug and licks a paw with the delicacy of a little old lady patting her brow on a hot summer day.

"Hey, old girl," I whisper in a voice hoarse with tears, glad no one is around to hear me talking to my treasure of a calico. "I'll miss you when you're gone."

Delta stares at me with eyes the color of spring grass and saunters off for a long winter's nap. All is right in her world now, until the next time she wanders around a corner and loses her direction.

~Ruth Jones

79

The Ingredients of Happiness

Three grand essentials to happiness in this life are something to do,
something to love, and something to hope for.
~Joseph Addison

Since last March, I have been visiting a wondrous place where dogs and cats play, people tell funny stories and pets show off their goofiest tricks. It's a medical facility for animals in northern Massachusetts, about two hours from our home on Cape Cod. It's the only clinic in the state that consists solely of veterinary oncologists. I expected it would be terribly depressing but it's just the opposite. I have been so surprised at what I have learned there: the ingredients of happiness.

Cancer treatment, including chemotherapy, does not have the same side effects for pets as it often does for humans. Our cat, Eddie, was referred to the medical facility because he has lymphoma. I was worried that he would hate the car rides but he loves them. I was also worried that the treatment would cause him further suffering. It doesn't in the least. He is happy and doing great, and by that, I mean as of right now. "Right now" is the only way people think at the clinic.

I believe that one ingredient of happiness is love in any form. If I've ever known an angel, it is Keri, Eddie's technician. Both Eddie and I are under her loving care. She gives Eddie his medicines. She gives me emotional guidance.

She asked, "Would you like to be with him for his infusion?"

Of course I would. Ever since Eddie's been a baby, I've calmed him by singing a lullaby, a silly song I made up to the tune of our old Westminster chime clock. When Keri placed Eddie on the table, I held his paw and slowly sang to four chimes, making his name into two syllables, "Who loves Ed-die?" Keri began administering the medicine. I whispered four more chimes, "I love Ed-die." He closed his eyes and started purring. I sang the hourly chimes that ring at four o'clock. "I love Ed-die." When Keri was through, I kissed Eddie's forehead. Then I kissed Keri's too.

I can often tell when it's someone's first visit. They're usually crying. I think the reason the rest of us don't cry has nothing to do with hope. I think it has to do with another ingredient to happiness: living in the present moment. When we think about our pet's distant future, even if they're healthy, we envision darkness and death. Keri, in her soothing prayerful voice says, "Focus on loving Eddie right now."

Today, our trumpet vine was flourishing with orange blossoms. Then, so typical of me, I thought of how quickly time passes. All too soon the vine will be winter barren. But because of Keri's wisdom, I stopped my thoughts and instead cradled one beautiful blossom in my hand. I have spent way too much of my life missing what is right in front of me.

In the waiting room of the hospital, we don't mention what we do for a living. It's not important. What is? Another component of happiness: connection. Can you picture a New York City subway where riders are crowded together, yet in their own separate worlds of talking on cell phones? Try picturing that same scene, but instead the riders are looking at each other, often touching hands and talking openly from their hearts. That instant connection is what happens in the waiting room. I think helping others makes us happier. We join together to tenderly lift a lame dog. We take turns distracting a cat with sparkly toys so she doesn't chew her bandage. Nobody asks for help. Nobody offers. We just do it. When the end of life is very near, owners often prioritize that their pet's happiness is more important than things like a strict diet.

A young fellow brought Leo, his Golden Retriever, to the scale. He gained seven pounds. Leo's owner feigned surprise.

He laughed as he whispered to me, "Last night we both had sirloin steaks." He patted his old friend. "He can have anything he wants now." So I guess an element of happiness is not so much the length of a life as it is the joy and peace that living that life contains.

Leo started nosing around in my purse. He could smell Eddie's treats. His owner said he could have a few. Leo was in ecstasy tasting the tuna-flavored treats. With that big goofy grin Golden Retrievers are known for, Leo was on cloud nine. So was his dad. So was I. In that moment.

It's been said that cancer is the great equalizer. Leo's dad was wearing chains and a "Mike's Truck Stop" T-shirt. Next to him was a seventy-ish woman wearing a silk dress and sapphire jewelry. I was dressed like I had spent the day cleaning a pig barn. If we only see the exterior of a person, such as their clothing, physical attributes or skin color, then we do not experience the real person inside. At the clinic, stereotypes and prejudice fall by the wayside. When a dog has a missing limb, we regard that as merely a characteristic in the same way that a pet has whiskers. But when I see disabled humans, their disability is primarily what I see. I'd be a better and happier person if I saw everyone as a dog. At this wondrous place, the focus is not about dying, and it's not about living. The focus, for pets and for people, is on living well and the ingredients of happiness.

~Saralee Perel

80

Tiger One, Vet None

Always the cat remains a little beyond the limits
we try to set for him in our blind folly.
~Andre Norton

Tiger, like many middle-aged cats and humans, had definitely begun to chunk up. One pound. Two pounds. Three pounds. The vet suggested I cut back on her food but it didn't help. Middle-age spread continued to spread. Then during her thirteenth year, I noticed that she seemed a bit lighter. Pleased, I petted her.

"You are a beautiful cat," I told her, "at any weight." Tiger gave me a look that said, "Was there ever any doubt?" Then she blinked twice and jumped up onto the wall unit for a nap. Over the next few weeks, Tiger grew increasing slimmer until she had regained her lithe youthful figure. My first reaction was envy, since even my youthful figure had been stocky. If I could figure out her secret to weight loss, I could package it and make a million. But when Tiger went from lithe to gaunt and fragile almost overnight, I knew something was seriously wrong. I hesitated taking her to the vet, not wanting to hear that my thirteen-year-old cat was dying. But guilt won out over fear, and three weeks before Christmas I made an appointment.

The vet took one look at her. "Hmmm," he said. "I know I wanted her to lose some weight but this is too much and too fast. We'll need to take blood and urine samples."

He picked her up and brought her to the back of the clinic where I heard a low growl and an "ouch." After a few minutes, both returned. Tiger had a satisfied look on her face while the vet sported a Band-Aid on his hand. I figured that round went to Tiger. The vet handed her back to me.

"We'll have the test results in a couple of days, but I'm pretty sure we're looking at advanced kidney disease," he said. "I'll call you as soon as I know."

Tiger slipped back into her carrier and we went home. She decided a nap was in order and hopped onto the dining room table. I hit the chocolate to calm myself down. Two days and about a pound of chocolate later, the vet called.

"Are you planning on being away for Christmas?" he asked.

"I was going to visit my parents," I said slowly as I processed the information. Then it hit me. "That fast?"

"I don't know, but her numbers were off the chart and she also has a bladder infection. It's not looking good. We can treat the bladder infection but we can't cure kidney disease," said the vet. "Still, there are special foods for cats with kidney disease. And if it comes to that, we can hydrate her with subcutaneous fluid therapy."

"Sub what?" I asked.

"Subcutaneous fluid therapy," he said. "It's a bit like reverse dialysis in which we're putting fluids into the cat rather than taking them out. Some cats do well on weekly treatments, and others need daily ones. And some cats won't stand for it. As for Tiger…" he said, his voice trailing off.

"Ah, Tiger," I said. "I can't even give that cat a pill. The thought of trying to give her daily or weekly transfusion of liquids is scary. But so is her dying."

The vet didn't answer for a moment. "It comes down to you and Tiger. If it makes both of you miserable…"

"Then it's not worth it," I finished. "I'll come in for the antibiotics and special food. Then we'll see."

That night I called my parents to give them the news. "Forget about visiting us," my mother said. "You have to stay with her. We understand."

The holidays were a quiet time around my house—just me,

Tiger and my other cat Sammy. I knew Tiger was sick when she didn't fight me as hard over the antibiotics and only scratched me twice. Luckily, she liked the new food. Although she didn't gain weight, she didn't lose any more. I know because I started to weigh her every two days. I also checked on her at least ten times a day, often waking her up to make sure she was still alive. Each time she glared at me I said a silent prayer. I'm pretty sure what she thought was a lot less angelic. One month went by. Then a second and a third. At the end of the first year, Tiger and I went back to the vet. He looked her over and smiled.

"I wouldn't have believed it if I hadn't seen it. This is one time I'm pleased to be wrong," he said. He ran his fingers along her ribs, and then listened to her heart. "She's still skinny but her heart is strong. That is one determined cat. She'll probably outlive us all."

I could swear Tiger smiled. In the end, she was so determined that she lived another six years before her failing body finally proved too much for her spirit. But some days, as I walk past the dining room table, I could swear I can see a black and brown tabby smiling at me.

~Harriet Cooper

81

Steps of Dignity

Never interrupt someone doing something you said couldn't be done.
~Amelia Earhart

For a few years, there was a set of stairs to nowhere in my apartment. Thirteen inches high and covered in faux lamb-skin, they led right into the wall in my living room. On the box, they had been advertised as a set of pet steps designed to help elderly cats and dogs climb to places they could no longer reach, and in theory they were an excellent idea. However in reality, in my home, they collected dust. My cat, Chewie, was not interested in pet steps.

My mother had purchased the steps for Chewie as a Christmas present. She thought that since he was officially a geriatric cat he might appreciate them. But I wasn't sure how I felt about the pet steps. As far as I was concerned, Chewie wasn't getting old and he was certainly never going to die. I ignored all the signs that Chewie might be slowing down. He did, too. At fourteen, his coat was glossy and his eyes were bright. His veterinarian remarked that he looked and acted well for his age, and his blood work showed no major cause for concern.

If he didn't jump and run about the house as much as he had before, well, he obviously had better things to do. He still attacked his toys every day, he still occasionally got stuck in the closet, and he continued to follow me everywhere. Physically and mentally, he seemed fine, and the very idea that he might have trouble jumping seemed ridiculous to me.

Nevertheless, I accepted Mum's Christmas gift and set up the steps for Chewie. He was deeply interested in the construction efforts, and hovered around as I arranged the pieces of plywood into a staircase. However, once the steps were assembled and placed by the side of the bed, Chewie turned up his nose and made it clear that he considered it all to be a serious affront to his dignity. Who was I to tell him that he needed steps to get anywhere?

Chewie snubbed the steps. When I picked him up and tried to place him on the fabric-covered riser, he wriggled out of my arms and ran away. When I tried to coax him to use the steps by bribing him with treats, he turned his back to me. Eventually, I gave up and moved the offensive apparatus to the living room, where Chewie continued to ignore it. He was old, but he was still Chewie.

When he was sixteen years old, Chewie was diagnosed with lymphoma completely by accident. If the vet hadn't felt the single enlarged lymph node during Chewie's annual checkup and decided to investigate, it would probably have gone unnoticed. He didn't know he was ill, and he certainly wasn't going to act that way. I cried, did research, and had serious discussions with Chewie's kind vet. We put him on a treatment protocol that was designed to fight the cancer while preserving his quality of life.

For a while, it seemed to work. Chewie fought with me when I gave him his lymphoma medications every day, ate voraciously, and tore around the house. Every night when I returned from work, he met me at the door. When he went for his follow-up visit with the vet, she discovered that his cancerous lymph node had shrunk. He continued on his lymphoma protocol, but the idea that cancer was going to harm him somehow seemed as ludicrous as the idea that he needed pet steps to jump up to the bed.

Then came one terrible night, shortly after Thanksgiving, when Chewie did know he was sick. He refused to eat and staggered around the house, crying and vomiting. I cradled his carrier on my lap as we sped across the city in a taxi, headed for the emergency room at the 24-hour animal hospital.

The vet quickly whisked Chewie away to run tests, leaving me to sit alone in the empty exam room. I paced the corridors and watched the clock turn from midnight to one, and then to two, and then to three. When I returned to the exam room, I tried to ignore the photo collage directly opposite me, a tribute to some of the hospital's former patients. Even though I made an effort not to notice, it stayed with me: the wall covered with pictures of cats and dogs, their names written with markers; the knowledge that it was a memorial, and that every single pet I was looking at had passed away.

The memorial wall forced all of my fears about Chewie to bubble to the surface of my mind, and suddenly they were no longer ridiculous. Chewie was old. He had cancer. I was sitting in an animal hospital in the middle of the night waiting for the vet to figure out why Chewie was crying in pain, and given the extenuating circumstances, it was entirely possible that the prognosis was not going to be good. I had to confront that and all that it meant.

However, Chewie bucked all expectations again. When the vet finally did return after reviewing the tests and imaging studies, she had good news for both of us. Chewie's cancer hadn't progressed. In fact, his condition was improving. He simply had a nasty infection that was entirely treatable, so she gave him fluids and a shot for pain relief, and sent him home with a bottle of antibiotics. In the morning his regular vet prescribed painkillers to hold him over until the infection subsided.

He might have been comfortable, but he was also completely worn out. I watched Chewie gingerly plod around the apartment, weak and woozy from his illness and the strong pain medication, and my eyes fell on the neglected pet steps. Maybe, just maybe, he'd finally want to use them. I set up the steps by the side of the bed and waited. Chewie stopped in front of them, looked at them, and then looked up at me with his eyes narrowed in disgust. If he were human, he might have sneered. And then he stepped back, crouched, and jumped right over the offensive steps. He landed on the bed gracefully, turned in a circle, and settled down for a nap.

~Denise Reich

82

A Simple Princess

When you are sorrowful look again in your heart, and you shall see that in
truth you are weeping for that which has been your delight.
~Kahlil Gibran

I opened the door to my five-year-old daughter's bedroom and peeked in. Liz was always sneaking my accessories into her room. I half expected to find her bedecked in my grandmother's pearls and covered in make-up. Instead our silver and gray cat, Princess, with pearls draped around her neck, was being treated to a royal tea party. She lay on a pink velour blanket with her white paws delicately crossed like a lady. She flicked her tail at the sight of me and then resumed resting her head on a plush purple pillow. In front of her was a spread of pink and purple plates full of cat food, water and plastic cookies. I tried not to laugh as Liz poured water into her teacup and offered it to Princess. Liz turned around and looked up at me with a wide toothy grin, lipstick smeared across her face. Her cheeks were covered in bright pink powder that matched her eyelids.

"What are you doing?" I asked.

"Having a tea party, Mama. Want some tea and cookies?" She stood up and handed me a pink teacup. How could I resist? I took the teacup and sat down with my two beautiful princesses.

Princess looked at me with bright green eyes. She truly deserved to be treated like royalty. Especially after all the harsh medications and doctor visits she had been through recently. Her body was beginning to fail her, and I had taken on the new role of being a nurse. Dispensing medicines every possible way and cleaning up unsightly messes was a small price to pay to keep Princess alive and somewhat pain-free.

For the past thirteen years Princess had watched my life blossom from being a single woman to getting married and having children. She was always there, purring at the end of my bed. One stroke of her soft fur could melt away my frustrations. She was a constant reminder of the simplicities of life, like catnaps in the sun and frolicking in the grass. Only recently she frolicked less and napped more.

I ran my hand down Princess's sharp spiny back. All the questions that I had tried not to face began to surface. Was I cruel for keeping her alive? Did I have the right to put her to sleep, even if she did still seem to enjoy parts of her life?

"Why isn't kitty eating?" Liz asked.

"She's sick," I said. "Her body is getting old. You know how we pick flowers and we put them in water, but after a few days they start to die?"

"You mean she's dying?" Liz asked.

"Yes baby, she is," I said.

"Can't we just stick her in more water like a flower?"

"No honey, she doesn't want any more water," I replied.

"What does she want?"

"She wants to sleep," I said.

"But flowers don't sleep."

"Kitties do," I said. "They sleep their way to heaven, and one day that's where she'll wake up."

Liz nodded, as if she understood. I wanted Princess to enjoy the things she loved before she left us, but I wasn't sure when I should play God. Maybe I was selfish, or just too scared to face the truth, but her time was coming and soon there would be no other choice.

I picked her up and set her down in the grass outside. The sun beat down on her back as the wind ruffled her fur. Her nose wiggled as she took in the spring air. The smell of grass and earth was comforting. She purred as I stroked her back and neck. I wanted her to go peacefully under the sun, lying in the grass as the wind caressed her face, but that was not my choice to make.

The next day, Princess did not greet me for breakfast. I found her curled up in the closet, barely able to lift her head. Liz brought Princess her pink blanket and put it by her side. I walked to the phone with a dead weight in my heart. I would never be ready for this, but it was time.

We brought Princess to the vet's office and I held her in my arms wrapped in Liz's pink velour blanket. A light purr rolled off her chest. I stroked her back, and kissed her soft head one last time. "I love you," I said. Princess nuzzled my arm and closed her eyes. She was gone.

When we walked back outside, Liz looked up to the sky.

"I see Princess," she said, pointing up to a big round cloud. "She's in kitty heaven."

I looked up at the bright blue sky. I felt my spirit lift when I looked into Liz's big brown hopeful eyes, so full of love and certainty. She had hope for Princess, and all I could do was mourn her death. Through her eyes I began to hope. I looked up to the sky, and took a moment to remember the most simple and beautiful moments that Princess loved.

~Melissa Laterza

A Gentle Passing

Since each of us is blessed with only one life, why not live it with a cat?
~Robert Stearns

We named her Misty since her coat reflected all the colors of a misty night. And like a misty night, Misty was mysterious. During the day she would often sit like a queen upon the garden wall and survey her kingdom, pretending to be disinterested. With eyes almost closed she would recline with only the occasional wave of her tail exposing her true state. She was actually watching each leaf as it fluttered in the wind, ants busy carrying food to their nest, and birds flying out of her reach. Then suddenly she would spring to life and race off to challenge a creature. We never had to worry about rats or mice; rodents were never tolerated in her kingdom. Sometimes she would slip out at night to handle a rodent emergency and, even though there were coyotes, she returned promptly each morning without a scratch. It remained a mystery where she hid and how she managed to stay safe. We tried to keep her in at night but when she needed to be out she somehow found a way.

In contrast to her queenly demeanor, she could turn downright silly at the sight of a feather on a string. She would throw herself high into the air and flip around, landing on all fours, ready to jump again. At one point I realized that she loved to watch the Animal Planet channel on TV. One day there were lions on the screen and, crouching down, she slowly and quietly walked from the couch, up and over the ottoman, and stalked them, her eyes never leaving the screen. When birds or fish came on, her head would bob back and forth watching their every move. I never lost my fascination with how her mind processed what she saw.

Misty was a good companion for many years. As with most good companions, we came to almost know each other's thoughts. I would tell her I needed her to do something and, if she was in the mood, she would do it. If she was outside too long and I started to worry, I would just think that I needed her to come home and she would show up at the door. I learned to distinguish her different meows and could tell whether she was sad, lonely, hungry or, if I had gone away for a few days, just downright angry that I had abandoned her.

Unfortunately, there came a day when I realized I was going to lose my friend. I had taken Misty to the vet for her yearly checkup. She had never been sick so I thought it would be a routine visit. During the checkup, the vet's face changed to a look of concern and I knew something was wrong. She finished her exam and explained that Misty had a severe heart murmur. She wasn't in any pain, but there was nothing that could be done, and she had only months to live. I had noticed that she was slowing down, but thought it was just natural aging since she was fifteen years old. I soon began to notice other changes. She didn't eat as much and her activity level fell even more. She started to lose weight and spend more time sleeping. This period was hard on both of us. We both knew our time together would soon end. Her eyes were still clear and bright and our connection was still strong, but eventually she began to slip away. She had lost a lot of weight and had very little energy, and I realized I had to let her go.

One evening just before bed I decided to have a talk with Misty. I put her on my bed on a soft towel and told her it was probably time for her to go to kitty heaven. I explained that, since she hated trips in the car, and she hated leaving her garden to go to the vet or anywhere, it would be easier for her if she crossed over on her own. I had heard stories from many of my friends that people often fight passing on since they are concerned about the loved ones they will leave behind.

I wondered if that might also be the case with animals. I continued to talk to Misty, telling her that it was okay for her to cross over, that I would be okay. I thanked her for all the years that we had shared and that I would always remember and love her. After spending some time with her, I placed her on the bathroom floor on the towel and said goodbye. During the night I heard just one meow.

I found her body the next morning. Misty's ashes now sit on my mantle in a pretty copper urn—a reminder of a lovely sixteen-year friendship. I still miss her but feel blessed to have had such a wonderful friend.

~Cynthia Baker

My Cat's Life

Over the Rainbow

Miracle Cat

Miracles are not contrary to nature,
but only contrary to what we know about nature.
~Saint Augustine

Everyone has their superstitions about black cats. Some say they are bad luck and some say they are witches in disguise. Never has an old wives' tale been so disproven as in the case of Jinx and the love she showed our family.

October is the time for jack-o'-lanterns and witches on broomsticks. It was also a lucky month for a small, shy black cat. I was looking at a local shelter for a companion cat for my other fur baby, Onyx. I walked up and down the rows of kittens and cats, all of them purring or mewing to get my attention. All except for one were jumping at the chance to get a new home. The name tag on the reticent one's cage said "Angel." It also stated that this was her last day. Halloween was coming soon and the shelter would stop adoptions of all black cats. By the time the hold on the black female was to be released, her fate would be sealed. A stroke of bad luck turned into good because I could not turn away from her.

"May I see her?" I asked a shelter attendant.

"You don't want that one," she said. "She has been the meanest one in here yet. A real firecracker."

Not discouraged, I took her out of the small cage that had been her home for twenty-nine days and held her close. A faint purr emanated from deep inside this "mean" cat. Then to everyone's surprise, she licked my nose. From that day forward, Angel truly was a wonderful addition to my small family. Jinx, as I renamed her, was there for the birth of my daughter, and the deaths of Onyx and my horse Clover. She welcomed a new Poodle puppy named Winnie into her home and heart without any hesitation.

At the age of four, Jinx was diagnosed with cancer. The vet's words hit like a ton of bricks. So young and full of life; how could life be so cruel? I cried all the way home from the vet. I made up my mind not to worry about when she would leave us, but to focus on how much fun we could have while she still was here. Jinx spent the next year playing with gallon milk jug tabs and hair ties, and devising a plan to capture our fish. She tormented Winnie and let the Poodle chase her time and time again. After their sport, they would curl up next to each other and rest.

The moment came late one night when we had to say goodbye. Jinx went from bad to worse in less than a day. As I held her in my arms for the last time, I told her what a great cat she was and what an amazing friend she had been. As the pink liquid seeped into her veins, she sighed and was gone. No more pain for my baby Jinx.

While my husband and I were burying her in a beautiful wooded area, I said, through a flood of tears, "I don't think I could ever accept another cat in my life. She set the bar too high." Then I added, laughing with the absurdity of it, "Unless it's all white, the exact opposite of Jinx. Plus, it would have to have one blue eye and one gold eye."

Two days later we were at my mother-in-law's house and Winnie started whining at the sliding glass door. My husband said, "Take that dog out so she stops whining."

I walked to the door and saw, sitting on the porch with her tail curled around her paws, a pure white kitten with one blue eye and one gold eye. Gabby is a healthy, bouncy, mischievous little kitten who dried our tears and let us know that miracles happen. I believe that Jinx wanted us to love again. Her little message from the Rainbow Bridge reached our doorstep and our hearts. Jinx was truly an "Angel" after all.

~Angela Marchi

85

Grieving Together

Friendship doubles our joy and divides our grief.
~Swedish Proverb

"Oh no, not another cat," I exclaimed as my teenage daughter Mary carried the tiny white bundle of fur in the front door.

"Oh Mom, can we keep it? It's just a baby," she pleaded.

Having a huge heart for animals, especially strays, I knew we were going to be owned by another feline. I had seen the kitten outside earlier and asked the neighbors if there was a new family on the block, or if anyone knew who the owner was. No one had a clue. The kitten had picked us and unless we took it to the shelter, it would be ours. Word was out on the street among the cat population that for a decent meal, and possibly a lifetime of pampering, our house was the place to be.

"Okay, but you'll have to feed it and take charge of the litter box," I reluctantly conceded.

Mary went off to her room, cooing to our new family member.

Through the years we had sheltered many cats as our children brought home stray after stray. Now we were down to just one cat, Leo, an aging tabby. I looked forward to a break in the cat caretaking once the kids were all off to college. Oh, I knew I would always own a cat or two, but I relished the thought of a break, a little time to travel with my husband. The timing of this kitten couldn't have been worse. But then again I'm a sucker for furry creatures.

The kids named the kitten Fluffy since she was a ball of fluff. However, upon our first visit to the vet, I was informed that she was a he. When asked if we would like to rename the cat with a more masculine name, the cat got my tongue, so to speak, and in a flustered moment I blurted out the name "Studley." Studley missed his mother and adopted our cat Leo to fulfill the role. Never mind that Leo was a fifteen-year-old, overweight, arthritic male. He was "Mom."

At first, when approached by this strange new addition to the household, Leo gave Studley a wide berth. But things have a way of changing. As the days passed, I would see Leo sunning himself on the front windowsill, his tail swishing in agitation as Studley jumped all around trying to pin it down. At feeding time Leo sat and watched as Studley ate his own food and then proceeded to start on his. Leo had the patience of a saint. He never hissed or growled; he just tapped the kitten with his paw when he had had enough. Spring turned to summer and one afternoon I saw two fur lumps lying on the patio. My heart leapt with joy. It was Leo and Studley curled together, making it impossible to distinguish where one stopped and the other started.

When they weren't sleeping together, Studley would pester Leo until he joined him, however briefly, for a romp in the yard or a quick chase after a moth. As Studley matured, I realized that he and Leo had become best buds and were inseparable. Five years passed with Studley being raised by Leo. Then one afternoon Studley came to me, yowling at the top of his lungs. I tried to decipher the cause of his pain. I glanced around for his pal Leo, who was nowhere in sight. Letting Studley lead the way, I followed him outside. This time there was one lump of fur on the patio and it wasn't moving. I eased myself down on the concrete and put Studley in my lap. I caressed Leo's soft fur and told him I loved him and that I would see him on the Rainbow Bridge. Studley and I sat together rocking back and forth. I sobbed as we grieved for Leo—a braver cat there never was. He had managed to take on parenting, with all its accompanying challenges, in his old age.

In the course of the next months, I would seek Studley out daily just to hug and pet him. We would sit and chat, mostly about our happy times with Leo. He would purr and I would talk. We enjoyed our newfound bond. He seemed to know that I was grieving right along with him.

~Sallie A. Rodman

86

Oh, Romeo...

Cats look beyond appearances—beyond species entirely, it seems—
to peer into the heart.
~Barbara L. Diamond

Life can deal some real doozies and somehow even though you know they're coming, you're never quite prepared for them when they arrive. One morning I found myself sitting teary-eyed in the vet's office with the family cat, Romeo. I woke up earlier that morning to find him staring at me with his one blue eye and one gold eye. Something was definitely wrong. He was bleeding from behind, he looked ill in the face, and it was apparent by looking at my soiled bedding that it would mean an emergency trip to the vet. I got my boys off to school as casually as I could, worry gnawing at me inside. I think my younger son sensed something was wrong because he spent an extra few minutes with Romeo before he left for the bus stop. I knew it wasn't going to be good news. I felt it like you feel at the first drop of a roller coaster.

I sat listening to the vet's prognosis, yet not really hearing the words. She went over several different options, none of which I could afford, and none of them leaving much promise for a full recovery. I looked over at Romeo with bleary eyes as he lay quietly on the table, seemingly at peace. His eyes zeroed in on me. It was as if he knew. We both looked to each other for understanding. That's when I broke into tears.

Offering a kind shoulder, the veterinarian held me while I cried.

302 Over the Rainbow: **Oh, Romeo...**

After a minute or two the vet excused herself, leaving me alone for a final farewell with my cat—a special member of my family, the warm ball curled up at the foot of my bed at night. As I tried to control my emotions, I remembered a quote by Kahlil Gibran that I had read just the day before: "Love knows not its own depth until the hour of separation." Nothing felt truer, especially because for the past seven years that I had cared for this animal, a lot of it was spent complaining about his long white hair. I would find it pasted to all of my clothing, and I would blindly step in the disgusting hairballs at night. Also, the way he bit my ear at night so that I would let him out was annoying. And then there was his steady companionship, like the time he stuck by my side when I was down with the flu for two days.

Romeo was a romantic—thus the name. And he would always look at me like he was completely smitten, as if I were the most beautiful creature on the planet, and it never mattered that I looked like the walking dead after pulling all-nighters with sick kids. He was a true companion, loving me even at my worst.

The hardest part about losing him would be telling my two children, Billy and Alec. It's a huge life lesson to lose a pet, a true member of the family. The hardest thing that you will ever do in this lifetime is to love another soul because to love sometimes means having to let go.

Letting go of Romeo was one of the hardest things I've ever had to do. As I held my weeping children in my arms, after delivering the hard news to them after school that day, I realized that love—in the truest sense of the word—hurts like nothing you've ever known, but oh, in the end, was it worth it!

~Natalie June Reilly

87

How a Cat Came to Be Pavarotti

Love makes your soul crawl out from its hiding place.
~Zora Neale Hurston

Fifteen years ago, I noticed a white cat with unusual black markings crouched under the birdfeeder in my backyard. He appeared to be eating some of the dry bread that I had put out for the birds that morning. I was surprised to see a cat eating bread and was immediately struck by the fear that he was foraging for food. Being a passionate cat lover, I was devastated to see a cat abandoned without food or comfort.

The next day, I put out some bread again and, sure enough, the tiny white cat showed up. There was no doubt—he was clearly hungry. My mission to adopt him began that very moment. I fed him every day and talked to him, at first from a distance, then through a hedge, and finally from a few feet away. Eventually, he came to empty his bowl of food morning and night. A month later, he was sleeping in a corner of our backyard. He was adopting us. The fact that it was spring comforted me. He had obviously survived the harsh elements of winter and if my plan worked, he would never have to suffer again. It was May and I had plenty of time to build my bond of trust with him before winter.

Around that same time, I was looking forward to purchasing tickets for an upcoming concert by the opera star Pavarotti. It was a dream of mine to hear Pavarotti sing in person and I reminded myself daily not to forget about buying the tickets on May 25th. That day, I was out in my garden, engrossed by my new little friend. I sat on the grass and admired him from a distance, telling him that I would take care of him, that he had a feline friend waiting to welcome him inside the house and that he could trust me. And then we had a break-through! He communicated with me for the first time — a sweet and graceful meow. My heart was so filled with joy at our progress that I completely forgot about the concert tickets. By the time I remembered to call, they were sold out.

I phoned my sister Lorraine, upset and distressed that I had lost my chance to hear Pavarotti sing. And then my sister said the sweetest thing. "Oh, but you did hear him sing today. He was in your backyard. I think you found a name for your new cat!" And so it was. I had my very own Pavarotti.

He was a tiny, less-than-ten-pound, elegant cat, so our friends and family thought it comical that he shared a name with the cor-pulent opera singer. But as it turned out, my Pavarotti was vocal and expressive, and the name suited him well. By July, he trusted us enough to let us pick him up and hold him. Before welcoming him into our home to meet the resident cat, we took him to the vet for a checkup. Pavarotti was dirty and flea-infected but otherwise healthy. After a week of TLC at the clinic, my husband and I took him home to meet Cappuccino.

From then on, Pavarotti shadowed me everywhere — basement, bedroom, bathroom. He slept with me, curled up in my lap to watch TV or read, sat on my keyboard while I worked. When I became severely ill five years ago, he was even more insistent about our proximity. Housebound and oftentimes bedridden, I could always count on my devoted friend for warmth and love. He was a constant companion, but as it turned out, he was much more than that — he was a healer.

My dear, sweet Pavarotti passed away at seventeen years old, and he had not shown any signs of illness before the day he died. He had been asleep on our bed, as per his usual routine, while my husband

and I prepared lunch in the kitchen. I was setting the table when I heard my husband say in a worried voice, "Oh Pavarotti, what's wrong?" I turned around and saw my beautiful cat slip down to the floor, almost in slow motion, on his right side. He seemed to be having a seizure. We both immediately sensed that our cat was dying. We cradled him, kissed him, said his name and thanked him for everything. We saw him struggle for a second, take one last labored breath and, he was gone. In less than a minute, our lives had changed. Our hearts filled with grief and sorrow as we tenderly wrapped him in a soft towel. While my husband took him to the veterinary clinic close by, I stayed home and said a prayer for my cat's soul.

We spent the next few days in shock and we cried until our eyes burned. I was emotionally fragile and physically drained from five years of chronic illness and knew that grief could really set me back on my journey to recovery. I did not know how to move through the pain of our loss without jeopardizing whatever progress I had made in the last few months.

Three days after Pavarotti's passing, my friend Mehri came to visit. She listened to my sadness and comforted me with her compassion. I was grief-stricken, inconsolable, devastated. I described my relationship with my cat, told her how I missed his presence, his singing, his joy, his playfulness, and mostly, how I ached for the comfort and support he provided me all these years.

My wise and concerned friend said, "Your cat did a lovely thing for you. He worked very hard to bring you back to health. He knew you lacked energy and that is why he was always with you. He was working all these years to bring back balance for you. He knew that before now, you would not have survived his passing. He also knew that you are stronger, that you are on the road to recovery. He sensed that your energy was slowly coming back. But his heart was tired and his job was done. Fill your heart with gratitude because he did such a good job for you. You gave him a good life and he did the same for you. Because of this bond, you don't want his soul to struggle. Animals are like people. They have souls and their souls ascend to heaven. The love you exchanged was so pure that he came down from upstairs to be with you when he died. He did not want to die by himself. He wanted to be with you one last time. He has cared for you and now he is in another place. He is resting. Remember him with love and gratitude."

~Jeannine Ouellette

88

Where the Dandelion Grows

Cats are a tonic, they are a laugh, they are a cuddle, they are at least pretty
just about all of the time and beautiful some of the time.
~Roger Caras

"I'm sorry to tell you this, but Dandelion died during the night," said the cat sitter. I could hear her struggling not to cry at the other end of the phone, and I did my best to reassure her despite my own distress. Although the news didn't come as much of a surprise, I was immediately overcome with grief and guilt. I had been with Dandelion the night before at my parents' house, and then left him alone when I returned to my own apartment. Dandelion had been ill—ill enough so that my vacationing parents and I were considering having him put to sleep. I wondered: Would he have lived longer if I had stayed? Could he tell how much I loved him? Did he know that I couldn't help him? And how would I tell my parents?

Dandelion came into my life just when I needed him. My parents had just split up, and my mom and I had moved out of our sprawling house into a small apartment. Reeling from shock, hurt, and uncertainty, I didn't know how I would go on. But then we got a kitten. A kitten who, truth be told, was a little terror. Dandelion, named for his yellowish color, climbed up our drapes, swung back and forth on our screen door, and meowed nightly to interrupt our sleep. My mom and I were very close to finding him a new home—away from us. Fortunately, we didn't give up Dandelion, and he turned into the sweetest cat in the world and the best cat that I've ever had.

He loved to make us laugh. Dan, the man who would become my stepfather, was a customer service rep for JVC, and kept us flush with the newest stereo equipment. One day, Dandelion jumped into a box containing a battery-powered boom box, and turned it on. Looking satisfied with himself, he practically began to dance to the music. Another time, he sat on the box concealing my birthday cake, and didn't seem to understand why we were so upset as well as amused. Then Dandelion fell in love with the cat who lived in the apartment next door, and despite her rejection, continued to woo her. Every time we looked outside, he was making his way from our balcony to hers. Fearing for his safety, Dan constructed an elaborate blockade. Undeterred, Dandelion used a tree branch to reach his beloved, and he went on to court her until she pushed him off the balcony railing. We watched in horror as he sailed over to the floor below. We thought for sure he wouldn't survive the fall, but like a good cat, he landed on his feet and lived to tell the story.

Dandelion was compassionate, too. When he discovered a sick cat on his travels, he stayed with her until someone was able to come to the rescue. And once when Dan fell in the bathtub, Dandelion sat on the bathroom floor until my mom came home. But my favorite memories of Dandelion were when I would lie on the couch—usually with a textbook—and he would climb up the length of my body, kiss me, and then settle contentedly on my chest. He wasn't the kind of cat who would demand attention—he didn't try to knock my book away or sit on it. He was fine with being with me while I did something else.

Dandelion eventually grew older, and I eventually grew up. I had to leave him, but I continued to look forward to seeing him whenever I visited my parents. He always welcomed me, never holding a grudge that I had abandoned him. He led a happy and healthy life until the end, and lived to be an incredible nineteen years old.

My grief and guilt over his death lessened as the months went on.

I came to believe that Dandelion was okay with me not being there when he died. I think he didn't want me to have to go through that. He knew how hard it would be. And I think he knew he had done his job. He had turned me from an unhappy thirteen-year-old into a well-adjusted grown woman. Yes, Dandelion had raised me well.

~Carol Ayer

89

Uri's Story

Loss leaves us empty — but learn not to close your heart and mind in grief.
Allow life to replenish you. When sorrow comes it seems impossible —
but new joys wait to fill the void.
~Pam Brown

"**M**om, you'd better hurry. Uri isn't going to last much longer," said Holli. Returning from a weekend visit to my two siblings, I had placed a call home to my daughter to inform her of my arrival time. My ETA was off by an hour and I did not want her to worry. Her comment was a shock. Uri, my exceptionally beautiful cat of eleven years had cancer, and the cancer hit him early. I thought I had been protecting him from harm all this time — keeping him indoors, away from speeding traffic, feeding him only the best — giving him all the loving TLC any cat could desire. Cancer never even entered my mind. How could this happen to such a well cared for kitty?

When Uri first came to live with us, he was but three weeks old. Born the offspring of a successful Persian show cat and a passing vagrant, his mother's owner needed to part with the kittens as soon as possible. Holli and I accepted Uri and his little runt brother to bottle-feed. His feeble brother did not live long, but Uri was a fighter. In fact, at feeding time, he batted at the bottle with his front paws and often pulled the nipple out by tugging ferociously, bathing us in milk. A handsome mixture of black-and-white fluff, as he grew his eyes became comparable in size and color to those of an owl. Rather than the usual Persian face, he had what was referred to as a doll face. Uri was a true beauty, and he knew it.

Upon acceptance of the kittens, we promised to keep them indoors, as their natural instincts had been bred out of them. We witnessed this loss of feline savvy when Uri was several months old. He escaped the safety of the garage and was later found in the backyard, about fifteen feet up our pine tree. Holli tried coaxing him down, cooing with gentle words, not expecting it to work. Uri let go of the limb to which he clung, emitted a loud "Mmmeeeeooooowww!" (which in cat means "Geronimo!"), and dropped the distance directly into Holli's outstretched arms. Taking the ultimate leap of faith, he trusted that she would catch him.

Uri would never respond to the common phrase, "Here, kitty-kitty." He refused to come to anyone unless they whistled the theme from *The Andy Griffith Show*. Then he would come at a run. This little mystery was never solved. Uri was about five years old when Max the dog joined our family. Max, a mix of Chow, Collie, and Australian Shepherd, was eight weeks old when I brought him home. Cute and cuddly, he displayed a high intelligence from a young age, mixed with a charming sweetness. Over the next six years, Max and Uri became best buddies. They could be found at any given time napping together or cleaning each other's faces. Their mutual affection was heartwarming, and our little family lived in harmonious bliss.

When Uri turned ten, he began to sleep more than usual. At first I attributed this to his age, but as he worsened, I became concerned. Since I work in the medical profession, the symptoms made me think that Uri had cancer. Watching his life slip away was devastating. I was losing my exceptional friend. Still, when presented with the opportunity to spend precious time with my siblings, I had to go. And since Uri's cancer was progressing slowly, I chanced my weekend excursion. Now I prayed I would not be too late to say goodbye.

When I arrived home, Uri was still hanging on. Holli and I both thought that he had waited for me. I sat on the loveseat and held my sweet, sweet Uri in my arms. He expired within the hour. Hard as this was, Max's reaction was not any easier. He nudged his friend's still body with his nose, whining and turning his head from one side to the other. It was a heartbreaking scene. I hurt not only from the loss of one beloved pet, but for the obvious distress of the other. I vowed then and there to never adopt another cat. It could never compare to Uri anyway. I felt sure Max agreed with me.

Time passed and life went on. Still, I couldn't get over losing Uri. There was an empty void that nothing seemed to fill. Then one day my daughter inherited a litter of two-week-old, dehydrated kittens. The party that found the felines knew of Holli's healing gift for animals and figured that she was their best chance for survival. The litter consisted of two red males and one dark calico female. My mistake was looking into the box and seeing those minute miracles. The first thing I saw was a little dark face with love radiating from her enormous green eyes.

"Mom," Holli said, hesitating before continuing. "We all know that you can never replace Uri, but it would probably help Max if you adopted a kitten. Not as a replacement, but to remind you of the better times, the younger times with Uri. Besides, this little miracle survived for a reason." When did my daughter get so smart?

I held Benicia for the first time and was hooked. At eight weeks old, Benicia came to live with Max and me. Max seemed to come to life, despite his advanced years. And Benicia? Well, she was definitely no Uri. For the first year of her life, she literally climbed the walls, taking down decorations as well as the hands on my cuckoo clock, but still, her frustrating antics were nothing short of endearing. Uri will never be replaced in our hearts, but Benicia has definitely filled the void. I thank Holli on a regular basis for sharing her wisdom.

~Christina M. Ward

90

Whiskers and Me

A beating heart and an angel's soul, covered in fur.
~Lexie Saige

I have known a lot of grief in my lifetime. As a child, my home was dysfunctional and abusive. "Why don't my parents love me, and what's wrong with me?" I used to cry to myself over and over again. It would take me decades to figure out that there was nothing wrong with me, but that there was certainly something wrong with my parents.

When I was eight years old I was allowed to adopt a sweet white tabby kitten. I immediately named her "Whiskers" because her whiskers were so prominent on her tiny face. Whiskers was a special cat. From the very beginning she seemed almost human. Whiskers did not like my parents and stayed away from them as much as possible. It felt like she was taking my side and standing up for me, and for the first time in my life I had another living thing who loved me unconditionally.

Whiskers gave me love, companionship and security throughout my teenage years. She gave me something positive to come home to every day. She taught me what love was. Days turned into months, and months turned to years as Whiskers and I grew up. She began to slow down. She began to sleep more. She even began to get a few gray hairs. It was difficult for me to see my precious little friend aging at a much faster rate than I was. When I had finished a year of college, and was ready to move out of my parents' house, Whiskers passed away quietly in her sleep one night as she lay next to me in bed. It was almost as if she were waiting for me to get out of my unsafe and unhappy environment before she let herself pass on.

The grief I felt when I woke up and found Whiskers' lifeless body next to me was more painful than any of the grief I had felt as a child. Whiskers' death hurt more than any abuse I had experienced. Whiskers was an angel sent from heaven and I was devastated by her passing. I stayed home for four full days after Whiskers died, sobbing and crying out for my forever friend. I knew I had to get on with my life—I knew that's what Whiskers would want—but I was depressed and lonely for a very, very long time. I couldn't tell people how I felt, since when I tried they didn't seem to understand. No one I talked to seemed to have ever experienced such a deep love and connection with a cat before. It took me a long time to realize that I could love another cat, perhaps not as much as Whiskers, but I had love inside of me that was aching to get out. I decided to give love to a new kitten.

When I was settled in my first apartment I adopted a kitten. I hovered over that kitten, mothered and protected her, and somehow the strong grief I felt for the loss of Whiskers faded. Sure, I knew that I would probably have to go through the death of Snickers someday too, but I also came to realize that it would be selfish to waste years of loving because of my fear of death and grief. So, although I still mourn the death of Whiskers and all the pets I have had since her, I still have their loving memories and the comfort each one of these precious cats has brought me. I keep them buried deep within my heart. They nourish me. And my life is much richer for having loved my many feline friends.

~LaVerne Otis

91

Remembering Twist

There is no such thing as "just a cat."
~Robert A. Heinlein

When my two small children—Alice, six, and Eric, four—finally wore me down with their pleading, I agreed to consider adopting the stray calico kitten that a neighbor could not keep because her daughter was allergic to cats. I knew my husband, Dick, would object to an animal in the house, but telling the kids this fell on deaf ears. I decided to let them convince their father that they were old enough to care for the kitten. I dreaded the confrontation. The moment he walked in the door that evening, they were shouting the news to him in unison: "Daddy, Daddy, we've got a kitten and her name is Twist!" They ran to fetch the frightened animal from the kitchen while my husband shot me a displeased look that asked, "What's going on here?" The children returned with the cat, a small ball of fluff wriggling in Alice's arms. I watched Dick's expression melt as both kids nuzzled and petted their kitten, and I knew that Twist had found a home.

Over the years, as the children grew, Twist was there for them as playmate and comforter, a loyal friend always ready to entertain or listen to their problems. To be honest though, it wasn't just the kids Twist served. Dick and I also laughed at her antics and found solace in stroking her warm, purring body when she rested on our laps. Twist considered herself in charge and supervised everything. When I was in the kitchen preparing meals, she was on the counter checking that I did it right. I could not train her not to jump up, and I finally gave up trying. It was easier to train myself to always put down wax paper where I worked with food to be sure that Twist's footprints did not contaminate it.

When I dressed, Twist was there, making sure my outfit was put together properly. She would perch on the bed, her eyes following my every move. When I combed my hair in front of the mirror, she would leap from the carpet to my left shoulder, always making a perfect soft landing, and wrap her head around my neck as I primped, so she could lift a paw and re-arrange my coiffure if the styling didn't please her. I never cared for her versions and a battle of wills usually followed as we revised each other's handiwork.

One morning, a couple of weeks before Twist's seventeenth birthday, I had finished dressing for work and started combing my hair. As usual, Twist leaped toward my shoulder to help—but missed. I'm not sure which of us was more shocked. I looked down at her on the floor and she stared up at me, puzzled looks on both of our faces. I turned my attention back to the mirror and waited, but she did not try again. Other changes followed. I began finding wet spots on the carpet as well as in the kitty litter box. Twist stopped emptying her dish, no longer devouring every last scrap of her favorite cat food. She was slowing down, mellowing with age, I decided. My son Eric came home a few weeks after the missed jump incident and I was surprised to receive a phone call from him shortly after I arrived at work. He usually liked to sleep late when he was on a visit. I could tell from his voice that something was wrong.

"Mom, Twist was in my room." He choked back a sob, then continued in one long agonized rush. "She started to shake and foam at the mouth and fell down on her side and I called the vet and he said to come right over and I put Twist in the car and we went to his office but she wasn't moving at all and then he said she was gone."

He was having trouble keeping his voice steady and so was I. We talked for a while. I felt so sorry he had to be there all alone when this happened. If there had only been a clue before I left for work, but she had seemed all right when I set out her breakfast and fresh water. I said I would have to call Alice and Dick, but Eric felt that he should, since he had been the one with Twist when she had her seizure and died. I hung up, put my head in my hands and sobbed. I couldn't stop. The door to my counseling office opened and one of the teachers came in. She rushed to my side, put her arm around my shoulders and asked what was wrong. I felt suddenly foolish for causing such alarm.

"I'm sorry," I said, lifting and drying my face. "My son just called to tell me our cat died."

Her face filled with alarm and she rushed to hug me again. "Oh that's so terrible! I know how you feel," she said and began to cry with me. I had found another cat person, and we sobbed together for several moments before she rushed off to meet her first class. I felt better and stronger because she had understood. Twist was not just a cat, an animal, to me or to my family. She came to us when Alice was in first grade and Eric started pre-school. She was there to supervise their packing for college and to greet them when they returned home for visits. Twist was family and we felt diminished by her loss.

It has been twenty years since I last had a cat and almost thirty since Twist passed away, yet I still place wax paper on any surface where I'm preparing food. Sometimes a visitor will ask me why I do this and I'll smile, remembering Twist. "Old habits are hard to break," I'll say and tell them about my in-charge cat who insisted on supervising my cooking up close. I don't tell them that I don't really want to give up the practice. I like remembering Twist.

~Marcia Rudoff

Buster

Another cat? Perhaps. For love there is also a season; its seeds must be
resown. But a family cat is not replaceable like a wornout coat or a set of
tires. Each new kitten becomes its own cat, and none is repeated.
I am four cats old, measuring out my life in friends that have succeeded but
not replaced one another.

~Irving Townsend

t's my fault, I said to myself as I watched Mike try to comfort his cat Buster. If I had not insisted that he get Buster spayed this would not be happening. Mike leaned down, speaking soft encouragement to the dying animal as Buster continued his seizures.

"Come on buddy, you can do it. You can get through this," Mike said.

Mike had just picked up Buster that morning from the vet. He appeared to be fine and ready to go home. The vet said to call if there was a problem, but he didn't foresee any complications. And now here it was, our first Christmas Eve together, and I was indirectly responsible for possibly killing my boyfriend's pet. Buster growled softly as he started another seizure, his eyes wide and dilated. Large pools of black stared blankly into space. Mike started to pet him again, and I couldn't watch any more.

"I'm sorry," said the vet, finishing his examination. "It's a complication from the anesthesia. There's nothing that we can do for him. You need to consider his suffering and let him go."

Mike nodded in agreement, unable to speak as Buster's seizure came to a stop. I can still hear the soft growls coming from the exhausted animal. Buster's life came to an end, leaving me riddled with guilt.

I remember the day I had insisted that something be done. Buster seemed to delight in spraying my clothes. His jealousy towards me was obvious. He always nudged his way in between us when we were on the sofa. I tried to ignore his constant efforts to get Mike's attention when he was home, but when he backed up that day to spray my purse, that was the last straw.

"Mike, you have to do something about that cat," I said, anger filling my voice. "He won't stop spraying my clothes."

"He just doesn't know you," Mike said in Buster's defense. "He has never done this before. I'm sure it will stop once he gets to know you."

We continued to argue over it and evidently I won. An appointment was made at the vet's for Buster to be neutered, and within a week Buster was on his way for his overnight stay.

"Do you want us to dispose of the body?" the vet asked, his voice breaking into my thoughts.

Mike's voice cracked. "Yes, I have no place to put him."

Paying fees for a vet visit takes a long time when you are trying to keep your composure. It wasn't until we were safely in the truck that Mike spoke to me.

"I know what you're thinking and it's not your fault," Mike said, pulling out of the driveway onto the snow-covered road. He reached over and grabbed my hand, his voice cracking. "No one could have known that he would have responded this way," he said. My shoulders shook as I began to cry.

"I'm so sorry," I said as I dug through my purse for a tissue. "I never meant for it to come out this way."

Several months passed before I felt that Mike might be open to the idea of a new kitten. My friend Gina knew that her parents' cat had a litter of kittens ready to leave their mother. I was determined to get one from the litter for Mike.

"Gina's parents have a litter of kittens that are ready to go," I said as I finished setting the dinner table.

Mike leaned against the counter as he waited for the microwave to finish warming up the vegetables.

"What kind are they?" he asked, pulling the hot bowl out of the microwave and setting it on the table.

"A mixture. Gina says we can take a look if you want on Saturday." I watched him out of the corner of my eye. "But only if you want to."

Gina was right. There was a variety to choose from. A little calico female romped and played with another kitten with tuxedo markings. Grabbing the tuxedo, Mike scratched it behind the ears.

"That one is a male," said Gina's mom. Reaching down she scooped up the little calico. "These two are the little troublemakers of the litter."

Mike continued to inspect the rest of the litter, but it was obvious that the tuxedo was the one that drew his attention the most.

"What do you think, should we take the pair? They would have each other to play with during the day," Mike said as he reached out for the calico.

We left that day with two kittens. The little tuxedo sat upon the console of Mike's truck all the way home.

"Have you thought of a name yet?" asked Mike. The little calico's head was buried in the crook of my arm.

"I think she looks like a Bella," I said. Reaching down I petted the small back of the cowering kitten.

"What about him?" I asked, glancing at the kitten still sitting on the console.

"I think I'm going to call him Bubba," Mike said glancing over. "He looks like he's going to grow into a big cat."

Buster could never be replaced, but with Bubba and Bella, Mike and I created a new family and new memories together.

~Talia Haven

Chapter 11

My Cat's Life

I'll Always Love You

Jack's Friends

Cats are designated friends.
~Norman Corwin

Fourteen years ago a friend popped over and thrust a gift into my husband Bill's hands. "You two need this," the friend said.

"We need a cat?" Bill scratched behind its steel gray ears.

Bill and I had recently married, but owning a pet was not on our list of things to do. For one thing, I had no prior experience caring for living things. I didn't come from a family that took in creatures or marveled at anything with fur. We had the requisite short-lived fish that kids with pet-phobic parents were destined to acquire, but that was it. Bill hoisted the ten-pound beast, with its creamy front paws and milky shirt, into my arms. The moment I cradled it and made eye contact, a mother was born.

"Is it a girl or boy?" I asked. Its green eyes and contented purr mesmerized me, and then it smiled. Bill huddled close, pulling its legs this way and that.

"Looks like a boy to me," our friend offered.

"So you're a boy," I said holding the cat up. The sun spilled over his back, his legs dangled downward as his eyes closed into another happy purr. This was going to be fun, I thought and I re-snuggled him, christening him Jack. Jack the cat. Well, one trip to the vet for our happy family and we learned Jack was a Jill. However, after a week, we weren't going to change her name. This was no ordinary cat. She was outgoing and intelligent and we were sure she would be happier with a boy's name than if she realized her parents weren't as bright as she was.

Jack started out as an indoor cat. We never planned to let her out of the house, but she grew bossy. She sat in the window screaming. She begged at the door, and slipped out whenever the opportunity presented itself. We came to realize this adventuresome side was just a part of who Jack was. She never went very far, only exploring our property, our neighbors' yards, their porches and the yards across the alley, and all it would take from Bill or me was, "Come on Jack, come on home," and she would be back on the porch and in my arms.

Bill and I knew a large group of people in our diverse city neighborhood, but it turned out Jack knew many more than we did. She was the family ambassador.

"That cat of yours, she's like a dog!" a neighbor we hadn't met bellowed out of her second floor window.

"Jack stopped in the other day and we shared a bowl of milk," another would lean over the porch railing to report. "You'll have to come for lunch!"

Jack's favorite yard to visit was Dave the gardener's. Jack filled a void in Dave's life as he struggled through sadness. Watching Jack leap at phantom mice and teeny insects while he tended his roses brought joy to our dear friend. Jack even tried to make friends with the crotchety couple across the alley. They lived in a giant, romantic Victorian with a lush garden and were not interested in making friends with human or furry beings.

"Jackie was in the garden today," the wife would say over her fence, scowling. "We're not animal people, you know!"

Jack wasn't only partial to humans. When we adopted a tortoiseshell kitten, Jack welcomed her with extended paws and allowed little Amelia to soothe herself by pretending to nurse from Jack. Though Amelia would never set foot outside the house, Jack continued to thrive by gallivanting around the neighborhood in the late afternoon. When night would begin to settle I would call for Jack and she would be there. Until the day came that Jack wasn't. I walked around the backyards that connected to each other.

"Jaaack! Come on Jack, time to come home! Time to come in, Jack…" I called.

I listened between each call, hearing a quiet version of Jack's voice. But I couldn't find her. I had a feeling something was wrong. Everyone searched for her. One day passed. I knew I heard her voice in the backyard, yet she wasn't there. Another day passed. Another evening of waiting. And as the sun began to set, there was a knock at the door and the gardener Dave was there. He stood, fingers woven together, kneading them. His eyes were wet. Someone must have died.

"Is your mother okay?" I asked. He shook his head.

"It's Jack," he said. "Mark next door found her."

My face lit up for a second before my mind put together what he was saying. I followed him to the backyard, behind the house that was joined to ours with a common brick wall.

"She's under there." Dave pointed to the lattice that enclosed the space under the stairs.

I couldn't look. Bill came quickly behind. He couldn't look either. We didn't need to. The sour smell said it all. What had happened? No one could tell. The hot summer days had taken their toll on her. So, in the dark night, Bill dug a hole in the backyard and laid Jack's body in it. He tossed the dirt back in the grave while Dave and I looked on, unable to speak. Silently we said what we needed to. We took a beautiful stone from our retaining wall and set it on the spot where Jack would lie for eternity and said a little prayer for the greatest cat who ever lived.

Two weeks later the male half of the crotchety couple across the alley appeared at the door. He shoved a small white envelope into my hand and disappeared down the steps.

Inside, a card read:

In loving memory of Jackie
A donation to Animal Friends of Western Pennsylvania
A Good Friend Gone.
Love,
The Thompsons

I knew that although Jack's life was far too short, she had been a happy cat. And more than that, she had been the kind of creature that people don't forget, the kind of being that makes people see the world a little differently, even if it is for just a minute or two.

~Kathleen Shoop

94

Loss and Peace

While we are mourning the loss of our friend,
others are rejoicing to meet him behind the veil.
~John Taylor

My cat Bandit died recently. She was a wonderful, loving companion for eighteen years, wandering quietly through the halls of my house, stretching languorously on the back of the sofa. Often she sat on the carpet and stared at me lounging in an armchair.

"What are you thinking?" I would ask. She answered my question with that inscrutable gaze cats are famous for. "Figure it out for yourself," she seemed to say. Bandit had a wonderful serenity. I could come home from work exhausted and tearful, and she never altered her attitude or her behavior. She simply sat on my lap or next to me, as if to say, in spite of what happened today, "All will be well." No matter how frazzled my life was, her peacefulness comforted me.

When she grew close to the end of her life, I needed that tranquility, the feeling that all would be well, for it was the exact opposite of what I was feeling: dread at the impending loss of my beloved kitty. Given Bandit's age, I had decided that if she was not in pain, I would keep her at home and not take undue measures to keep her alive.

One day she stopped eating and slept almost continually. The next day she stopped drinking water and I sensed that the end was near. She would wake up, stand, wobble a few steps, then stop, lie down and sink into a stupor. I watched her eighteen-year-old body lose the last remnants of its energy. Soon she would be gone and my heart broke at the thought. I prayed that God would take her. Occasionally she cried out. I rushed to her and she lay in my arms like a blind creature, alive but diminishing. I petted her head and murmured comforting words but I was crying too. I stopped myself because Bandit was not used to hearing that voice, filled with tears. I said, "I love you, Bandit," over and over again. Did it help? Did she hear me? I hoped so.

The next day Bandit lay on the green carpet in the living room where she had spent so much of her life. Her breathing was shallow, her eyes dull and unfocused. To make her more comfortable I covered her with a fuzzy green throw that she loved. Trying to control my tears, I petted her head with two fingers and murmured, "I'm here for you, baby, I won't leave you." Throughout the day I walked from my desk to my cat, then back again, over and over, waiting, waiting. I was sitting next to her when she took a breath, then quietly stopped breathing. I placed my hand gently on her thin ribs. Her heart had given up the battle. She was gone.

I lined a cardboard box with a towel, wrapped her lifeless body in another towel and picked her up. I winced at the lightness—she must have weighed four pounds. I cried at her frailty, her vulnerability and how I loved that and everything else about her. I covered the box, wrote Bandit's name, the date and time of her death, and "Beloved by everyone who knew her."

The following morning Michelle, the owner of a local crematorium, came for Bandit's body. Michelle opened the box, looked down at her sweet face and said, "Yes, she is beautiful." We talked briefly about Bandit's life, my house, how long before I received the ashes. I touched the lid one last time and said, "Goodbye, my love." Then my Bandit left this house for the last time. The cat who hated to climb into her carrier for a trip to the vet, who preferred a life of quiet indoor comfort, left the only home she had ever known.

As Michelle was carrying Bandit to her van, I said to her, "I think the day is sunny and beautiful because God is opening His door to Bandit. He's welcoming her to heaven." I waved to Michelle as she drove away, the little box on a silk cushion in the back of her SUV, and whispered, again, "Goodbye."

The next day at dusk I walked on the golf course across from my home. When I approached the area where I could see the sun sinking over the horizon, I stopped in awe. Huge, deep pink clouds crowded the sky, backed by dark blue ones. They created a mass of splendor, providing a foreground for the setting sun. Slim pink rays broke through the clouds, which were as dense and mystical as the clouds in a Renaissance painting. I stared at the sight. I hadn't seen a sunset like that in years. Then I thought, God is telling me that Bandit has arrived safely. This is the world she will live in. I burst into tears, wildly happy, knowing that my cat had made the voyage and was now home. This radiant place was hers.

I knew the spectacle would last only a few moments so I watched it through my tears. The clouds, some of them unusually small, stuttered in round and jagged puffs across the sky and became a swirling marble backdrop as the sun went down.

When it was over I continued my walk, noticing that the pink puffs and streaks were still visible in the twilight, and I felt deeply that this was God's gift to me, my Bandit and the world. I was at peace.

~Patricia McElligott

95

My Gardening Buddy

A single rose can be my garden... a single friend, my world.
~Leo Buscaglia

When my friend Lynn crept into my office with a loudly mewing straw tote bag, it was obvious that I was about to be played like a fiddle. My cat Slugger had recently died, and Lynn knew I was in a vulnerable kitty-less state. The latch opened and out popped a gray-and-white face, with a tiny pink and brown nose in the shape of an upside-down triangle, long white whiskers and large emerald green eyes. One look at him and I was a goner.

"Oh how cute!" I exclaimed.

That was his cue to begin peddling his best shtick, rubbing and weaving around my legs while noisily purring. He didn't have to peddle very long before I put him back into the tote bag and took him home. Since he was the color of a summer rain cloud, I named him Stormy.

The new kitty wasted no time defining his role in our household. A mere ten minutes after we pulled into the driveway, he escaped through a patio door left slightly ajar. As I anxiously searched for him, I spotted a few weeds and bent over to pull them up. Just then Stormy leapt out of a bush and began digging at them too. From then on whenever I worked in the yard, my "Gardening Buddy" was ready to lend a paw. As he sat on the sidelines meowing amiably, scampering after bugs and lizards, chasing his tail, or cheerfully rolling around in the grass, the world seemed a brighter, happier place.

On hot Florida nights, Stormy kept cool by sleeping on the roof of our one-story house. Each evening he would leap onto the big ligustrum hedge alongside the patio. From there he would hop up to the aluminum awning where his claws scraped and screeched until he found his footing. Then he would cleanly catapult onto the shingled roof, landing with a pleasant thump.

However, his dismount was nothing short of a train wreck. Plunging from the roof, he would slide, scrape, and yowl down the awning until he plopped onto the hedge. There, more often than not he would lose his balance, tumble off and land with a graceless splat in the flowerbed below. Amazingly, the only injuries Stormy ever sustained were blows to his pride. If only my poor posies could say the same.

I had always planted annuals and perennials in that particular spot because it had the perfect blend of sunlight, shade and humidity. It was the one place in our yard where everything flourished. During summer months, when many plants wilted or burned to a crisp, it was the only bed that could be counted on for plenty of blooms. Thus, I hoped that rooftop snoozing was merely a phase that Stormy would quickly outgrow. No such luck. After each "accident" I would drive to the garden center and buy replacement annuals. Nurseryman Bob would see me approach the cash register with six packs of flowers, and ask, "Stormy again?"

"Yep."

"You know for all the money you've spent on annuals, you could have bought some nice, sturdy, permanent flowering bushes right?" he said.

"I know Bob. But I don't want to put flowering bushes in an annual bed, because it would cease to be an annual bed."

He would sigh, shake his head and take my money, no doubt believing that I wouldn't recognize expert advice if I tripped over it. But then Stormy changed his diet and my annual bed was doomed for good.

Our next-door neighbor Mrs. Slark had taken quite a shine to Stormy, who in turn eagerly poured on the charm in a quest for handouts. She rarely disappointed him, often giving him tidbits of whatever she was fixing for dinner. Then one day Stormy hit the mother lode when Mrs. Slark gave us four cases of canned herring purchased by her late husband Vern. She correctly assumed that Stormy would love it as much as Vern had, but warned us of its malodorous properties.

"That stuff is so stinky that I had to leave the windows open for two days to get the smell out of the house when Vern ate it," she advised.

Stinky was an understatement. Every time I opened a can, the fumes made my eyes water and my throat gasp. It was worse than the hold of a shrimp boat in August, but it didn't bother Stormy in the least. He wolfed down can after can with the enthusiasm of a famished football player. From then on, whenever I used the electric can opener Stormy assumed that a helping of herring was on its way. If he was on the roof, he would pulverize practically all of the plants in the annual bed in his haste to get down.

I would hear a shrieked "Meow!" and my silly cat would sail past the window on his way to terra flora. Clearly, I had created a monster. I tried closing the window before using the can opener. I even threw a towel over it to muffle the sound, but there was no duping Stormy. After two weeks of replacing crushed flowers, I gave in and bought some hibiscus bushes, much to the amusement of Nurseryman Bob.

"I knew sooner or later you'd see reason," he snickered. Smart aleck.

Life with Stormy was never dull. He was my own court jester, so corny and adorable that I giggled each time I looked at him.

Over time my madcap Gardening Buddy began to slow down, succumbing to old age. He was less inclined to rush after every fluttering butterfly that crossed his path. His appetite began to fail, and he even quit sleeping on the roof. Clearly the sun was setting on our friendship.

One autumn day I cuddled Stormy as he purred his last purr,

and laid him to rest in my former annual bed. After all the time he spent there it belonged to him more than it ever did to me. Blinking back tears, I felt alone, really alone, a feeling I hadn't known for years. I wanted my Gardening Buddy back. He had made the most arduous chores seem fun and brought me such happiness.

By springtime planting, another Gardening Buddy meowed his way into my life. Though no one could ever replace Stormy, little Simon quickly filled my heart with joy. A soft, warm, white-and-black bag of spots, he irresistibly made me the center of his universe, dogging my footsteps, spooning against my back at night and becoming my constant companion. As Simon wriggles in the grass, beckoning me to put down my trowel and smother his plump, fuzzy tummy with kisses, I'm reminded that a loving cat is one of life's greatest gifts, with the ability to heal old wounds and soften the sharp edges of a harsh world. My grandmother once told me, "A good cat will cure what ails you." If that's true, my Gardening Buddies have made me an exceptionally healthy woman.

~Michelle Close Mills

96

One of a Kind

Every cat is special in its own way.
~Sara Jane Clark

Throughout my career as a veterinary technician, hundreds of kittens and puppies have passed through my hands, some just a few hours old. But from the day Bucky was dropped into my hands, I knew he was special. Maybe it was his huge blue eyes or the way he was growling at me, or maybe it was the fact that he had somehow managed to get twelve pieces of dog food stuck in his throat. Yes, he was a special boy.

As he grew, Bucky's uniqueness grew along with him. He developed a habit of playing fetch with a green sponge soccer ball that he inherited from one of my many fosters, and when he wanted to play he meant business. If I was working on the computer, he would climb up behind me and throw the ball onto my keyboard. If he still couldn't get anyone to play with him, he would carry it in his mouth to the top of the recliner and drop it over the side so he could run after it.

This determination and ability to make the best of a situation were what I would remember most about him, long after he left me. When he was four months old, Bucky developed asthma. We found this out after a three-hour drive to a cardiologist in Madison, thinking he had heart disease. He took to the inhaler surprisingly well and was soon back to playing fetch with no wheezing, but it wasn't to be his last trip to the hospital by far.

At eight months, Bucky started losing weight rapidly and having diarrhea. Soon after that he began vomiting and refusing food. I was in Chicago at the time and he was still in Wisconsin, so I advised his caretaker to get him to the doctor immediately. They called me to say he was severely dehydrated, underweight and hadn't been grooming himself properly. I agreed that he should be admitted and he spent a long weekend on fluids, being poked and prodded by every doctor in the practice. Dr. Burton called me regularly and assured me that although they were no closer to finding out what caused him to be ill in the first place, he was still purring and cuddling everyone who got close enough. He went home early the next week, only to be readmitted two days later, weaker than before.

That was the beginning of a stay in the hospital that lasted two weeks and saw every test known to veterinary medicine performed on him. His caretaker visited every day and brought him a stuffed duck that smelled like home, then sent me photos and text messages telling me that he was still snuggling and purring in spite of his rapidly progressing mystery illness. The technicians told me he was happy to be brushed and groomed, and he was something of a hospital mascot. I was hoping that he would hold out long enough to follow me to Chicago to see specialists if no one else could find an answer, but an emergency call at work requesting permission to do an exploratory surgery on his intestines changed everything. I was in surgery myself at the time, overseeing anesthesia, when another tech called me out for a phone call. Dr. Burton told me that they found a blockage and asked for my consent to have a surgeon remove the last third of his colon. I agreed and waited by the phone for the next three hours. The next time she called, he was awake, stable, and trying to get someone to rub his head. We agreed the next step was to send the sample to the lab and see if we could get some answers.

Over the next few days, his caretaker told me Bucky was doing worlds better and even sent me photos of him happily eating his canned food and putting his face into the camera. We were all confident that he was on the road to recovery until the test results came back and confirmed all our worst fears. Bucky had feline infectious peritonitis, a virus that destroys the systems of the body by way of an immune system reaction. There is currently no cure and almost all cats diagnosed by way of a biopsy like Bucky's do not survive.

Though I was calm on the phone, once I hung up I couldn't stop crying. It didn't seem possible that the sweet kitten that was still charming every person who met him might not see his first birthday. I brought him to Chicago as soon as possible after his diagnosis so he could be with me and see the feline specialists I worked with. We came up with an aggressive regimen of treatments designed to keep Bucky as comfortable as possible.

Everyone fell in love with Bucky. Every time I walked into the treatment area someone was cradling him like a baby or rubbing his shaved belly, and Bucky loved every minute of it. It didn't matter if he was getting brushed or if I was giving him fluid treatments and injections at night. As long as he had a friend he was happy.

Just a few weeks later, surrounded by those same friends, Bucky lost his fight with FIP. The pain I felt was immeasurable. Every time I turned around, the place in my life he had occupied was more and more evident. Through illness, unemployment, happiness and tears, he had been a constant for me since he was only a few weeks old and his absence made my heart ache. Working helped, but anytime I was home it was as if I was too tired to move. My other cats seemed to understand and snuggled around me, but we all knew that it wouldn't be the same without Bucky.

Then one day, about a month later, I was packing up some of his things and came across the stuffed duck that had been by his side at the hospital. I remembered one of the techs telling me that the only time he ever got angry he bit his duck instead of the doctor, and I started to laugh for the first time since he died. It took me a moment to realize that I wasn't just laughing at the memory, I was laughing at myself. If there was one thing that spunky little cat would never have wanted, it would be for me to think of him with sadness. There was never a point in his life, no matter how painful or dark it might have been, when he didn't face whatever might have been before him with anything less than bravery, optimism and a determination that someone, somewhere, wanted to pet him. Even on his very last day he was happy that I was holding him, loving him, and oh yes, leaving the lid off the yogurt for him.

In his short life Bucky taught me that even though things might be sad or painful, there is always a little happiness to be found—in your friends, your passions, or even just a book that you really enjoy. Sometimes it's hard to find, and sometimes it takes everything you've got, but in the end it's worth it because each day you're alive, as Bucky taught me, is one of a kind.

~Natalie Smothers

97

Guardian Angel Cat

Pay attention to your dreams—
God's angels often speak directly to our hearts when we are asleep.
~Quoted in The Angels' Little Instruction Book
by Eileen Elias Freeman

My dreams are vivid even after all these years. In my dreams I can still feel the twelve-pound weight of his body curled against me on the couch, hear the pitter-patter of his feet trotting down the hallway behind me, and anticipate his "ambush" from under the dining room table.

For nine years, he ruled the roost, overseeing my every move. He even supervised me as I weeded the flowerbeds, and often tried to help by scratching alongside me. Thinking perhaps he had an ulterior motive, I would gently shoo him away.

He was a big boy, but fast, beating me to my favorite chair on a daily basis. At one point I considered changing his name to Velcro. He was always that stuck to me.

But cats are no match for cars, and early one sunny summer morning, his time on this planet was up. The driver of the car that hit him stopped and moved his body to the shoulder of the road. I am grateful for that.

When I found him later that morning, he was warm with the sunshine. I lifted him reverently with both hands and brought him inside the garage. I called, of all people, my ex-boyfriend. "I'll be right there," he said. The cat was special to him, too. During the months my then-boyfriend had studied for his commercial electrician's test, the cat was his constant study partner, nestled between his thigh and the arm of the chair.

It was only fitting that we buried the cat together. He dug a very deep hole in the woods on my property, and I solemnly bent down to place the cat inside. The hole was so deep I had to just let go the last couple of inches.

"Look," he said, pointing into the hole, "when he landed, he turned his head toward home." We held each other and wept. After a time, and a few words of praise for our feline companion, we replaced the dirt and camouflaged the grave to keep other animals from disturbing it.

As we walked to the house, a Monarch butterfly flitted twice around our heads and led the way. I smiled through my tears. "It's him, you know," I said, motioning to the butterfly.

"Your guardian angel," he said, taking my hand and giving it a squeeze.

Now it doesn't surprise me when I'm out weeding the flower-beds and I find a Monarch butterfly flitting about my head. Also, it doesn't surprise me that my dreams are still so vivid, and in them my senses are always fully engaged. Last night in my sleep I heard his special meow, telling me it was time to get up. "Not yet," I groggily whispered. "Let me enjoy your company just a few minutes more."

~Jan Bono

The Million-Year Promise

No heaven will not ever Heaven be
Unless my cats are there to welcome me.
~Author Unknown

"Will Tiger go to Heaven?" I held the small kitten in my lap and looked up at Mother. She looked back at me, a frown between her brows. I could feel my heart beating. I was eight years old and the kitten was a gift, mine alone, that Mother had given me after my father died. I didn't realize until years afterward that she hoped the small life would help heal the loss of the larger one.

She had told me, as we walked along holding hands, "Daddy went to Heaven." I don't remember exactly what that meant to me—I had an image of the sky, very blue, and clouds—but I knew he wasn't coming back, and I knew I was very still inside.

The kitten came a few weeks later. Ignorant of the nuances of gender, I named her Tiger. She was an ordinary tabby with green eyes, thin and unprepossessing, but I thought she was the most beautiful thing I had ever seen. I loved her from the first moment. I marveled over all the wondrous parts of her, from her tiny toes and velvety ears to the tawny color of her belly, prattling over each remarkable feature to Mother. But mainly I looked at the black stripes on her forehead. The pattern clearly made an M. It stood for million, I told her, as she sat on the carpet in front of me, her green eyes wide and solemn. It meant that she would live to be a million years old, I said. The thought that she might die was terrifying.

I found Mother in the kitchen. "Will Tiger go to Heaven?" I asked. It was very important. Mother had said we would see Daddy again someday, and I needed to know. There was a pause.

"No, animals aren't eternal," she said at last. It must have been difficult for her to say it, but not as hard as it was for me to hear. I was shattered. I went back to the living room and sat on the floor again, Tiger in my arms, tears in my eyes. I couldn't bring myself to disbelieve Mother, but I never quite forgave her. The M became a totem, a promise. I told Tiger she must promise to stay with me forever, a million years, and I promised to always take care of her.

Tiger did her best. She gave herself to me as wholly as I to her, deigning only to be petted by someone else. Mother called her Madame because of her regal aloofness. With me she let herself go, purring and rubbing and rolling over to let me stroke her belly. At night she slept in the curve of my knees. She kept her promise and stayed with me through school and college and well into my adulthood. When I got married, I decided it would be best to leave Tiger at home in my bedroom for a week until the new apartment acquired familiar smells. The night before, she sat quietly on my bed watching me pack, green eyes following me around the room. The next day, honeymoon or not, Mother called.

"I think you should come get this cat. She's pining and I'm afraid she's going to die," she said.

The only person beside myself to whom she ever gave her love was my husband Pat. It was instant. The minute she came into the apartment she was home. She made the usual cat rounds, signaled her approval, then sat down against his leg and looked up for his hand.

She was old by then and settled down contentedly to an inside life, though she had come and gone at will all the years before through my bedroom window. She kept her eye on the neighborhood from the windowsill, curled on the desk while we worked, and slept long hours on the bed. As I had as a child, I would have long conversations with her while she lounged on my lap.

Six years passed. All too quickly, it seemed, the inevitable happened and her kidneys began to fail. Now she spent most of her time on the bed. When she lost interest in eating I cut raw liver, her favorite, into small pieces and fed her by hand. As long as one of us was close by she seemed content, but soon even the liver failed to work, and one day I found her standing in front of her litter box with a vacant look in her eyes, urinating on the floor. I knew what it meant. In time uremic poisoning affects the brain and there is nothing to be done. I sat up with her that night, holding her and stroking the glossy M on her forehead. We had our last conversation. I released her from her promise. "It's okay," I said, and told her that I loved her and knew she had gone as far as she could. I talked quietly to her for hours. I don't know what she understood, but the quiet purr under my hand was as steady as it had ever been, and just as comforting. It was enough.

A few weeks later Pat and I were walking in the neighborhood, trying not to dwell on the small absence that seemed so large. "Wait, what's that?" he asked, stopping under a large tree next to an apartment building. As my eyes adjusted to the deep shade, I saw a small cat sitting by a door stoop in the mud created by a dripping water faucet. With its long gray fur tangled and sticking out in all directions, it looked like nothing so much as a trodden thistle or ragged piece of dandelion fluff. The mud and the door stoop told a clear story—the cat's need for companionship was more important than a more congenial spot. As we knelt down, a woman opened the door.

"It's been there for days and no one seems to know where it belongs," she said. "I've given it some food."

Pat looked at me. I shook my head. "I don't think I want another cat," I said. But what I thought didn't count. The cat pressed its rough, damp body against my leg and mewed, a remarkably polite little sound considering its plight.

We named her Amber and she cleaned up wonderfully. It took her no time to settle in. She discovered an old toy mouse of Tiger's under the sofa and laid claim to it immediately. She also laid claim to us. It was impossible not to respond wholly to this new life. As Tiger had so many years earlier, Amber bridged the painful loss with her own needs and demands and unbridled affection.

When Mother picked a kitten to help a little girl through a hard time, she gave more than she perhaps knew. And regardless of what she said that day in the kitchen, I am certain a thin striped cat with solemn green eyes is in Heaven, waiting, keeping our promise.

~Juliann Stark

Noah's Angel

*I will always remember the olive-eyed tabby who taught me that
not all relationships are meant to last a lifetime. Sometimes just an hour
is enough to touch your heart.*
~Barbara L. Diamond

W e didn't mean to keep her. She was in a basket in front of the grocery store and I really just stopped to gawk at the teeny kittens, but I took one look at her lying in my four-year-old son's arms and was a goner. Noah is deaf and really needed a friend. His hands fluttered excitedly, describing how soft and sweet the little cat was. This tiny furry friend was just what he needed.

I somehow knew that the little black kitten would be his best friend. She seemed complacent and purred in his chubby arms. Signing "mine," Noah already proclaimed the kitten to be his. The weeks and months flew by, and "Angel" became Noah's constant shadow. I often wondered how she tolerated his slinging her under his arm and carrying her everywhere, sometimes locking her in his room with him, or "teaching" her how to jump from his top bookshelf to his race car bed. Angel seemed to take it all in stride, and despite Noah's special brand of torture for his new kitty, every night I would find her fast asleep tucked under his arm or sprawled across his back. Nothing hurt me quite as much as knowing my little guy had no playmates, and Angel filled in wonderfully. Noah glowed with joy when his little black shadow was near. Spring came and Angel began

Noah's Angel : I'll Always Love You   347

to venture outside more and more, chasing butterflies and threatening the birds from afar, her shiny black coat glinting in the sunlight. Noah played outside with her and they remained inseparable—until one Monday.

Monday morning came and Angel had been out all night. It was warm and she had been staying out more and more. My older son, Nick left for junior high school, but in less than a minute was back in the door.

"Mom, Angel got hit by a car," he said, his chalk-white face revealing the worst. "She's dead, Mom."

"No, no!" I cried, racing outside to help her. Angel's small lifeless body lay on our lawn, blood coming from her head. I reached out to feel for a pulse and there was nothing. She was gone. Her body was still warm and I realized that it had just happened minutes earlier. "If only" ran through my mind repeatedly. If only I had made her stay inside last night. If only I had let her in earlier that morning. But nothing could bring her back and Nick and I gently laid her body in a box so we could bury her later.

I had no words for my young son, who had lost his best friend. I held off telling Noah until after preschool so that I could think of the best way to tell him. At the age of four, some things are harder to grasp and harder to explain. After school, I sat him down in the backyard, Angel's box next to me. We had already dug the hole for her little grave. I told Noah how Angel had played in the street, how dangerous that is, and that a car had hit her. His eyes grew huge as he watched my hands and my face. Anguish filled his eyes and understanding dawned. We talked about heaven and that her spirit was now there, but her body was dead. I felt hot tears pouring down my face as I saw the pain in his sweet blue eyes. I opened the box so Noah could see that she was indeed gone.

"Wake up, wake up," Noah signed over and over to his lifeless buddy. He softly stroked her fur, crying. He understood. Noah then placed a special blanket over her body and we solemnly held a heartbreaking funeral for the little angel who had brought us so much joy.

I cried for my son the rest of the night. I prayed for comfort for Noah and for a way to give him a new friend.

Both prayers were answered the next day. Together my husband and I finally reached a decision that had been causing me sleepless nights for months. Now the answer was perfectly clear. We would be moving in a few months to an area where we had other deaf friends and Noah would flourish with other deaf children to play with. It was a peaceful feeling, knowing that this was the right thing. I doubt that we would have seen it so clearly had we not lost little Angel when we did. My other prayer was answered when Noah woke up and began talking about his kitty dying. What he said next both shocked and amazed me. My young son told me that he misses his little shadow but that he knew she was in heaven and that God was holding her hand. I am so thankful for Noah's little angel and for the short time she was with us because I know that her passing was necessary for me to see what Noah really needs. We all look forward to the new start and new friends, especially Noah. And I have a feeling a little angel with a shiny black coat will be watching over him.

~Susan Farr-Fahncke

The Sun Worshiper

If there is one spot of sun spilling onto the floor,
a cat will find it and soak it up.
~J.A. McIntosh

For her entire life, Suki the Siamese cat had a thing for the sun. In Texas, that is no trivial matter. From May to September, the sun can be a formidable presence to be respected and protected from, usually with hats, sensible clothing, and lots of sunscreen. But Suki seemed to have no limits to the amount of sun she could tolerate. Unlike the rest of us mere mortals seeking the cooling shade, Suki seemed to revel in the sun, absorbing its rays and transforming them into her very life force. If there was ever a solar-powered cat, it was Suki.

Living with Suki was like living with a feline sundial. Her morning would start in an eastern window, washing her face after breakfast in the gentle glow of my office or bedroom, checking out the early birds on the balcony and stretching out against the glass for her pre-lunch nap. At noon she would take a break, checking on the progress at my desk, balancing herself on my forearms as I typed, sleeping in my inbox, or organizing (chewing) my interview and research notes. By this time the sun was overhead and there was no way to access it directly. No matter. Suki was patient.

After lunch, she would head for the living room to wait for the sun to start its western descent. While I was racing to lower the thermostat to prepare for the mid-afternoon onslaught that would turn the front of my home into a giant sauna, Suki was poised by the front windowsill ready to greet her blazing friend. As the long strips of sunlight crept along the carpet, Suki would stretch out full length so that every inch of skin and fur could catch the rays. I would sweat just looking at her. How, I would implore, can you lie in that hot sun? She of course ignored me as only the regal Siamese can do. Nothing could deter Suki from her sun-worshiping. As the sun sank, she would begrudgingly move to wherever she could catch the best sunspots, following them until they faded into the same warm glow that began her day.

Needless to say, Suki was not fond of gloomy, rainy days, looking accusingly at me as if I had something to do with taking her beloved sun away. Ever resourceful, she would find the nearest light source and plant herself like a hamburger under a heat lamp. Once, when she was very young, she sat on a candle. Yes, it was lit. It singed the hair on her kitty buns but she was undeterred. To Suki, there was no such thing as too hot.

As Suki aged, the sun became even more of a welcome friend, as the warmth penetrated her old bones and seemed to give her new life. She was never happier than when she hit the trifecta—curled up with me, on my lap, in a sunny spot. I sweltered in silence, treasuring every golden moment as the days got longer, but never long enough when a cherished companion is headed toward twilight.

In her final hospital stay, the reason for Suki's love affair with El Sol finally came to light. In addition to receiving all of the traditional treatments for chronic renal failure, Suki also had the caring and professional touch of a veterinarian certified in acupuncture. He mentioned that she had an excess of yin, or cold energy, and I listened incredulously before regaling him with tales of how much Suki loved heat and light.

Four days before her death, as Suki slept on my chest, I had a dream. We were in the car, as we had been so many times, and Suki was on the back ledge, trying to climb the back windshield. In the dream there had been a horrible storm, but it was over and the sun was out, warm and brilliant through the glass. Suki was climbing higher, saying "sunny, sunny," over and over. I turned and asked, "What is it, Suki? What's wrong?" She responded, "Why do my legs feel like rocks?" I said, "I don't know baby, but I'm so sorry."

She then looked at me and in a voice as crystal clear and pure as a ray of light, said, "Thank you for giving me a nice place to live." I have no doubt that in addition to all the food and toys and treats and trips, the hugs and kisses and photographs and parties, she was talking mostly about those sunspots.

On the morning of Suki's last day, there was a horrible storm, just like in the dream. By the afternoon, the sun was shining on a crystal clear spring day, warm and brilliant in a cloudless blue sky. I took her on the balcony for what would be her last time in the sun, watching her stretch and soak up the light as she had for so many years, while I hoped for a miracle that never came. As the sun set on the day and on Suki's life of almost twenty years, I held her close to keep her as warm as I could, but never as warm as she wanted, I'm sure. She struggled to keep her place in the sun, but in the end we had no choice to but say goodbye. At the hospital I insisted they keep her wrapped even afterwards. I could not bear the thought that she would be cold.

The sun went out for me that day, and in our home Suki's sunspots are empty now. I look at them with grief and love, both unending, and with smiles and tears at memories that will never fade. Sometimes I can still see the outline of a brave and beautiful Siamese shining in the golden light, and I know in my heart that wherever Suki is, she is still following the sun.

~Julie Catalano

Achilles' Gift

People that don't like cats haven't met the right one yet.
~Deborah A. Edwards, D.V.M.

I've never been a cat person. All of the cats I knew when I was growing up were cold, aloof and some were just plain mean. They weren't the kind of pet I wanted. Or so I thought. About eighteen months ago, I was in the midst of a hard time in my life. Emotionally I was having a tough time living on my own, but I knew that I didn't want a roommate. One of my work colleagues suggested that I foster kittens. Kittens? Those antisocial mini-tyrants? No thanks. But the idea gradually began to make sense and a few weeks later I found myself picking up three kittens, two females and a male, to be fostered. They were young—only about seven weeks old—and within a week of having them, I grew to see a different side of cats. But did I want one for my own? The male of the bunch decided to answer that for me.

One day while playing with them, he climbed into my lap, stood up on his back legs, put his front paws on my chest, and stared into my eyes, as if looking deep into my soul. After a moment he got down from my chest, meowed in a rather confident tone as if to say, "I pick you," curled up in my lap and went to sleep. He had picked me, and I realized then that I had just picked him too. I scratched his ears as he slept there on my knee and his purr matched the vibrations he had started in my heart. He was home and we both knew it.

He had always been the little daredevil of the bunch, so I

considered two names for him—Achilles and Apollo. He seemed to think he was a little hero, and he had definitely saved me in a few ways, so Achilles it was.

Achilles would meet me at the door when I came home from work, nuzzle my cheek, wipe away my tears when I was upset, sleep beside me on the bed at night, and play with my fingers and toes when I was happy. I looked forward to a happy coexistence with my sweet boy. Unfortunately, things wouldn't turn out that way.

One evening, about two months after I had first picked him up for fostering, I came home from work and found no Achilles at the door waiting for me. Immediately alarmed, I found him in the bathroom lying on the rug and knew right away that something was wrong. He was pale and his kidneys were swollen. He looked at me, barely able to lift his head, as if asking me to take away his pain. For all the times he had comforted me, I was at a loss for how to comfort him. I stayed awake all night, sitting with him, talking quietly and stroking his fur.

I was at the vet's door when they opened the next morning, and as the technician took Achilles, she looked at me with a sad expression and said, "He's very sick." I looked at my kitten in her arms, and realized how small he was. He looked back at me with sad eyes as if to say, "I'm sorry." Holding back tears I said, "I know." But to this day I'm not sure if I was answering the technician or Achilles' unspoken apology.

The news from the veterinarian wasn't good—feline leukemia. Achilles had probably been born with it. At three months of age, I had my little hero put down to end his obvious suffering. And it devastated me, ripping apart my heart. He had done so much for me—wiped away many tears, offered many nuzzles and licks, and provided the other side of many silent dialogues in our short time together. And even though I was assured that there was nothing I could have done differently, I still felt as if I had failed him.

As time went on people consoled me, told me I had given him a happy life, and started suggesting that I get another kitten. But I couldn't do it. I wasn't a cat person. Achilles had been different, special. Eventually people stopped suggesting it and I moved on with my life, a little piece of my heart closed off.

A year after losing Achilles, something pulled at me to look at The Humane Society website. I gave in and surveyed the different cats and kittens that needed homes, and a part of me wanted to give one just that, but none of them jumped out at me. The same feeling that had pulled me to the website seemed to tell me to give it time, but not give up, that my kitten was out there.

I was again fighting depression, and didn't even know if I had it in me to care for another animal. Besides, did I really want to risk getting hurt again? The answer came one day when I was looking at the website and he jumped out at me. He looked exactly like Achilles, and to top it off his name was Apollo—the second name I had considered a year ago when my first kitten touched my heart. He was the one for me. I went to the shelter the very next day to see him.

He was ten weeks old, and when I saw him in his cage, my heart melted. I was cautioned that he was semi-feral and had not had much socialization, but this didn't bother me. I took him home that very day, of course keeping the name Apollo. At first Apollo hid behind the couch, and he didn't eat for the first day I had him. But I was patient and allowed him the space that he needed.

One day I came home from work feeling completely dejected after a tough day and just flopped into my chair, forgetting that I even had a kitten. I laid my head back and closed my eyes, but a moment later I heard this tentative "meow." I opened my eyes and looked down at my little Apollo.

"Well, hello there," I said. Apollo promptly jumped into my lap and nuzzled my cheek, purring softly as I held him. At that moment, he became my little man.

It's been four months since I brought Apollo home from the shelter. He meets me at the door every night, and I immediately pick him up and hug him as he nuzzles my cheek and purrs. "And how is my little man today?" I ask, and he meows his response as we go to get him dinner. In the short time that I've had him, my life has turned around. Apollo doesn't let me forget that even when life seems dark, there's always that little ray of sunshine—in this case, my ray of sunshine is Apollo, named for the Greek Sun God.

When I get upset, he curls up beside me, quietly purring, his tail wiping away my tears. When I'm happy he turns into a little vampire and play bites my fingers. How did this little kitten come into my life? Is it possible that he is a gift from Achilles who had to leave me so young? I like to think that Achilles guided this kitten to my heart, but whatever force was at work, I'm grateful. Apollo is happy and healthy, and has warmed my heart and saved me all over again. I'm not a cat person, but I am a cat lover.

~Tara Scaife

Meet Our
Contributors

Cate Adelman currently lives in the Midwest and serves as an advocate for people with disabilities. She has completed a bachelor's degree from NLU, and religious studies with the Servants of the Holy Heart of Mary. Her passions include issues of peace and justice, the arts, and the Spiritual journey.

Monica A. Andermann lives on Long Island with her husband Bill and their cat Charley. She is a frequent contributor to the *Chicken Soup for the Soul* series, and in between tending to and generally spoiling her feline friend, she has produced writing which has been published in various anthologies, newspapers, and journals.

Elizabeth Atwater is a small town Southern gal who discovered the joy of writing as soon as she was old enough to grasp a pencil in her hands and form a cognitive thought in her head. She lives on a horse ranch with her husband Joe, who is another absolute joy in her life.

Carol Ayer lives in Northern California. Her credits include previous *Chicken Soup for the Soul* volumes, *Woman's World* magazine, *Poesia*, *Poetry Quarterly*, and *flashquake*. Her romantic novella, *Storybook Love*, is available from Wild Child Publishing. Visit her website at www.seaaircarol.com.

Suzanne Baginskie recently retired as a paralegal/office manager at a Florida law firm after twenty-eight years. She has been published in several *Chicken Soup for the Soul* books, *A Cup of Comfort* books, mystery anthologies, *True Romance* and *Woman's World* magazines. Suzanne is currently writing a legal thriller novel.

Cynthia Baker received her B.S. in Education from Millersville University. She was a counselor for group homes, managed bookstores for B. Dalton, and is currently a Realtor in Southern California. She supports efforts for child abuse prevention. She is currently working on a novel. E-mail her at Cynthia.Baker@camoves.com.

Nikki Studebaker Barcus is a licensed teacher and freelance writer who lives with her husband and their three children on an Indiana farm. She writes about the lessons God teaches her through her kids on her blog, Lessons from the Carpool Line. www.nikki-studebaker-barcus.blogspot.com.

Garrett Bauman is retired from a career in teaching at Monroe Community College in Rochester, NY. He and his wife live a mile from the nearest country road in upstate New York. E-mail him atMbauman@monroecc.edu.

Joan McClure Beck is a college instructor whose hobbies include painting and writing. She and her husband love spending time with their children and grandchildren. They share their home with several cats, including Lizzie, who, given the chance, would still ride in the hood of that old sweatshirt. E-mail her at deejoanb@yahoo.com.

Jan Bono lives on the Long Beach peninsula in Southwest Washington State. She is a life coach, writing coach, Law of Attraction presenter, and freelance writer. Jan has numerous articles, one-act plays, and several books to her credit. Check out her blog at http://daybreak-solutions.com/blog.

Debra Ayers Brown, a marketing professional, received her B.A. with honors, from the University of Georgia and her MBA from The Citadel. She is the creator of My Yellow Bluff and Southern Deb blogs. She loves traveling, birding, and spending time with her daughter Meredith and husband Allen. E-mail her at dabmlb@comcast.net.

Dave Carpenter has been a full-time cartoonist since 1981. Besides the *Chicken Soup for the Soul* books, his cartoons have appeared in *Harvard Business Review, Reader's Digest, Barron's, The Wall Street Journal, Good Housekeeping, Woman's World, The Saturday Evening Post* and numerous other publications. E-mail Dave at davecarp@ncn.net.

Julie Catalano is a former dancer and has been a freelance writer since 1980, with articles on travel, health, profiles and pets published in regional and national publications and online. She is a member of the Authors Guild and the American Society of Journalists and Authors. E-mail her at julie@juliecatalano.com.

Robert Chrisman graduated from college and took a job with Social Security. Thirty-two years later he retired early to try his hand and heart at writing. Currently he is hard at work on a memoir of the last five years of his mother's life.

Lynn Cole enjoys painting, reading and writing. Her mother, Norma Favor, and sister, Renee Hixson, also have stories published in *Chicken Soup for the Soul* books. Lynn's father, Roy Favor, was a Baptist minister for many years before his death.

Harriet Cooper, a freelance writer/humorist, is owned by four delightful, though sometimes terrifying cats. When not rubbing furry tummies, she writes about health, diet, exercise, family and cats. Her work has appeared in magazines, newspapers, anthologies, newsletters, radio and even a coffee can. E-mail her at catladywrites@hotmail.com.

Rebecca Davis is a third-year communications major at Northeastern University. She would like to be a screenwriter when she graduates. E-mail her atbecdavis15@gmail.com.

Regina K. Deppert lives near Indianapolis, IN. She graduated from Florida Metropolitan University in 2006 with honors. She currently lives with three shelter cats, Louie, Shelby and Jasper. Regina enjoys reading, writing and working with those less fortunate. This was her first experience writing a story and submitting it to be published. E-mail her at gina92262@msn.com.

Karen Donley-Hayes holds an M.A. in interdisciplinary studies, is an editor at Hiram College, and is earning her MFA in creative writing from Ashland University. When she's not writing professionally, for school, or for fun, she spends her time with her remarkable husband, a plethora of cats, and one horse.

Cheryl Dudley received her B.A. in creative writing and M.A. in literature. She works as a writer and editor for Washington State University and also freelances. She is the author of *The Legendary Appaloosa, Horses That Save Lives, Rescued by a Horse*, and *Wrangling Snakes*. She lives in Pullman, WA, with her husband, three horses, and two mules.

Washington, DC author **Dr. Sheila Embry** holds three nationally accredited degrees: Baccalaureate in Business Administration, Master of Arts, and Doctorate of Management. She is a Unit Chief at a federal agency and enjoys beaches, sailing, reading, and writing. Currently working on her second novel, she can be reached at drembry@ymail.com.

Anne Erickson is a writer and freelance television producer who lives on Washington's Olympic Peninsula. She's documented on video or in print everything from painting a 747 to digging geoducks, and has concluded that Everything's Fascinating. Mr. Whiskers is currently relaxing and looking for an agent. Reach Mr. Whiskers at elvis@olypen.com.

Susan Farr-Fahncke is the founder of www.2TheHeart.com, where you can find more of her writing and sign up for an online writing workshop. She is also the founder of the volunteer group, Angels2TheHeart, the author of *Angel's Legacy*, and contributor to over seventy books, including many in the *Chicken Soup for the Soul* series.

Donna Gephart writes funny books for kids. Her recent book from Random

House is *How to Survive Middle School*. Be on the lookout for her new book, *Olivia Bean, Trivia Queen*. To learn more, visit Donna at www.donnagephart.com.

Sharon Grumbein graduated from Craven Community College in 1986 with her Associate of Arts. She works part-time with the elderly. She has been a homeschooling mother for sixteen years. She lives in Havelock, NC, with five of her children, four cats and a very trusting hamster.

Lauren Gullion currently teaches English composition and is an MFA candidate at Colorado State University. She writes both fiction and nonfiction, often with her cat Mau at her side. Lauren is also a passionate yoga instructor and blogs about her favorite inspirations at www. LuluLoveAndLightYoga.com. E-mail her at laurengullion@sbcglobal.net.

Patrick Hardin is a freelance cartoonist living in his hometown of Flint, MI. He earned a B.A. with dual majors in Philosophy and Psychology from the University of Michigan-Flint. His work appears in a variety of books and periodicals around the world. E-mail him at phardin357@aol.com.

Juliana Harris recently published her first novel, *The Fork in the Road*. She is a singer/songwriter who lives in Guilford, CT. This is her second appearance in the *Chicken Soup for the Soul* series. Contact her through julieharrismusic.com.

Born in Michigan, **Talia Haven** has been writing short stories for several years. Current works include "Speak for Us," a short story in the *Mertales* anthology published in 2010 from Wyvern Publishing. "Buster" is her second story published in the *Chicken for the Soul* series.

Marti Hawes is a retired business owner who began writing in high school and college. She enjoys camping, hiking, bicycling and RVing. She and her husband Ken share their country home with their dog Shiner, cats Rosey and Rocky, and a myriad of wildlife. E-mail her at marticar@embarqmail.com.

Cara Holman lives in Portland, OR, with her husband, youngest son, and two mischievous but lovable cats. Her personal essays and poetry have been featured online and in anthologies, including *Chicken Soup for the Soul: Count Your Blessings* and *Chicken Soup for the Soul: True Love*. She blogs at: http://caraholman.wordpress.com.

Teresa Hoy lives in rural Missouri with her husband and a large family of rescued cats and dogs. Her work has appeared in the *Chicken Soup for the Soul* series, *The Ultimate* series, and other anthologies. Visit her at www.teresahoy.com.

Nan Johnson is pursuing her bachelor's degree at Taylor University in Upland, IN, and loves her little sister, Rebecca Johnson, with all her heart. She has two dogs and two cats, all of whom are like family members. E-mail her at nan.johnson89@gmail.com.

Ruth Jones lives in Cookeville, TN, with her husband Terry. She is hard at work on her second novel.

Ron Kaiser, Jr. lives, teaches, and writes in the beautiful Lakes Region of New Hampshire. No one really knows how he managed to convince an absurdly beautiful woman to marry him, but it did in fact happen. Ron is currently seeking representation for a novel and a book of short stories. E-mail him at kilgore.trout1922@gmail.com.

April Knight is a freelance writer and the author of several novels. She enjoys riding horses and traveling; her favorite destinations are Hawaii and Australia. She has just completed her latest novel, a romance titled, *Stars in the Desert*.

Nancy Kucik is the editorial assistant for a medical journal in Birmingham, AL. She and her husband share their home with two dogs and a cat. Laser unexpectedly passed away in December 2010, but lives on in the memories of everyone whose life he touched. E-mail Nancy at nancykucik@yahoo.com.

Francesca Lang lives in Orlando with her husband Richard and son Aiden, along with Bailey the cat and Jazmine the dog. She holds a degree in Intercultural Communications and Sociology, however, her passion lies in health and wellness and she's working towards a license in exercise physiology and personal training.

Renee Lannan, with a B.A. in English and M.Ed in teaching English, freelances for magazines on parenting, health and faith-related topics. Many of her online articles are accessible at www.triond.com/users/Renee+Lannan. She considers every article completed a miracle while raising small children.

Melissa Laterza is a freelance writer and college student in Florida. She has publications in *Senior Times*, *GRAND Magazine* and *Elektraphrog* literary magazine. She loves the beach, walking, swimming and spending time with her friends. She plans to write fiction for young adults and adults.

With a B.A. from Amherst College and an MALS from Dartmouth College, **Leigh B. MacKay**, left New England in 1977 for Atlanta, where he taught English and coached golf for thirty-one years. Now retired, he plays golf in Port St. Lucie, FL, during the winters and in Plymouth, MA, during the summers.

Australian born author **Grant Madden**, immigrated to the United States in 2005, and resides in San Diego. He has written cover stores in international publications, *Sailing, Catamaran Sailor*, and is a feature writer for the *San Diego Reader*. Grant can be contacted through his website www.grantmadden.com.

Shawn Marie Mann lives in Central Pennsylvania with her husband and three children. She is a trained geographer who writes about family adventures in Pennsylvania on her website www.amusementparkmom.com. This is her second Chicken Soup for the Soul story to be published. E-mail her at shawnmariemann@yahoo.com.

Angela Marchi is a college student and a married mother of a four-year-old daughter. She is planning on receiving her B.S. in Nursing by 2013. Angela enjoys spending time with her family and pets. E-mail her at windsong81@aol.com.

Timothy Martin is the author of four books and nine screenplays. His children's novel, *Scout's Oaf*, was published in 2010 by Cedar Grove Books. Tim's work has appeared in numerous *Chicken Soup for the Soul* books. He lives in McKinleyville, CA, and can be reached via e-mail at tmartin@northcoast.com.

Patricia McElligott, a writer of fiction and nonfiction, is currently working on her second novel. She lives in Pittsburgh, where she shares her life with her family, friends and two beloved cats. E-mail her at Patmc255@yahoo.com.

Avril McIntyre is a showroom manager and lives on a mountain. She enjoys traveling, friends and is passionate about animals. Her plans are to continue writing inspirational animal stories and finishing her book.

Peter Medeiros is a student at Arcadia University in Pennsylvania, where he studies literature and creative writing. He enjoys very specific forms of folk dance. Peter is currently writing a fantasy novel.

Terri Meehan grew up in Ohio before moving to England nineteen years ago. The inspiration for her stories evolves from her childhood memories, along with a mixture of her current lifestyle in the UK. Terri is employed by LexisNexis publishers, but her weekends and any leisure time are devoted to writing. E-mail her at dstout@iuk.edu.

Michelle Close Mills' stories have appeared in many anthologies including *Chicken Soup for the Recovering Soul: Daily Inspirations*, *Chicken Soup for the Soul in Menopause*, *Chicken Soup for the Soul: Devotional Stories for Mothers*, as well as *The Ultimate Gardener* and *The Ultimate Bird Lover*. Learn more at www.authorsden.com/michelleclosemills.

S. Kay Murphy is the author of *Tainted Legacy: The Story of Alleged Serial Killer Bertha Gifford*. She lives in the San Gabriel Mountains of Southern California with her best friend, Sugar Plum, and can be contacted through her website at www.skaymurphy.com.

Every time **Julie Neubauer** returns home, Mr. McKitty greets her at the door. He has the sweetest purr, and he's never, ever hissed at anyone. Julie, Mr. McKitty, her husband Ken and their son John, live in a suburb of Chicago.

Born and raised in Port Alberni, BC, among friends **Louise Nyce** is jokingly referred to as the crazy cat lady. She has always had a love of the written word, finding comfort and a place to hide in the magic that all stories, be they fact or fiction, can provide.

Tracie O'Braks has been writing since she was a young girl. She has a book of poems in the works, and is currently working on a novel. She enjoys spending time with her family.

LaVerne Otis lives in Southern California where she loves writing, photography, bird watching, reading and spending time with family. LaVerne is recently retired, taking classes at a local community college. She has been published several times in *Chicken Soup for the Soul* books and various magazines. Contact her via e-mail at lotiswrites@msn.com.

Jeannine Ouellette received her B.A. in Psychology and a Master of Education from the University of Ottawa. In 2000, she won the Laura Jamieson Prize for her book on women's ways of learning. She is currently writing and producing inspirational DVDs. E-mail her atjeannine@triyana.ca.

Mark Parisi's "off the mark" comic, syndicated since 1987, is distributed by United Media. He won the National Cartoonists Society's award for Best Newspaper Panel in 2009. His wife/business partner Lynn and their daughter, Jen, contribute with inspiration (as do three cats, one dog and an unknown number of koi). Mark's humor also graces greeting cards, T-shirts, calendars, magazines, newsletters and books. Learn more at www.offthemark.com.

Saralee Perel is an award-winning columnist/novelist and multiple contributor to Chicken Soup for the Soul. Her current book, *The Dog Who Walked Me*, is about her dog who became her caregiver after Saralee's spinal cord injury, the initial devastation of her marriage, and her cat who kept her sane. Contact her at sperel@saraleeperel. com or www.saraleeperel.com.

Charles Pettingell is a Bostonian, and a retired federal labor-management specialist; **Patria Pettingell** is a native of Ponce, Puerto Rico. They were married during WWII in P.R. where Charles served with the Army Air Force. They settled in California. Patria's first novel, *Island Fury*, was published in 2005.

Luanne Porper received her B.A. in English at Northeastern Illinois University. She enjoys writing poetry and essays and has a story appearing in an upcoming issue of *I Love Cats* magazine. She is married and has a son, two cats and a dog. E-mail her at luanneporper@yahoo.com.

Marsha Porter has written numerous short stories and nonfiction articles. She co-authored a video movie guide that reviewed over 20,000 films. She perfected the 500-word essay in grade school when it was the punishment du jour. Currently she teaches high school English.

Felice Prager is a writer and a multisensory educational therapist from Scottsdale, AZ. Her essays have been published locally, nationally, and internationally in print and on the Internet. She is the author of the book, *Quiz It: Arizona*. To find out more, visit www.QuizItAZ. com. To find more of her essays visit www.writefunny.blogspot.com.

Darlene Prickett lives in Chippewa Falls, WI, with her husband BJ and their daughter Sandra. They are in the process of adopting more children through the Special Needs program. Darlene received her first award for writing when she was ten years old and she has been writing ever since.

Denise Reich practices flying trapeze, travels a lot, and has seen the B-52s in concert eight times. Her work has appeared in publications in the USA, Bermuda and elsewhere, such as *The Royal Gazette* (Bermuda) and *Chicken Soup for the Soul: What I Learned from the Cat* and *Chicken Soup for the Soul: The Gift of Christmas*.

Natalie June Reilly is definitely a cat person. She is also the mother of two extraordinary young men, Billy and Alec, and the author of the children's book, *My Stick Family: Helping Children Cope with Divorce*. She is a student at Arizona State University and can be reached via e-mail at natalie@themeanmom.com.

David Alan Richards is passionate about writing and martial arts. He lives in North Jersey with his wife, Rosetta, and works in the computer field. He frequents bookstores and is an avid reader. He loves the cinema. E-mail him atwriter@davidalanrichards.com.

Sallie A. Rodman received her Certificate in Professional Writing from California State University, Long Beach. She lives with her husband Paul, Mollie the dog and her big boy, Inky the cat. Sallie feels very fortunate for all the cats she has had the privilege of loving. E-mail her at sa.rodman@verizon.net.

Maureen Rogers is a transplanted Canadian living in the Seattle area with her husband and two feisty felines. Her writing projects include fiction, poetry and essays. She has been published online, in newspapers, anthologies and in *Chicken Soup for the Coffee Lover's Soul* and *Chicken Soup for the Soul: My Resolution*. E-mail her at morogers@gmail.com.

Marcia Rudoff, author of *We Have Stories—A Handbook for Writing your Memoirs*, has been teaching memoir writing classes and workshops for over a decade. A freelance writer, her columns and personal essays have been published in various newspapers and anthologies. Marcia lives and writes on Bainbridge Island, WA.

Patricia Sabengsy is an inspiring freelance writer. She currently resides in Southern Illinois with her husband. Patricia enjoys writing, reading, boating, and hiking with her two Labs.

Arthur Sánchez is a writer residing in sunny Florida. As an employee of an animal rescue group he learned what many people know—that often the pet chooses you; you do not choose the pet. For more information on Arthur's work visit www.ArthurSanchez.com.

Theresa Sanders loves contributing frequently to *Chicken Soup for the Soul* books. A Springfield, MO, native and a University of Maryland graduate, she was an award-winning technical writer before turning to creative endeavors. She has four grown children and lives with her husband near St. Louis. E-mail Theresa at TheresaLSanders@charter.net.

Tara Scaife has a Psychology degree from the University of Toronto and is currently a public servant. She has always loved writing and started with poems, branching out into short stories. Tara is currently working on her first novel. She resides in Toronto with her cat, Apollo.

Leslie C. Schneider grew up in Montana where she and her husband of forty years raised their two sons. She has four grandchildren and currently resides in the Denver area. E-mail her at Leslie@airpost.net.

Margaret Shaw received her B.A. in English Literature from the University of Hawaii at Hilo. Margaret enjoys spending time writing poetry and short stories, reading, cooking and spending time with her grandchildren. She is currently working on a collection of poetry and a cookbook.

Kathleen Shoop, PhD is married to Bill and a mom to Beth and Jake—oh, and mom to two dogs named Bob and Izzy! When she's not writing historical fiction novels and articles, she works with teachers and lunches with ladies. Kathleen can be reached at www.kshoop.com.

Ava Siemens lives on beautiful Vancouver Island with her husband, Jeff, and their two cats, Lydia and Opi. She is an avid photographer who also enjoys hiking, and cheering for the Vancouver Canucks. When not watching hockey, you will find her collecting beach glass and sea shells.

Everyone has a story to tell. Some have many. "Crippy" is **David Michael Smith's** third published story in the *Chicken Soup for the Soul* series. The author, from Georgetown, DE, proudly gives God all the glory! Contact him at davidandgeri@hotmail.com or on Facebook.

Natalie Smothers has worked as a Registered Veterinary Technician for the last seven years and has lived in places as diverse as Colorado, Wisconsin and Chicago. In her spare time she writes fiction and tends to her numerous pets. Her first novel, *Plans*, was published this year. E-mail her at chickiepants@gmail.com.

Besides having graduated from Bible college in Three Hills, Alberta, Canada, **Helen Splane-Dowd** has received certificates from two international writing courses and from business college. She spends her time at her computer, writing stories about pets and life in general. Her writings can be found on her website: www.occupytillicome.com.

Juliann Stark and her husband Ron have headed S/R Laboratories, the world's only animation art conservation, for over thirty years. She is an accomplished writer and book editor and has authored numerous articles. Tiger was the first of a long line of extraordinary cats with whom she has shared her life.

Pamela Tambornino, Cherokee, Wolf Clan, works full-time for Haskell Indian Nations University. She received her MA in English in 2010. Her four cats and two dogs allow her and her husband to live with them. E-mail her at bookwormbugg2002@yahoo.com.

Jayne Thurber-Smith is an award-winning writer for various publications. She has had the pleasure of interviewing Christian athletes for *Faith & Friends* and *Sports Spectrum* magazines, and has also contributed to *The Buffalo News*. She and her husband enjoy being the unofficial cheerleading squad for their four children's extracurricular activities.

Sandi Tompkins, an award-winning journalist and Pulitzer Prize nominee, has edited fifty books and two study Bibles as part of her work with Youth With A Mission (YWAM) in Kona, HI. She also writes articles, teaches writing, and mentors authors.

Deborah Van Dyke has two wonderful daughters. She was a stay-at-home mom for twenty years and is now an assistant librarian at Duniway Middle School in McMinnville, OR. She loves all kinds of books, kids of all ages, all types of animals and any activity outdoors.

Ann Vitale lives in the Endless Mountains of Northeast Pennsylvania. She has been a microbiologist, a new car dealer, a master gardener, and a dog trainer. Past publications include educational books, flash fiction magazines, and *Chicken Soup for the Soul: What I Learned from the Dog*. E-mail her at ann.e.vitale74@gmail.com.

Beverly F. Walker lives in Greenbrier, TN, with her retired husband and beloved cat Audrey. She enjoys scrapbooking, photography, and spending time with her grandchildren. Beverly loves to write and has stories in many *Chicken Soup for the Soul* books and in *Angel Cats: Divine Messengers of Comfort*.

Christina Ward is a retired medical transcriptionist. She enjoys gardening and spending quality time with her beloved Yorkshire Terrier Megan, cat Benicia and thirty-pound tortoise Otis. Christina is a member of Quills of Faith Writers Group and enjoys attending workshops and critiques, writing poetry and other inspirational works. She's working on her first novel.

Arthur still lives on in **Susan Ward's** heart, but she's made room for Louie and Precious. Louie and Precious are just as loving and affectionate and snuggly as Arthur, but they are not nearly as vocal as Arthur was.

Pam Williams is a freelance writer and pastor's wife. She enjoys traveling with her husband to visit their children and grandchildren. Pam's stories have been included in four other *Chicken Soup for the Soul* books as well as numerous magazines. Pam is head of the housekeeping staff for their Maine Coon, Baxter.

Peter Wood is the author of *Confessions of a Fighter: Battling Through the Golden Gloves* and *A Clenched Fist: The Making of a Golden Glove Champion*. He teaches English at White Plains High School in New York. When not writing, he enjoys painting, running and yoga. E-mail him at peterwood05@aol.com.

Joanna G. Wright is a freelance writer from Indianapolis, IN, where she resides with her husband and two daughters. She enjoys reading, gardening, drawing and quilting.

Sandy Wright leads Joy Writers and is a member of Royalty Writers, both with North Texas Christian Writers. Her writing has emerged from church newsletters and GT curriculum to freelance devotionals and articles with such publishers as Chicken Soup for the Soul. She has completed her first book and is working on a second.

Elisa Yager is a human resources guru by day and freelance writer by night. She is "Mom" to two awesome teenagers and shares her home with cats, Cassidy and Smoke, four aged goldfish and a bunny named Ms. Elmer. Elisa would love your feedback. E-mail her at Proud2blefty@yahoo.com.

Sue Young is originally from England and now makes her home in Florida. She works in the corporate world and in her spare time loves to read, write and travel to the far corners of this beautiful world.

Melissa Zifzal worked in public relations as a writer and designer before beginning her most important job as a stay-at-home mom. She also contributed to *Chicken Soup for the Soul: Devotional Stories for Mothers.* Melissa, her husband, Dwayne, and their children, Ethan, Lindsey, and Caleb, live in Bloomingdale, OH.

Patti Wade Zint is the owner/mother of very spoiled kitties who have graciously chosen to live with her and her family. She and her husband are the proud parents of three wonderful children, one of whom is a United States Marine. E-mail Patti at pwzint@cox.net or visit her blog at pattiwadezint.wordpress.com.

Chicken Soup for the Soul

Meet Our Authors

Jack Canfield is the co-creator of the *Chicken Soup for the Soul* series, which *Time* magazine has called "the publishing phenomenon of the decade." Jack is also the co-author of many other bestselling books.

Jack is the CEO of the Canfield Training Group in Santa Barbara, California, and founder of the Foundation for Self-Esteem in Culver City, California. He has conducted intensive personal and professional development seminars on the principles of success for more than a million people in twenty-three countries, has spoken to hundreds of thousands of people at more than 1,000 corporations, universities, professional conferences and conventions, and has been seen by millions more on national television shows.

Jack has received many awards and honors, including three honorary doctorates and a Guinness World Records Certificate for having seven books from the *Chicken Soup for the Soul* series appearing on the New York Times bestseller list on May 24, 1998.

You can reach Jack at www.jackcanfield.com.

Mark Victor Hansen is the co-founder of Chicken Soup for the Soul, along with Jack Canfield. He is a sought-after keynote speaker, bestselling author, and marketing maven. Mark's powerful messages of possibility, opportunity, and action have created powerful change in thousands of organizations and millions of individuals worldwide.

Mark is a prolific writer with many bestselling books in addition to the *Chicken Soup for the Soul* series. Mark has had a profound influence in the field of human potential through his library of audios, videos, and articles in the areas of big thinking, sales achievement, wealth building, publishing success, and personal and professional development. He is also the founder of the MEGA Seminar Series.

Mark has received numerous awards that honor his entrepreneurial spirit, philanthropic heart, and business acumen. He is a lifetime member of the Horatio Alger Association of Distinguished Americans.

You can reach Mark at www.markvictorhansen.com.

Jennifer Quasha is an award-winning writer and editor. She is a published author of more than 40 books, including three dog books: *Don't Pet a Pooch... While He's Pooping: Etiquette for Dogs and their People, The Dog Lover's Book of Crafts: 50 Home Decorations that Celebrate Man's Best Friend*, and *Sew Dog: Easy-Sew Dogwear and Custom Gear for Home and Travel*.

She graduated from Boston University with a B.S. in Communication and has been writing ever since. Jennifer has been a contributing editor at *Dog Fancy* and *Dogs for Kids* magazines, and has written monthly columns on rescue dogs, etiquette, and travel. Jennifer has also been published in Chicken Soup for the Soul books and is thrilled to be a co-author of *Chicken Soup for the Soul: My Dog's Life* and *Chicken Soup for the Soul: My Cat's Life*.

In her free time Jennifer loves to read, travel and eat anything anyone else prepares for her. She lives with her husband, kids, and two dogs, Sugar and Scout. You can reach her by visiting her website at www.jenniferquasha.com.

About
Wendy Diamond

Since adopting her Maltese, Lucky, along with a rescued Russian Blue cat named Pasha, **Wendy Diamond** has dedicated herself to animal rescue and welfare. She launched Animal Fair—a lifestyle media company in support of fairness to endangered animals and animal rescue—in 1999.

When Animal Fair launched, 12 million animals were euthanized in shelters. Since then, that number has decreased to 6 million. Animal Fair is dedicated to highlighting non-profit animal organizations, giving them the opportunity to tell their inspirational stories and to provide information so the community may be involved.

Wendy is a frequent pet lifestyle contributor to NBC's *Today Show* and has starred in television shows on CBS, NBC, Style Network, Fox, and Animal Planet. Wendy and Lucky Diamond were judges on CBS' primetime hit *Greatest American Dog!* Wendy has also contributed and has appeared on CBS' *The Early Show*, *The View*, Fox News, CNN, *Extra*, *Good Morning America*, E!, VH1, MTV among many others. She has been featured in numerous publications including *The New York Times*, *Forbes*, *Time*, *People*, *The New Yorker* and *Vogue*.

She also has written three books—*How to Understand Men Through Their Dogs*, *How to Understand Women Through Their Cats*, and *It's a Dog's World*, a lifestyle guide to living with your dog.

For the last decade Wendy and her team have created and executed numerous original events with Animal Fair including Toys for Dogs, Paws for Style (the first-ever pet charity fashion show), Mutt Makeover, White House Pet Correspondents Benefit, Halloween Pet

Costume Benefit, and Yappy Hour, raising hundreds of thousands of dollars for local animal rescue.

Currently, Wendy serves on the board of advisors for the United Nations Millennium Development Goal Achievers and World Entrepreneurship Day. She continues to extend her wealth of animal knowledge serving as a keynote speaker on numerous pet lifestyle topics at seminars across the world from Harvard University to the United Nations.

You can find more information about pet lifestyle, animal rescue, and Wendy's work at www.animalfair.com.

Thank You

hank you cat lovers! I owe huge thanks to every one of you who shared your stories about beloved cats that have touched your lives. You have made me laugh, cry and nod my head. My heart brightened when you got a new kitten; I chuckled at your teenage cat's shenanigans; I was touched by the amazing variety of ways that your adult cats love and share your lives; and I promise that I cried with you when old age or sickness took your best friend from you. I know that you poured your hearts and souls into the thousands of stories and poems that you submitted. Thank you. All of us at Chicken Soup for the Soul appreciate your willingness to share your lives with us.

We could only publish a small percentage of the stories that were submitted, but at least two of us read every single submission—and there were thousands! Even the stories that do not appear in the book influenced us and affected the final manuscript.

A special thank you goes to Chicken Soup for the Soul editor Kristiana Glavin, who read all the stories and poems with me. This book could not have been made without her diligence, input, and well-oiled knowledge of what makes a great Chicken Soup for the Soul story. Amy Newmark, Chicken Soup for the Soul's whip-smart publisher had my back during every stage of creating this book and guided me gracefully and with quick replies. I also want to thank Assistant Publisher D'ette Corona for managing the whole production process, and editors Barbara LoMonaco and Madeline Clapps for their proofreading assistance.

Thank you to cartoonists Mark Parisi, Patrick Hardin and Dave

Carpenter for giving us twelve reasons to giggle throughout the book. Lastly, I owe a very special thanks to our creative director and book producer, Brian Taylor at Pneuma Books, for his brilliant vision for our covers and interiors. Finally, none of this would be possible without the business and creative leadership of Chicken Soup for the Soul's CEO, Bill Rouhana, and president, Bob Jacobs.

Keep writing, friends. I can't wait to hear from you again!

~Jennifer Quasha

Improving Your Life Every Day

Real people sharing real stories—for seventeen years. Now, Chicken Soup for the Soul has gone beyond the bookstore to become a world leader in life improvement. Through books, movies, DVDs, online resources and other partnerships, we bring hope, courage, inspiration and love to hundreds of millions of people around the world. Chicken Soup for the Soul's writers and readers belong to a one-of-a-kind global community, sharing advice, support, guidance, comfort, and knowledge.

Chicken Soup for the Soul stories have been translated into more than forty languages and can be found in more than one hundred countries. Every day, millions of people experience a Chicken Soup for the Soul story in a book, magazine, newspaper or online. As we share our life experiences through these stories, we offer hope, comfort and inspiration to one another. The stories travel from person to person, and from country to country, helping to improve lives everywhere.

Share with Us

We all have had Chicken Soup for the Soul moments in our lives. If you would like to share your story or poem with millions of people around the world, go to chickensoup.com and click on "Submit Your Story." You may be able to help another reader, and become a published author at the same time. Some of our past contributors have launched writing and speaking careers from the publication of their stories in our books!

Our submission volume has been increasing steadily—the quality and quantity of your submissions has been fabulous. We only accept story submissions via our website. They are no longer accepted via mail or fax.

To contact us regarding other matters, please send us an e-mail through webmaster@chickensoupforthesoul.com, or fax or write us at:

Chicken Soup for the Soul
P.O. Box 700
Cos Cob, CT 06807-0700
Fax: 203-861-7194

One more note from your friends at Chicken Soup for the Soul: Occasionally, we receive an unsolicited book manuscript from one of our readers, and we would like to respectfully inform you that we do not accept unsolicited manuscripts and we must discard the ones that appear.

www.chickensoup.com